PROGRAMMING DELPHI CUSTOM COMPONENTS

Fred Bulback

M&T BOOKS

Associate Publisher: Paul Farrell

Managing Editor: Cary Sullivan   **Copy Edit Manager:** Shari Chappell
Editor: Michael Sprague   **Production Editor:** Stephanie Doyle

To my dear wife, Kim.

To the memory of my grandfather, Fred Bulback II.

CONTENTS

Chapter 1: Introduction to Delphi 1

Chapter 2: Creating a Simple Nonvisual Component 53

Chapter 3: Serial Communications with Delphi 89

Chapter 4: Creating Dialog Box Components 177

Chapter 5: Creating a Visual Component 195

Chapter 6: Creating an Interactive Component 223

Chapter 7: Inheriting Existing Functionality 281

Chapter 8: Components That Print 303

Chapter 9: Property and Component Editors 349

Acknowledgements

Writing this book was an enormous task that I could not have hoped to complete without the help and guidance of several individuals.

At the top of the list are Charlie Calvert and Danny Thorpe, both of whom work for Borland. They went way beyond the call of duty in answering my numerous questions—most of which were obscure to say the least. Guys, I hope I didn't get too annoying.

The denzians of the Delphi Beta forum on CompuServe—far too many to mention by name—also proved to be invaluable. I have never before encountered a group of people who were so willing to roll up their sleeves and get their hands dirty for a person they never met.

My development editor, Michael Sprague, took a big chance when he approached me with the offer of writing a book about Delphi components. I hope that gamble pays off. While in the early pre-outline stages, he forewarned me that writing a book was much different than writing an article. He was right, but failed to let on exactly how it was different... at least until the contract was signed. Then he told me that I was in peril of falling meteors and earthquakes. Thankfully, there were no meteors and the earthquake was minor, but I did have my fair share of unusual events during the time. If anybody personifies patience and understanding, it is Michael.

The whole team at M&T did an excellent job overseeing the final stages of preparing my manuscript for publication. In fear of leaving somebody out, I will not even attempt to name them all. Nevertheless, with their skill and coordination the rough spots—and there were many—have been beautifully polished over.

Last, but by no means least, is Jeff Duntemann, editorial director of the Coriolis Group. Whether he knows it or not, and I doubt he does, it is because of him and his former magazine, PC Techniques, that I became aware that writing was something that I wanted to do. The relaxed style of that magazine was a far cry from the all-too-typical stuffy magazine of the time; you read PC Techniques not because you had to but because it was thoroughly enjoyable to do so. I have tried to adopt the same casual style here, which I can only hope remotely approaches that of *PC Techniques*.

I can not possibly express my thanks to all of the above people adequately. They are the ones ultimately responsible for this work, and the meager mention here cannot even begin to repay them for their unique contributions to the successful completion of this book.

CHAPTER • 1

INTRODUCTION TO DELPHI

On February 14, 1995, Borland International released Delphi, an exciting new product that is bound to leave its mark on the programming community for years to come. The reason for all the excitement is that Delphi is a *Rapid Application Development*, or *RAD*, programming environment for both Microsoft Windows 3.1 and Windows 95. A RAD programming environment allows a programmer to quickly build fully functional, solid applications in typically less than half the time and for half the expense it would take to program the same application using a traditional text-based programming environment. This fact alone has immediate appeal both to programmers, who quickly grow bored working on the same code day after day, and managers, who are anxious to see the product out the door as soon as possible with the least expense possible.

Professional RAD environments have been available for years, but they are generally known for their exceptionally high cost and the poor quality support available. In the more recent past, a low-cost product, Microsoft's Visual Basic, has attempted to fill the desire for good RAD tools and has indeed managed to produce a huge and committed following. Despite this, Visual Basic falls flat on its face when more than a small- to medium-size project is attempted, or when speed of execution is a critical factor. In contrast, Delphi is a low-cost package that has had formidable support available since its early beta stages, with knowledge bases growing by the day. It wields all the power contained in Borland Pascal version 7.0 and can more than adequately handle big projects. As an example, it may be of interest to you to know that Delphi was built with itself!

One feature that most RAD environments have in common is that the programmer selects a control, such as an edit box for displaying and editing text or a button for clicking on, from a list and then proceeds to draw it onto his display. This is repeated until all the desired controls are on the display, at which point the user interface is *done*. After this, all that remains is to write code to implement the functionality of the project. As you may gather, the power a RAD environment comes from the controls available to it; without the controls, all that remains is a lackluster traditional programming environment. It is therefore desirable to put as much functionality into the controls as is possible, which is where Delphi again comes to the rescue.

Delphi has an intimidating arsenal of controls, or *components* as they are known, at its disposal. These components range from lowly text labels right up to OLE and database components that allow *thousands* of lines of code to be dropped in quickly and conveniently. All this functionality is contained in the *Visual Component Library*, or *VCL*. The VCL as it comes with Delphi contains most of the components that you will require for a project. You will probably find that, on occasion, it would be nice if you could either buy or create your own component. This is where Delphi goes off the well-beaten RAD path. From day one, Delphi was intended to allow the easy creation of new components, and the interface for doing so is elegant and efficient.

This is where this book fits into the big picture. It is my goal to teach you how to design and program useful components for Delphi. I will do this by providing many real-world examples of where components can and should be used rather a typical brute-force programming approach. To accompany these examples will be in-depth discussions of the techniques used to create them and how the same techniques can be put to work for your own components.

What I Expect From You

Before we begin this journey, I should mention that I assume you are somewhat familiar with the Pascal programming language, at least the Borland Pascal 7.0 implementation of it. If you are not, you may have some difficulty with basic concepts such as units and object-oriented programming. If this is the case, I suggest that before you attempt to read this book you purchase one of the many good beginning Delphi programming books available and read through it to acquaint yourself with the basics.

I will also assume that you have at least a basic understanding of the Delphi environment itself. For example, you should know how to add components to a form and compile a program. Again, if you don't feel comfortable with Delphi at this level, you should seek out additional sources of information. You will only be making things harder on yourself and wasting your time in the process if you attempt to jump into this book without knowing the basics.

In the past, it was necessary to have a firm working knowledge of the Windows API to even remotely consider programming a Windows project. With Delphi, the emphasis on the API has diminished to a point that it is rarely required. This is due to the VCL, which encapsulates many of the API calls for drawing, printing, copying, pasting, and so on. This is fine if you are just a user of components; however, if you are programming them, you will find that the VCL often does not provide a level of control low enough for what you want do. For example, the project I will talk about in Chapter 3 is a component for serial communications. To implement this component, it is necessary to know about API calls such as **BuildCommDCB** and **PurgeComm**. This is not to say that you have to be fluent in the Windows API, just knowing that it exists and how to call functions in it is enough to be a programmer of Delphi components.

Before moving on to the fun stuff, I will devote the remainder of this chapter to telling you about Delphi and the VCL and how they compare to other programming environments available.

Delphi Compared to Borland Pascal 7.0

Delphi is the successor to the very popular Borland Pascal 7.0. Although at the core Delphi and Borland Pascal are very similar, there are some dramatic differences between the two. The most predominant difference is the appearance of the integrated development environment, or IDE.

Changes to the IDE

The IDE that accompanies Borland Pascal consists of a main window housing child windows, which contain Pascal code. All programming is done in these windows in a strictly text-oriented fashion. Delphi, on the other hand, does away with the client-child scenario, with its main window being short and horizontal, as shown in Figure 1.1. This gives Delphi a definite Visual Basic flavor. Like Visual Basic, this window contains a menu that provides access to the commands necessary to program and compile and a toolbar that allows frequently used commands such as **Open File**, and **Run** to be quickly selected by clicking the proper button. Unlike Visual Basic, however, is the addition of components to this window. The components are arranged in groups such as Standard, Additional, Data Access, and so on. To access a group, all that is required is to click on the named tab and all the components in that group are visually depicted as bitmaps. At this point, it is only necessary to click on the appropriate component to use it.

Unlike Borland Pascal, which requires that controls be created at run time, Delphi permits the visual layout of a window to occur at design time, see Figure 1.2. To be fair, it must be noted that Borland Pascal does allow some design-time layout in the way of dialog boxes contained in resource files, which in turn are created with the Resource Workshop or a similar resource editor. This is hardly unique to Borland Pascal however, as most compiled languages for Windows support the use of resource files. The difference in resource files and the design-time support that Delphi provides is that the Delphi's support is tightly integrated with the code, whereas a resource file has no knowledge of code whatsoever. To provide this design-time layout, Delphi uses the concept of *forms*, which are windows that can contain components.

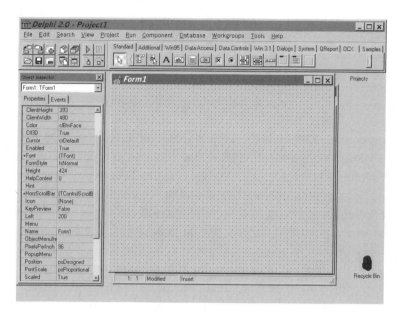

Figure 1.1 The Delphi IDE.

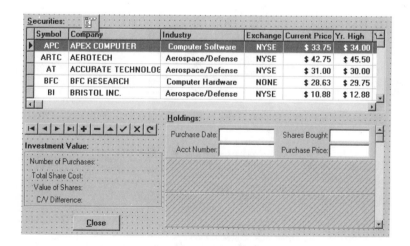

Figure 1.2 Creating a window at design time.

To aid in the design of forms, Delphi has an Alignment Palette, as shown in Figure 1.3, that allows components to be aligned with each other in a number of ways. Using the Alignment Palette, it is possible to do otherwise time-consuming tasks, such as creating equal vertical spacing or setting a common edge for a group of components.

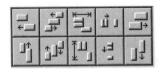

Figure 1.3 The Alignment Palette.

Also unique to Delphi is the Object Inspector, as seen in Figure 1.4. The Object Inspector is a small window that displays the properties and methods that belong to a component. A *property* is an attribute of the component, such as its height, width, font of any text that may be in it, or its color. A component's method is similar to a Borland Pascal function or procedure that is called when something happens to the component. For example, someone may click on it, or its size may change as a result of the user resizing the main window. By clicking on a component contained in a form, the Object Inspector fills with information that pertains to it. This information can then be edited to suit the values appropriate for the component's purpose.

Figure 1.4 The Object Inspector.

Similar to Borland Pascal, Delphi contains a window that allows the editing of code. The window, shown in Figure 1.5, is multipaged, and different files can be switched to by clicking on the corresponding page tab. This is an improvement over Borland Pascal, which cascades all the edit windows, which, if your project is large and you have many windows open, will result in an awful mess. Sometimes, however, it is useful to view more than one file at the same time, something that is impossible with the multipaged scheme just discussed. To accommodate the need for this, it is possible to have more than one edit window open simultaneously.

```
CtrlForm | Unit2 | Unit1 |

    unit CtrlForm;

    interface

    uses
        Windows, Messages, SysUtils, Classes, Graphics, Controls, Forms,
        DBCtrls, StdCtrls, ExtCtrls, Mask, DBTables, DB, Grids, DBGrids,
        DBCGrids;

    type
        TFmCtrlGrid = class(TForm)
            DBCtrlGrid1: TDBCtrlGrid;
            DBGrid1: TDBGrid;
            DBEdit1: TDBEdit;
            DBEdit2: TDBEdit;
            DBEdit3: TDBEdit;
            DBEdit4: TDBEdit;
            Label1: TLabel;
            Label2: TLabel;
            Label3: TLabel;

82: 1                           Insert
```

Figure 1.5 The Delphi Code Editor.

One major addition to Delphi, and one that Borland Pascal should have, is an integrated debugger. Currently, Borland Pascal programmers have only two options available to them if they want to debug the program:

• Including **WinCRT** in their uses statement and sprinkling **writeln** statements around their program in an attempt to monitor the flow of execution or watch the values of a variable. Borland does not recommended this when programming a true Windows project, however, because one side effect is that it creates another message loop in your program, which often causes more problems than it solves.

- Using Turbo Debugger. Turbo Debugger is a very powerful debugger that is great for hunting down those hard to find bugs; but for most bugs, it is overkill and a pain to use. First of all, Turbo Debugger is a separate program, which requires you to compile and link your program with debug information. This makes it incredibly easy to forget that this information is present in your program, and you may end up shipping some secret information to someone who knows what to do with it. Besides, it makes your executable quite a bit larger than without it. Being a second program, Turbo Debugger has to load into memory every time you want to debug something. I wish I were a perfect programmer and did not require a debugger, but I am not, and I find the wait for loading the debugger to be distracting. Finally, Turbo Debugger is by necessity a text-based application, which means that while you are debugging your program, the screen keeps changing back and forth from text mode to graphics mode. With some monitors, this change can be on the order of several seconds, truly adding aggravation to an already unpleasant situation.

The integrated debugger shares many of the features of Turbo Debugger and does not have to be loaded in every time you want to do some light debugging or watch the value of a variable.

Changes to the Implementation of Pascal

With the release of Delphi came some big changes to Borland's implementation of the Pascal language. The result of these changes is known as Object Pascal. Object Pascal remains completely compatible with Borland Pascal, but to do so, it was necessary to make a questionable compromise.

The New Object Model

The compromise in question is the new object model. In Borland Pascal. An *object* is defined with the keyword **object**. In Delphi, however, the keyword **object** still exists, and its functionality remains unchanged from

Borland Pascal. In order not to "break" existing code it was necessary to create a second object model with the keyword of **class**. That is correct, Delphi supports two distinctly different object models! If you're like me, you may find this slightly distasteful and a bit of a kludge. On the other hand, I am not about to give it up because it allows me to take old Borland Pascal projects and continue to work on them with all the features that Delphi offers.

Another reason that the new object model exists is because Borland wants Delphi to be known as an easy to use product, much like Visual Basic. To avoid eating up precious data segment space, the old object model relies heavily on pointers and dynamic memory allocation, which many programmers find confusing. The new object model, on the other hand, still relies on these, but they are hidden from the programmer. Consider the following old style object model example:

```
Type
  PMyObject=^TMyObject;
  TMyObject=Object(TObject);
    Procedure DoSomething;
  end;


Procedure TMyObject.DoSomething;
Begin
  {Do something}
End;


Var
  MyObject:PMyObject;


Begin
  New(MyObject,Init);
  MyObject^.DoSomething;
  Dispose(MyObject,Done);
End.
```

Notice how **MyObject** has to specifically be created and destroyed through the use of the **New** and **Dispose** keywords. Also notice that access to members of the object require the use of pointers, which are prone to bugs and create code that is difficult to read. Object Pascal streamlines this process:

```
Type
  TMyObject=class
    Procedure DoSomething;
  End;


Procedure TMyObject.DoSomething;
Begin
  {Do Something}
End;


Var
  MyObject:TMyObject;


Begin
  MyObject:=TMyObject.Create;
  MyObject.DoSomething;
  MyObject.Free;
End.
```

The functionality of this example is exactly the same as the previous one, and indeed the object declaration is nearly identical. The difference lies in the way the object is created. In Object Pascal, all objects are descended from **TObject**, regardless of whether you specify it next to the **class** key-word. **TObject** itself is responsible for allocating memory; and to achieve this, a new type of member function, called a *class method*, is required. A class method is special because it is called using an object type instead of an object instance. This means that a class need not be initialized to call a class method, and as such, a class method should never attempt to access members of its own class. The class method that **TObject** uses to produce an initialized instance of itself is called **Create**. Once the instance exists, member functions can be called without resorting to pointers.

Other Changes to the New Object Model

Predeclaring Objects

Often, a programmer will want to make two objects aware of one another. With the old object model, the only option available is to create pointer types, which can be declared before the declaration of their corresponding object. If a pointer type is created for each object that is to have knowledge of another object and then placed in the other object's declaration, it becomes possible to access members of that object, albeit indirectly. This is not an elegant solution for a such a common problem. Fortunately, the new object model permits classes to be *predeclared*, much like the pointer method just described, but without having to resort to pointers.

Member Scope

Private and **public** are keywords that indicate how members of a class may be accessed. For example, a **private** member is known only in the unit in which it has been declared; whereas a **public** member is known to all units. Object Pascal puts a new twist on this by providing the **protected** keyword, which is a hybrid of the other two. By declaring a member **protected** it is still inaccessible from any unit except the one in which it has been declared, much like the **private** keyword, *unless* a descendant of its class is being created, at which point it will behave like a **public** member.

In addition to **protected**, there is also the new keyword **published**. The **published** section of a class behaves exactly like the public section *except* that it generates additional information that is available to an application at run time. This is how the Object Inspector is aware of certain properties and events of components. We'll return to this topic and explore it in greater detail when we begin to design and program components in Chapter 2.

Abstract Methods

Sometimes a class is the building block for several other descendent classes. This base class will usually define the functionality and provide the support necessary to encapsulate the idea it contains; but it rarely will it apply the idea in some real-world manner. Instead, the class provides placeholders for descendants to override with the routines that actually put the base class to work. These placeholders are known as *abstract methods*.

Looking at it another way, let's suppose that for your birthday you got a cordless screwdriver. Upon opening it you would see that It contains things like a battery, a motor, and some gears. On the outside, you find a big red switch to turn on the thing and a hole to plug in all the various bits that came with it. This hole is just like an abstract method; you can flip that switch and watch it go round and round, but without a bit in it—the descendant—it doesn't do very much for you. Although this analogy is flawed at best, you get the idea.

To create an abstract method with Borland Pascal, it was required that you create the method procedure normally, and then call the procedure **Abstract** that would generate a run-time error. Delphi does away with this mess, and simply tacking on the new **abstract** keyword to the end of your method will suffice:

```
procedure TurnScrew;virtual;abstract;
```

Properties

Members of old-style objects can either be variables that hold data or functions that manipulate it. Good programming practice dictates that all variable access, outside of the object itself, should be done through member functions:

```
Type
  TMyObject=Object(TObject)
  Private
    MyVariable:Word;
  Public
    Function GetMyVariable:Word;
    Procedure SetMyVariable(MyVar:Word);
  End;


Function TMyObject.GetMyVariable:Word;
Begin
```

```
   GetMyVariable:=MyVariable;
End;


Procedure TMyObject.SetMyVariable(MyVar:Word);
Begin
   MyVariable:=MyVar;
End;


Var
   MyObject:TMyObject;


Begin
   New(MyObject,Init);
   MyObject^.SetMyVariable(10);
   Writeln(MyObject^.GetMyVariable);
   Dispose(MyObject,Done);
End;
```

The purpose of this is to hide the variable from the programmer, making future changes impact only the one object, rather than dozens of locations scattered around the program. For example, it may become necessary at some point to scale the return value. If this was done in the object, there would be only one change that would serve to enhance maintainability and reduce code size compared to the alternative of changing every affected line of code in the program.

The downside to this layer of protection is that variables are treated as functions and consequently, the purpose of a section of code becomes less clear:

```
MyObject^.SetMyVariable((Sum+OldSum) div 2);
```

You could probably make a fairly good guess at what was happening here, but the other option available is much more obvious:

```
MyObject^.MyVariable:=(Sum+OldSum) div 2;
```

Object Pascal has addressed this matter and came up with an elegant solution that provides the same level of protection, while allowing the intent of the code to be conveyed more efficiently. This solution consists of creating a new type of class member called a **property** that, for all things considered, works just like a member variable. There is, of course, a trick involved.

A **property** member is merely a means for telling the compiler what other class member—be it a variable or function—to access for operations such as reading from it or writing to it. Examine the following section of code:

```
Type
  TMyObject=Class
  Private
    FMyVariable:Integer;
  Public
    Property MyVariable:Integer read FMyVariable write FMyVariable;

  End;
```

Notice the property declaration for **MyVariable**. The only thing you may be familiar with is the **:Integer** part that indicates its type. The **read** keyword is followed by a member variable, **FMyVariable** to indicate that it will be accessed during attempts to read **MyVariable**. The **write** keyword is similar because it indicates that **FMyVariable** will also be accessed during a write operation on **MyVariable**.

Things start getting interesting when you have to do more than simply access a variable. Earlier, I told why you should always access variables through member functions and presented the example that explained that maybe the value would have to be scaled before it was returned. To perform an operation on a property before the value is returned, it is a simple matter of replacing the variable with a function, and doing the operation inside it:

```
Type
  TMyObject=Class
  Private
    FMyVariable:Integer;
    Function GetMyVariable:Integer;
  Public
```

```
    Property MyVariable:Integer read GetMyVariable write FMyVariable;
  End;
Function TMyObject.GetMyVariable:Integer;
Begin
  GetMyVariable:=FMyVariable*2;
End;
```

Here, **read FMyVariable** has been replaced with **read GetMyVariable**, referring to the newly added member function. Now, whenever **MyVariable** is accessed during a read operation, the member function **GetMyVariable** is being called instead:

```
WriteLn(MyObject.MyVariable);
```

In this case, the value printed out would be twice as much as **FMyVariable**, thus performing the necessary operation, but maintaining a variable-like access.

More often, it is necessary to do some sort of action upon setting a variable. For example, let's say that a complete recalculation is required whenever a member variable of a class changes, a very common situation. The code would look something like this:

```
Type
  TMyObject=Class
  Private
    FMyVariable:Integer;
    Procedure SetMyVariable(NewValue:Integer);
  Public
    Property MyVariable:Integer read FMyVariable write SetMyVariable;
  End;

Procedure TMyObject.SetMyVariable(NewValue:Integer);
Begin
  FMyVariable:=NewValue;
  Recalculate;
End;
```

Because the **write** portion of the property has been changed to **SetMyVariable**, this procedure will be called whenever **MyVariable** is assigned a value:

```
MyObject.MyVariable:=12;
```

During the course of the call to **SetMyVariable**, the **FMyVariable** variable is set to the new value, and the procedure called **Recalculate** is called, ensuring that the newly set value is taken into account for other parts of the class that rely on it.

Array Properties

Array properties are similar to regular properties except that they have an index or indexes associated with them —just like an array. Actually, it is a bit unfair to refer to the indexes as indexes because there is no restriction placed upon their type; it is just as acceptable to have an index that is a **Real** or a **TObject** as it is to have one of an ordinal type, such as **Integer**. The trick involved here is not to think of them as indexes, but rather as parameters of a function, which is what they ultimately are anyhow and how we'll refer to them from this point on. All this becomes clearer upon inspection of a typical array property declaration:

```
Type
  TMyObject=Class
  Private
    Procedure SetMyVariable(Index:Integer;NewValue:Integer);
    Function GetMyVariable(Index:Integer):Integer;
  Public
    Property MyVariable[Index:Integer]:Integer read GetMyVariable
      write SetMyVariable;
  End;
```

The array property **MyVariable** has a single parameter called **Index**, whose value is transferred to the **Index** parameter of **GetMyVariable** upon attempts to read and on **SetMyVariable** upon attempts to write. The declaration of the parameter is notably different from declaration for ordinary function parameters because it is flanked by brackets instead of parenthesis; but despite this, the functionality is otherwise identical. As with normal properties, the **read** function returns the value for the property. In addition, it requires a parameter list that is identical to the parameter list of the property itself. The **write** function is similar because it also needs to have the same parameters as the property, but it also still requires a parameter for the actual value that is being written and that goes right after the properties parameters.

Unfortunately, it is not possible to have the **read** or **write** parts of the property indicate an array variable instead of a function; any attempts to do so will result in a compile-time error. To work around this minor problem, simply have the **read** and **write** functions manipulate the array for you:

```
Type
  TMyObject=Class
  Private
    FMyArray:array[1..10] of Integer;
    Procedure SetMyArray(Index:Integer;NewValue:Integer);
    Function GetMyArray(Index:Integer):Integer;
  Public
    Property MyArray[Index:Integer]:Integer read GetMyArray
      write SetMyArray;
  End;


Function TMyObject.GetMyArray(Index:Integer):Integer;
Begin
  GetMyArray:=FMyArray[Index];
End;


Procedure TMyObject.SetMyArray(Index:Integer;NewValue:Integer);
Begin
  FMyArray[Index]:=NewValue;
End;
```

Array properties posses the unique capability of being permitted to be declared as **default**, as shown in the following declaration:

```
Property MyArray[Index:Integer]:Integer read GetMyArray
  write SetMyArray;Default;
```

The **default** keyword after the property declaration allows accesses to the property without having to specify it:

```
MyObject.MyArray[12]:=43;
```

Can now simply be written as:

```
MyObject[12]:=43;
```

With this, the object-oriented features of Object Pascal take a huge leap forward because it permits inner workings to be totally hidden from the programmer. For example, consider a hypothetical object called **TFile** whose purpose is to allow the reading and writing of individual bytes in a file. The interface could not be simpler:

```
MyFile:=TFile.Open('SOMEFILE.ABC');   {open the file}
MyFile[1050]:=74;                       {write 74 to file at offset 1050}
Writeln('The value is ',MyFile[14])    {read value from file at offset 14}
MyFile.Close;                           {close the file}
```

The code is compact and yet it does not suffer in readability—you really don't need the comments to understand what is going on.

Method Dispatching

With the old object model, it is possible to declare a member function **virtual** to invoke a process known as *late binding*, which means that the function's actual address is not known until run time. This allows different objects to be derived from a base object and have member functions that override those in the base object. When code from the base object attempts to call one of its own member functions, the replacement member function will be called. This is the basis of *polymorphism*, which refers to the capability to call a member function without knowledge of the type from which it is declared.

Old-style virtual member functions can also have an optional index included with the declaration, at which point they become *dynamic methods*. The index makes it possible to search through a list of all dynamic method indexes and attempt to match one to a desired index number, thereby allowing dynamic methods to be called without regard for their name, but rather their index. The Object Windows Library, or OWL, that ships with Borland Pascal relies heavily on this feature; and indeed, the same functionality would have been next to impossible to create without it.

Object Pascal classes do not force multiple functionality upon the **virtual** keyword. Instead, there are now four keywords that allow the same power to be dished out as it is needed. The first keyword, **virtual**, is identical to the old object model's implementation of it, with the exception that adding an index to it will not create a dynamic method. This is where it gets a bit confusing. **Dynamic**, the second new keyword, does not permit an index to be used like a dynamic method of the old object model—though one is used internally—but is unavailable to the programmer except by obscure backdoor techniques. The question that now arises is what is the difference between **virtual** and **dynamic** methods? The proper answer is a long and complex one dealing with how the methods are dispatched and not of much relevance to our discussion. The short answer is much more to the point: virtual methods are much faster than dynamic methods, but they produce slightly larger code. So if you anticipate that a method will be called frequently, it is best to make it **virtual**; whereas methods that hardly ever get called can be made **dynamic**.

Overriding a member function no longer requires repeating the **virtual** keyword. The new way of doing this is by specifying the member as **override**, the third of the newly added keywords, which is applicable to both **virtual** and **dynamic** methods.

Because member functions declared **virtual** or **dynamic** are not permitted to have an index of any sort associated with them, the final keyword, **message**, takes on the role of the old object model's dynamic methods. By calling **Dispatch**, which is inherited from **TObject**, it is possible to call a member function declared as **message** without regard for its actual name. This is accomplished by passing the index value that follows the **message** keyword in the call to **Dispatch**. Consider the following example:

```
Type
  TMyObject=Class
    Procedure MyMessageHandler(Var Msg:Word); Message 100;
  End;


Procedure TMyObject.MyMessageHandler(Var Msg:Word);
Begin
  Writeln('MyMessageHandler has been called with a message index of
  ',Msg);
End;


var
  MyObject:TMyObject;
  Msg:Word;


begin
  MyObject:=TMyObject.Create;
  Msg:=100;
  MyObject.Dispatch(Msg);
  MyObject.Free;
end.
```

In the call to **Dispatch**, the variable **Msg**, which is of type **word**, is passed. This variable holds the value 100, which corresponds to the message index of **MyMessageHandler**. However, the parameter to **Dispatch** is by no means limited to type **word**; it can be any type you wish, the only restriction being that the first two bytes are used to pass the message index. Further, whatever variable type you do pass to **Dispatch** is also passed as a parameter to the message handler. Because the parameters of both **Dispatch** and the message handler are declared as **var**, it is possible for the handler to modify the contents of the variable type, which will remain modified when the call to **Dispatch** is completed, allowing values to be returned from the message handler.

As a final note on message handlers, **TObject** has a member called **DefaultHandler** that is called whenever a call to **Dispatch** fails to locate a message handler with the proper message index. It is possible to override this member and perform some sort of default handling of your own, providing a fail-safe mechanism for your program. This is very much like how Windows operates. Windows sends messages to a program that only responds to the ones that it requires, calling **DefWindowProc** to handle all the rest.

Open-Array Parameters

Delphi now supports open-array function parameters. This allows you to pass an array to a function without regard to its size, which is a major improvement over Borland Pascal's strictness of requiring that every function parameter have an exact type. Previously, passing an array to a function required one of two approaches:

- Declare the array variable and the function parameter from the same type:

```
Const
    MyArraySize=10;

Type
    TMyArray=Array[1..MyArraySize] of Integer;

Function AddThem(AnArray:TMyArray):Integer;
var
    i:Integer;
    Sum:Integer;
Begin
    Sum:=0;
    For i:=1 to MyArraySize do
            Inc(Sum,AnArray[i]);
    AddThem:=Sum;
End;
```

```
Var
    MyArray:TMyArray;
    MySum:Integer;

Begin
    MySum:=AddThem(MyArray);
End.
```

This works well, and has been used by many programmers in their projects. There is a serious limitation to the code as presented, however. Suppose that you want to use procedure **AddThem** with another array, one that isn't of type **TMyArray**; what do you do? It may be tempting to duplicate the procedure, rename it, and change the type **TMyArray** to something like **TMyOtherArray**—tempting, but wrong. Code duplication is as tasteless as a rice cake and should be avoided with equal enthusiasm. Happily, an alternative exists:

- Pass the pointer to the array:

```
Const
    MyArraySize=10;
    MyOtherArraySize=20;

Type
    TMyArray=Array[1..MyArraySize] of Integer;
    TMyOtherArray=Array[1..MyOtherArraySize] of Integer;
    TIntegerArray=array[0..0] of Integer;
    PIntegerArray=^TIntegerArray;

Function AddThem(PAnArray:PIntegerArray;  Elements:Integer):Integer;
var
    i:Integer;
    Sum:Integer;
Begin
    Sum:=0;
```

```
{$R-}
For i:=0 to Elements-1 do
        Inc(Sum,PAnArray^[i]);
{$R+}
AddThem:=Sum;
End;

Var
    MyArray:TMyArray;
    MySum:Integer;


    MyOtherArray:TMyOtherArray;
    MyOtherSum:Integer;

Begin
    MySum:=AddThem(@MyArray,MyArraySize);
    MyOtherSum:=AddThem(@MyOtherArray,MyOtherArraySize);
End.
```

Here, the pointers to the arrays are being passed rather than the array variables themselves. This ensures that the compiler is unable to perform a type check, and as a result, both arrays are cast as **PIntegerArray,** which is a generic integer array and has both the upper and lower indexes set to zero. Normally, setting both indexes to zero would not allow us to use the array at all because an out of range error would occur the instant we tried to access it. By using the **{$R-}** directive, it is possible to turn off range checking and eliminate this potential error. Because range checking exists for a very good reason, it is shortly turned back on with the **{$R+}** directive, after the array accesses have been completed. Notice that it is also necessary to pass the size of the array because the compiler has no knowledge of it beyond the fact that it is an array of integer.

Delphi allows a much more informal approach:

```
Const
    MyArraySize=10;
    MyOtherArraySize=20;
```

```
Type
    TMyArray=Array[1..MyArraySize] of Integer;
    TMyOtherArray=Array[1..MyOtherArraySize] of Integer;


Function AddThem(AnArray:Array of Integer):Integer;
var
    i:Integer;
    Sum:Integer;
Begin
    Sum:=0;
    For i:=Low(AnArray) to High(AnArray) do
            Inc(Sum,AnArray[i]);
    AddThem:=Sum;
End;


Var
    MyArray:TMyArray;
    MySum:Integer;

    MyOtherArray:TMyOtherArray;
    MyOtherSum:Integer;


Begin
    MySum:=AddThem(MyArray);
    MyOtherSum:=AddThem(MyOtherArray);
End.
```

As you can see, the code is straightforward and easy to read. In the function **AddThem**, the **of Integer** portion allows the array to be passed without consideration for its size. The size, incidentally, does not have to be passed as an extra parameter; the Object Pascal compiler is smart enough to realize what array is being passed and look up its maximum and minimum indexes when required. This is what the **Low** and **High** functions do—or at least appear to do. In reality, **Low** always returns a zero, and **High** returns one less than the actual count of elements in the array. Don't worry about this though, because it does not mean that any array you pass has to be zero-based; it just means that is how the function with an open-array parameter will interpret them.

On rare occasions, it may be desirable to pass an array to a function without having to go through all the red tape required to declare and initialize it. This is accomplished in Delphi by the use of open-array construction:

```
MySum:=AddThem([10,15,7,24,10]);
```

As you can see, the array consisting of elements 10,15,7,24, and 10 is created without the need of a formal array declaration and is passed to the function **AddThem** in the same manner as a conventional array would be. One aspect of open-array construction that has interesting possibilities is that the elements of the array do not necessarily have to be constants—they are also permitted to be variables:

```
MyGrandSum:=AddThem([MySum,MyOtherSum]);
```

Suddenly, Pascal programmers have one of the more enviable features of C, the ability to pass a variable number of parameters to a function. However, the Pascal programmer gets the additional bonus of having the type of the parameter checked at compile time, reducing the risk of potentially hard to find bugs. Realizing this potential, the developers of Delphi included a new function, **Format**, which is similar to C's **printf** or Visual Basic's **Print Using**, both of which accept a string template and a list of variables. The template defines how the variables will appear in the returned string. Here is the declaration for the **Format** function:

```
function Format(const Format: string; const Args: array of
const): string;
```

The extension of the **const** keyword was introduced in Borland Pascal 7.0. When used as a prefix of function parameter, it ensures that attempts to change the value of the parameter in the body of the function will result in a compile-time error. We see this at work in the prior declaration for both the parameter **Format** and the open-array **Args**. You may, however, be wondering what exactly an **array of const** is. Simply stated, it is a place-holder that allows any type of variable to be passed in the open array, without type checking. To access the values in such an array, it might be your first instinct to index the **Args** parameter and then typecast it to the desired type. Although this is a reasonable assumption, it does not work. A working solution requires a better understanding of the makeup of the array itself. The most important thing is to realize that each element of the array is actually a **TVarRec** structure:

```
TVarRec = record
  case Integer of
    vtInteger:(VInteger: Longint; VType: Byte);
    vtBoolean:(VBoolean: Boolean);
    vtChar:(VChar: Char);
    vtExtended:(VExtended: PExtended);
    vtString:(VString: PString);
    vtPointer:(VPointer: Pointer);
    vtPChar:(VPChar: PChar);
    vtObject:(VObject: TObject);
    vtClass:(VClass: TClass);
end;
```

As you can see, this provides the placeholders necessary to access the values contained in the array. Also, it provides a field, **VType**, that indicates of what type the element actually is. With this knowledge in hand, it becomes a simple matter to get at the values contained in the array:

```
Procedure ShowArrayMakeup(MyArray:Array of Const);
Var
  I:Integer;
  PVarRec:^TVarRec;
Begin
  PVarRec:=@MyArray;
  For I:=Low(MyArray) To High(MyArray) do
  Begin
    case PVarRec^.VType of
```

```
      vtInteger:Writeln('Integer. Contents=',PVarRec^.VInteger);
      vtBoolean:Writeln('Boolean. Contents=',PVarRec^.VBoolean);
      vtChar:Writeln('Char. Contents=',PVarRec^.VChar);
      vtExtended:Writeln('Extended. Contents=',PVarRec^.VExtended^);
      vtString:Writeln('String. Contents=',PVarRec^.VString^);
      vtPointer:Writeln('Pointer.');
      vtPChar:Writeln('PChar. Contents=',PVarRec^.VPChar);
      vtObject:Writeln('TObject.');
      vtClass:Writeln('TClass.');
    end;
    inc(PVarRec);
  End;
End;
```

This simple procedure accepts an array and dissects it, showing the type of each element and, in some cases, the value it contains.

Return Values

Frequently, while programming a function, you will find that the return value is a collection of bit flags, or a set (see Chapter 3) with multiple members. As such, it is often highly desirable to manipulate only parts of it instead of the whole thing, as required by Borland Pascal, which requires that you do your manipulations on a temporary value, and when done assign it to the return value. Happily, Object Pascal removes this limitation through the use of the new **Result** keyword. Think of **Result** as you would an ordinary variable because not only can you assign values to it, as with assigning a normal return value, but you can also assign *its* value to another variable, including itself. This makes bit flags a breeze:

```
Function GetStatus:Byte;
begin
  Result:=0;
  if Condition1 then Result:=Result or 1;
  if Condition2 then Result:=Result or 2;
  if Condition3 then Result:=Result or 4;
  if Condition4 then Result:=Result or 8;
```

```
   if Condition5 then Result:=Result or 16;
   if Condition6 then Result:=Result or 32;
   if Condition7 then Result:=Result or 64;
   if Condition8 then Result:=Result or 128;
end;
```

This is considerably more attractive than the old-style alternative:

```
Function GetStatus:Byte;
var
   Status:Byte;
begin
   Status:=0;
   if Condition1 then Status:=Status or 1;
   if Condition2 then Status:=Status or 2;
   if Condition3 then Status:=Status or 4;
   if Condition4 then Status:=Status or 8;
   if Condition5 then Status:=Status or 16;
   if Condition6 then Status:=Status or 32;
   if Condition7 then Status:=Status or 64;
   if Condition8 then Status:=Status or 128;
   GetStatus:=Status;
end;
```

Often with code similar to this, I would forget the final assignment of **Status** to **GetStatus** and produce a bug in my program. Even though it was usually quick to appear and an easy fix, the new method ensures that this won't ever happen again.

Unfortunately, it is terribly easy to abuse **Result** by using it in a way that it was never intended. Consider this rather common chunk of code:

```
Function Average(Values:array of Integer):Integer;
var
    Sum:Integer;
    I:Integer;
Begin
```

```
    Sum:=0;
    For I:=Low(Values) to High(Values) do
            Sum:=Sum+Values[I];
    Average:=Sum div (High(Values)+1);
End;
```

This code is clean and self-documenting. Going overboard with **Result** would produce the exact opposite effect:

```
Function Average(Values:array of Integer):Integer;
var
    I:Integer;
Begin
    Result:=0;
    For I:=Low(Values) to High(Values) do
            Result:=Result+Values[I];
    Result:=Result div (High(Values)+1);
End;
```

Notice how **Result** is used in place of the variable **Sum** in the addition loop. This serves only to cloud the intended purpose of the loop, making it difficult to follow, and goes against everything a programmer has learned about writing clean, concise code. My advice is to avoid using **Result** as a "catch-all" variable and give intermediate values proper descriptive names.

While we are on the topic of function results, it is only appropriate to acknowledge that Object Pascal can permit nearly any type of variable to be returned, including structures. This is a long-awaited and very powerful feature and much more attractive than the alternative of passing a pointer of a structure to your function, and then accessing the structure through the pointer:

```
Type
  TRect=record
    Left:Integer;
    Top:Integer;
    Right:Integer;
```

```
    Bottom:Integer;
  End;
  PRect=^TRect;

Procedure OffsetRect(Rect:TRect;XOffset,YOffset:Integer;
  ReturnRect:PRect);
Begin
  ReturnRect^.Left:=Rect.Left+XOffset;
  ReturnRect^.Top:=Rect.Top+YOffset;
  ReturnRect^.Right:=Rect.Right+XOffset;
  ReturnRect^.Bottom:=Rect.Bottom+YOffset;
End;

Var
  Rect1:TRect;
  Rect2:TRect;

Begin
  OffsetRect(Rect1,5,13,Rect2);
End.
```

Notice how a procedure rather than a function had to be used, making it unclear that a value is actually being returned. Using the new functionality provided by Object Pascal, we can now write code that improves upon this:

```
Type
  TRect=record
    Left:Integer;
    Top:Integer;
    Right:Integer;
    Bottom:Integer;
  End;

Function OffsetRect(Rect:TRect;
  XOffset,YOffset:Integer):TRect;
Begin
  OffsetRect.Left:=Rect.Left+XOffset;
```

```
  OffsetRect.Top:=Rect.Top+YOffset;
  OffsetRect.Right:=Rect.Right+XOffset;
  OffsetRect.Bottom:=Rect.Bottom+YOffset;
End;

Var
  Rect1:TRect;
  Rect2:TRect;

Begin
  Rect2:=OffsetRect(Rect1,5,13);
End.
```

There is no question that **OffsetRect** returns a value, and that the value is being assigned to **Rect2**.

The only types that can't be returned are objects declared with the **object** keyword and file types such as **File of Integer** and **File of Text**. You will find that these are not severe limitations, however, because both are virtually unused in Delphi, in favor of the newer and better alternatives available.

Exceptions

New to Delphi and Object Pascal is the concept of *exceptions*. Simply stated, exceptions provide a means of responding to conditions, usually in the form of errors, that occur in your program. In the past, detecting an error condition usually required checking the return value of a function to see if it indicated an error:

```
Function Divide(Dividend,Divisor:Integer):Integer;
Begin
  If Divisor<>0 then
    Divide:=Dividend div Divisor
  Else
    Divide:=-1;
End;
```

```
var
  Result:Integer;
  Divisor:Integer;
  Dividend:Integer;

Begin
  Write('Enter the dividend ');
  Readln(Dividend);
  Write('Enter the divisor ');
  Readln(Divisor);
  Result:=Divide(Dividend,Divisor);
  If Result<>-1 then
    Writeln('The result is ',Result)
  Else
    Writeln('Error:  The divisor is zero!');
End.
```

The problem that arises in this example is that the value of **-1** is used to indicate an error, making all legitimate division results of **-1** appear as if they are incorrect. To circumvent this, sometimes the error is not returned as the result of the function and instead is assigned to a parameter that has been declared as **var**:

```
Function Divide(Dividend,Divisor:Integer;var Error:Boolean):Integer;
Begin
  If Divisor=0 then
    Error:=True;
  Else
  Begin
    Error:=False;
    Divide:=Dividend div Divisor;
  End;
End;

var
  Result:Integer;
```

```
  Divisor:Integer;
  Dividend:Integer;
  Error:Boolean;

Begin
  Write('Enter the dividend ');
  Readln(Dividend);
  Write('Enter the divisor ');
  Readln(Divisor);
  Result:=Divide(Dividend,Divisor,Error);
  If Not Error then
    Writeln('The result is ',Result)
  Else
    Writeln('Error:  The divisor is zero!');
End.
```

The same code can be rewritten to exploit exception handling:

```
Function Divide(Dividend,Divisor:Integer):Integer;
Begin
  Divide:=Dividend div Divisor
End;

var
  Result:Integer;
  Divisor:Integer;
  Dividend:Integer;

Begin
  Write('Enter the dividend ');
  Readln(Dividend);
  Write('Enter the divisor ');
  Readln(Divisor);
  Try
    Result:=Divide(Dividend,Divisor);
    Writeln('The result is ',Result)
```

```
    Except
      Writeln('Error:  The divisor is zero!');
    End;
  End.
```

Notice how there isn't any error detection in the **Divide** function. Because the **div** keyword is part of Object Pascal, it has been extended along with most of the other functions in the Run Time Library, or RTL, to generate, or *raise*, an exception when an error occurs. If left as it is, the program would halt when a division by zero was attempted, and a message would be displayed providing information on exactly what caused the exception. However, it is often desirable not to let things go that far, and some sort of handling is usually performed. This is where the **Try** and **Except** keywords come into play.

By beginning a block that you want to protect with the **Try** keyword, you are indicating to the compiler that you want to attempt to execute the instructions that follow it and be notified if they can't be. At the slightest hint of trouble, the flow of execution will leave the protected block and jump immediately to the first instruction after the **Except** keyword. At this point, you are given the opportunity to handle the error in some way, such as displaying an error message, as in our example.

Delphi 32 Changes

The changes that we have discussed thus far apply to both the 16 bit and 32 bit versions of Delphi. With the release of Delphi 32, however, additional significant changes have been made that will affect the way you program.

Strings and Things

Long Strings

At long last, Borland finally took the plunge, and Delphi's implementation of Pascal now supports (hold on to your hat) long strings. By long strings I mean a string whose length is limited only by the amount of memory you have in your computer. Given that the average computer has eight megabytes or so, plus whatever is available because of virtual memory, this can result in a long string indeed!

If you're a long time Borland Pascal 7.0 programmer, you may think that the arrival of long strings will be the devastation that PChar-type strings were. Think again—long strings are slick and well integrated into Delphi. So well integrated that you would need a darn good reason not to abandon other string types in favor of them. Here's the low-down:

- Compatible with both standard Pascal-style strings and with type-casting, PChar strings.

- Efficient memory usage. Unlike Pascal-style strings which used a fixed amount of memory regardless of the number of characters in the string, long strings are dynamically allocated in a block of memory that grows and shrinks depending upon the actual length of the string. Should the block of memory that the string occupies become too small to contain the it, the block will be abandoned for a different and bigger one that is capable of holding the string. The abandoned block then becomes available for other purposes, including other strings.

- If a long string variable is assigned to another long string variable, the string is not copied, but instead a reference is made to the original string. This situation persists providing that neither string changes during the course of it's lifetime. If either string does change, a copy has to be made to preserve the unchanged string. The main power of this feature reveals itself when passing string parameters to procedures and function. Consider the following function that accepts a string, evaluates any mathematical equation that may be embedded in it and outputs the resulting string:

```
function EvaluateString(InString:String):String;
var
  WorkString:String;
begin
  WorkString:=InString;
```

```
    if {math function in string} then
    begin
      {evaluate all equations}
    end;
    EvaluateString:=WorkString;
  end;

  begin
    writeln(EvaluateString('This will be evaluated: 10+20='));
    writeln(EvaluateString('This will not be evaluated'));
  end;
```

When the EvaluateString function is executed for either case shown above, the first thing that happens is that the parameter InString is assigned to the string actually passed to the function. Since this in no way alters the string, a reference is made to the original instead copying it. The same thing occurs when InString is assigned to WorkString. Next a test is performed to see if the string contains a equation that can be evaluated. In no way does the test modify the string, it only examines it. If the test fails, a final assignment occurs, this time assigning the WorkString to EvaluateString, the return value of the function. Because no modification to any of the strings took place, not one single cycle was wasted performing a needless copy. In the event that the test passed, indicating that the string could indeed be evaluated, a copy of the original string would be made in order to preserve it's contents.

Given the power of long strings, it should be no surprise that there are a few caveats:

- With standard Pascal strings, the zeroth character contains the length of the string (hence, the 255 character limitation of such strings). It is therefore not uncommon to encounter manipulations such as these:

```
StrLen:=Byte(MyString[0]);
```

or

```
Byte(MyString[0]):=12;
```

Long string do not support such brute force attacks, and a compiler error will result if one is attempted. Unfortunately, this may break existing code that you wish to port. All is not lost; there are functions included with Delphi specifically for these things. For instance, the length of a string can—and always could—be determined with the Length function. The real reason for accessing the zeroth character, however, is to set the length of a string, something that the new SetLength function excels at.

```
procedure SetLength(S;L:DWord);
```

Where S is the string and L is the length to set it to. Notice that the type for S is not given. This is because through the use of "compiler magic," SetLength can accept pascal-style strings, long strings, and wide strings. It cannot, however, accept zero-based char strings or strings of type PChar.

Length and SetLength make it possible to rewrite the above lines of code:

```
StrLen:=Length(MyString);
```

    and

```
SetLength(MyString,12);
```

- For PChar compatibility the long string must specifically be typecast to PChar.

- Long strings can not be passed to parameters of type OpenString. Similar to open arrays, an OpenString parameter permits a standard pascal-style string of any length to be passed to a procedure. Normally, the string being passed to a procedure must be identical in type to the parameter; OpenString does away with this restriction.

- A long string will not work if passed to a normal string parameter declared as var.

To get Pascal-style strings and long strings to coexist and at the same time promote the use of long strings, Borland *altered* Pascal—It's OK, they practically own it. The Pascal string as we know it is effectively dead; for the moment, however, it has been put out to pasture with a different name,

ShortString. As you may be able to guess, the String type now identifies long strings. Actually, if you are nostalgic and wish to resurrect the Pascal-style strings for a while longer, the $H compiler directive is just the thing for you, By including {$H-} in your program regain their full "power". This does not mean the prospect of using long strings is gone; they have a type all of their own, AnsiString.

In addition to SetLength, there are a few other new functions for string handling. The first is SetString:

```
SetString(var S;P:PChar;Count:DWord):String;
```

This function takes a null terminated string, P and copies it to the long string S. The amount of characters copied is limited by either the Count parameter, or by the length of P— whichever is shorter.

The next group of new functions remove "whitespace" from a string. In case you're confused with the term, whitespace is simply a name for the character produced when the space bar is pressed, or 32 in the ASCII table. The primary reason that you would ever want to do this is to clean up a user's input, which quite frequently will contain an extra space at the end, or somewhat less frequently, at the beginning. Here are the functions you would use for doing this:

```
function TrimLeft(S:String):String;
function TrimRight(S:String):String;
function Trim(S:String):String;
```

The functions TrimLeft and TrimRight do what their names imply: remove whitespace from the left side of the string, and from the right side. Trim is a combination of both, and removes whitespace from both sides of a string in a single operation.

Wide Strings

As you sit here reading this book, consider that it's entire content is represented by relatively few symbols. There are twenty six lowercase letters, twenty six uppercase letters, ten numbers and a small handful of symbols, all of which fit nicely into a single byte, with plenty of room left over for smiley faces, mathematical symbols, the odd foreign language characters and other graphical symbols. For the programmer of the 80's and early 90's, this mixture was a blessing because it did away with the horrors of having operate in graphics mode for what was otherwise strictly a text based application. When the Graphical User Interface, or GUI came into fashion with graphics mode being the norm, this was no longer an issue – any character could be represented by simply using the correct font. The problem was that some character sets could not be represented in their entirety because the number of unique symbols exceeded what could be represented by a single byte. The solution that arose was the double byte character set, or DBCS for short.

What the DBCS attempted to do was to arrange things so the most frequently used characters could be represented with only one byte, while the remaining ones would use part of the first byte and an entire second one. In short, this scheme resulted in headaches and despair because it couldn't be relied upon that a character would one byte or two bytes – it could be either. You certainly could not jump into a string at any old location and expect a valid character because you could very well be jumping on top of the latter part of character instead of it's head. Nor could you easily determine the length of a string; each character had to be individually counted. Remember, these were memory-tight times, so this quasi-compression was tolerated for the time being.

Times change though, and the DBCS has pretty much vanished from the mainstream. Besides, it never really acknowledged another problem, multiple languages in a single file. While it is indeed possible introduce multiple fonts into a single file, it doesn't really address the issue – real life information isn't dressed up in it's Sunday best, it's just data. This is where Unicode fits in. A Unicode character is sixteen bits in length – always. This means that a single Unicode character can be one of 65536 different values, enough to fit all of the characters of all of the languages in the world comfortably. Something in Russian will always be in Russian; even if you use a German font, the underlying data will still be in Russian. Because Unicode is always a fixed size, none of the coding problems from DBCS arise either; you can jump into a string anywhere you want, or determine it's size without having to count individual characters.

So where do Unicode and Delphi meet? That's a tricky question because Delphi 32 supports both Windows NT and Windows 95. The former has full support for Unicode, while the latter, not wishing to break Windows 3.1 applications, does not. This does not preclude the use of Unicode in Windows 95 applications, however, it just makes it somewhat more akward to accomplish. It would be most difficult to support both extremes, so Delphi makes no attempt to do so. What it does do though, is provide a new character type WideChar and a new string type WideString that allow you to implement Unicode as you see fit.

Compiler Optimizations

One feature of Borland's Pascal products that has always generated praise is it's efficient compiler, which can often generate optimized code that rivals hand-tuned assembly language. As good as it is, it has recently gotten better with Delphi 32, incorporating tricks and techniques previously reserved for assembly guru's.

The first optimization takes advantage of the fact that many variables in a program have a relatively short lifetime. The Index variable of a for loop and intermediate calculation values are good examples. Instead of storing such variables in slow memory, Delphi uses the CPU's internal registers to store the information. This results in an exceptionally quick access time, with the end result being that it produces code that executes much faster that the identical non-optimized code.

The next optimization is very similar to the prior one, except instead of storing variables in the CPU's registers, it allows parameters to be passed though them. Normally, parameters are passed using the stack, a horrendously time-eating mechanism, that requires slow memory accesses, and the incrementing and decrementing of pointers. By keeping everything internal to the CPU, the speed-up can be staggering. For example, in one test where I called a function with a parameter one million times, I managed to decrease the amount of time it took from 741 mS to 297 mS, or about 2.5 times faster.

Another optimization caters to the fact that some programmer—especially beginners—don't always write code as efficient as it could be. Sometimes, for instance, you will run across the following situation:

```
function Tan(Angle:Real):Integer;
var
  SinPart:Real;
  CosPart:Real;
begin
  SinPart:=Sin(Angle*PI/180);
  CosPart:=Cos(Angle*PI/180);
  Tan:=SinPart/CosPart;
end;
```

This small function incorporates the mysteriously missing tangent function, but in the process of doing so, some inefficiency has been introduced. The problem lies with the calculation for converting degrees to radians: It is done twice, once for the SinPart variable, and again for the CosPart variable. While a reasonable programmer would try to avoid such an error, often they slip by in the process of moving blocks of code around. Fortunately, Delphi eliminates this problem in it's entirety through the use of common subexpression elimination, Simply put, the compiler realizes that the same calculation is to be done more than once, and generates code so it only has to be calculated once, and then uses the same value in the other places where it is required.

The final optimization that I'll talk about concerns arrays, including strings, that are indexed inside of a loop, as shown in the following example:

```
type
  TS=String[5];
var
  i:Word;
  s:array[1..10] of TS;
begin
  for i:=1 to 10 do
    s[i]:='';
end.
```

Before Delphi 32, the compiler would generate code that required a multiplication to obtain the correct byte offset for s, detailed here in Pascal:

```
type
  TS=String[5];
  PString=^String;
var
  s:array[1..10] of TS;
  i:Word;
  ByteOffset:Word;
begin
  for i:=1 to 10 do
  begin
    ByteOffset:=(i-1)*SizeOf(TS);
    PString(LongInt(@s)+ByteOffset)^:='';
  end;
end.
```

Actually, saying that a multiplication is generated is a half-truth. While it is true that a multiplication is performed, the CPU's internal multiplication instruction is not used. Instead, whenever possible, it is emulated using faster shift and addition instructions. Even with this enhancement, Delphi 32's method of indexing arrays leaves the old methods behind in the dust.

What Delphi 32 does that is so amazing is a standard practice used by assembly programmers for decades. Instead of performing a multiplication for each iteration, a simple addition can be done in it's place. In the above example, the number of bytes occupied by the type TS is six— five characters and one size byte. By adding six for each iteration of the loop, the index is properly updated:

```
type

  TS=String[5];
  PString=^String;
var
  s:array[1..10] of TS;
  i:Word;
  ByteOffset:Word;
```

```
begin
  ByteOffset:=0;
  for i:=1 to 10 do
  begin
    PString(LongInt(@s)+ByteOffset)^:='';
    inc(ByteOffset,SizeOf(TS));
  end;
end.
```

Initialization and Finalization Sections

One of the smaller features that I failed to mention about the 16-bit version of Delphi is the Initialization keyword. Basically, it is used inside of a unit to create a section of code that is called whenever the unit is initialized. This functionality is nothing new, and could be accomplished in the past by simply forgoing the Initilization keyword and enclosing the initialization code between the begin and end statements at the end of the unit.

Sometimes, it is useful to uninitialize a unit, or clean up any loose ends. This is an awkward task under Borland Pascal because a pointer to the default exit procedure must be modified to point at a custom exit procedure, and when the custom exit procedure is called, it in turn must call the default exit procedure—much like intercepting an interrupt call. Thing got marginally better starting with Delphi 16. Rather than having to muck about with pointers, the function AddExitProc was introduced that did the mucking about for you provided you passed it the procedure you wanted to call instead of the default exit procedure.

Delphi 32 sticks it's tongue out at the methods just described, and provides the elegant Finalization keyword, which like Initialization is placed at the end of the unit. The only requirement is that it follows the Initialization section. Here is a short example of how the Initialization and Finalization keywords are used:

```
unit Test
  .
  .
  .
var
```

```
  Buffer:Pointer;
initialization
  GetMem(Buffer,2048);
finalization
  FreeMem(Buffer,2048);
end.
```

In this admittedly contrived example, a block of memory is allocated when the unit starts up, and is freed when the unit shuts down.

The Delphi Advantage

If you are a C or C++ programmer, I really have sympathy for you. You have chosen or have been forced to choose the hard path whether you know it or not, and sadly you probably don't. However, you are reading this book, so there must be hope for you yet! Let's see if I can put you on the path to Delphi. For the rest of you who may be thinking of sticking to Borland Pascal, Ada, or whatever, this is for you too.

Programming. What is it? When you write a program, there is one and only one goal in mind. Maybe it is to do accounting, determine the concentration of chemicals, or sort socks by color and age; there is only one purpose to the program. Without this purpose, your program would quickly fall to pieces, and you would have no market, no matter how many goodies you stuff into it. By goodies, I mean things like print preview, spell checkers, the capability to compile in the background while you play solitaire, and so on. None of these things contribute to the purpose of the program. The question that then remains is: Why do we put so many goodies into our programs? Of course, it boils down to the same old story—dollars and cents. This is fine, because both of our jobs depend upon it; but doesn't it strike you as a bit distasteful to be programming so many goodies when you could be concentrating on refining and enhancing the functionality of the sole purpose of your code? It bothers me; which is why I work mostly with VxD's, embedded systems, and most important, Delphi.

Delphi is chock-full of goodies in the form of components. As mentioned previously, components allow thousands of lines of tested and reliable code to be dropped into your program easily. These are thousands of lines of code that you don't have to write and debug yourself. There is the unfortunate tendency among programmers to think that their job performance is based upon how many lines of code they write. This simply isn't true. It wasn't even true in the not-so-distant past when programmers sat at their terminals keying in line after line of code, working into the early morning hours trying to meet the project deadline and still shipping with bugs in the end. Management cares only about two things: robustness of the product and how fast it can be completed.

I feel that Delphi gains a big advantage over its competition because it is built upon Pascal instead of another language like C or C++. Pascal is quite capable of holding its own against these other languages, and the resulting code is usually more readable, almost to the extent of approaching self-documenting, and as such, is easier to maintain.

Delphi Compared to Visual Basic

Delphi and Visual Basic share the common bond that both are visual programming environments. However, this is where the similarity ends. Despite its widespread use, the fact remains that Visual Basic just can't compete with all the powerful features that Delphi offers:

- Visual Basic requires a huge run-time DLL. This DLL contains most of a Visual Basic application's functionality, and without it the application cannot run. Delphi applications require no run-time DLL, and are completely standalone. This may or may not be an advantage depending on your point of view: On one hand, the presence of the run-time DLL allows many Visual Basic applications to share it, thereby reducing the amount of disk space required. On the other hand, the more files that ship with an application, the more likely it becomes that one will be forgotten in the final shipping version. Also, many applications don't always put the run-time DLL into the **\WINDOWS** directory as they should, but instead they put it into the application's directory, creating many duplicate run-time DLLs that serve only to use up hard drive space.

- As with its external run-time DLL, Visual Basic controls are external files—DLLs that merely have a **.VBX** extension. The same problems exist with these as with the run-time DLL, only more so because of potential version compatibility problems. For instance, suppose that you are installing an application that also installs a certain control. Further, suppose that you install another application that uses the same control, only newer. What happens to the first control? The only options available are to replace it or leave it as it is. Either way, chances are good that there will now be a problem running one of the applications. With Delphi, components are linked right into the executable, erasing any fears of compatibility problems.

- Visual Basic is interpreted. If you have ever looked at the size of a Visual Basic **.EXE** file, you probably observed that it is quite small. This is because the majority of the file contains tokens that indicate what function to call in the run-time DLL. These tokens require only a few bytes a piece to store, so a even a reasonably large project can be stored in a relatively small file. This is where Visual Basic takes a major performance hit—determining what function to call based upon a token takes a long time. Consequently, the same application written with Delphi will run much faster because the code generated by it is truly compiled.

- Visual Basic has gained a good portion of its popularity because of the vast library of controls available for it. But what if you want to make your own control? Well, you must learn C and become proficient with an API that will have little relevance to anything else you do. Chances are that the control you want to create is similar to something that already exists. Does this mean that you can build upon this existing control? Sort of. If you have mastered the Windows API and have stomach for it, it is possible to write a VBX that *wraps around* an existing VBX; but it is a very messy proposition. Whatever method you choose for creating a VBX inevitably you will have to do some debugging. Debugging a VBX is about as enjoyable as walking on hot coals. Not only do you have to run an application that uses the control, but you also have to use CodeView or a similar debugger. What comes out of this is an epileptic seizure provoking nightmares of screen flipping and a stream of angry growls with each inevitable reboot.

Delphi rises above all this by providing the capability to create and debug components *within* the IDE. In addition, it is a simple matter to take a pre-existing component and extend it to provide the functionality that you want. In fact, it is so simple to create a custom component that many new Delphi projects being developed are simply a collection of components all interlinked together. This makes these projects highly modular and permits ridiculously easy testing of individual pieces of the project. No one in his right mind would even think about trying do this with Visual Basic.

With these points in mind, it is easy to see why you would want to write any new projects using Delphi rather than Visual Basic. If you have already invested a lot of time and money developing a Visual Basic application, you may be understandably hesitant to switch over to Delphi. Relax; a product called Conversion Assistant, by EarthTrek, converts Visual Basic projects to Delphi projects. Firsthand experience shows it to be a reliable and robust product. All that is required is to feed it your Visual Basic source, and it will spit out Delphi source code and forms similar to their Visual Basic counterparts. In addition, it should be noted that Delphi 1.0 can use Visual Basic 1.0 VBX Controls, but Delphi 2.0 can't use *any* VBX controls at all. What this means to you , at least in the case of Delphi 1.0, is that you don't have to repurchase the same controls for Delphi, you can simply reuse them.

The Impact Delphi Will Make

We have just finished exploring what Delphi can do for you at the present. I will now take some time to speculate on the changes Delphi will make to our lives in the future.

According to a source at Borland, the response they received after the release of Delphi greatly exceeded all their expectations. I believe that this underestimation on their part is somewhat analogous to being so close to a painting that you can't see the beauty of what is on the canvas. This response came as no surprise to me and to others who had the privilege to beta-test or review Delphi and could see the dramatic impact that it was going to make.

The first impact was set in motion long before Delphi was released to the general public. Dozens of third-party vendors started and finished the task of building component libraries. Some components in these libraries are merely direct ports of Visual Basic controls; whereas others are built from scratch. Either way, it means that there is a huge existing code base available right now that you can use in your projects. This trend still continues, and as such the market will soon be saturated with low-cost component libraries of exceptional quality as one vender attempts to outdo the other. You will be the one to reap the benefit of these wars; and perhaps, if you are bold enough, decide to become an active participant in them. It only requires one idea to get started, and it really doesn't have to be your own, just choose something and improve upon it—there is always a way to make something better. Timing is everything though, and by the time you read this, it may already be too late. Remember, the competition will have the lead on you, and it may take months to get to point where they are, or at least *were* when you started, because they also had the same amount of time to improve upon their own product.

Although I have no knowledge of it, I predict the second impact is already underway—new Delphi-like packages from other companies. It is a sure bet that beta testers and reviewers were not alone when they saw how exceptional and revolutionary Delphi was. Borland's competitors were also watching. Like all good ideas, Delphi will not remain King of the Hill for very long. Maybe even by the time you read this the throne that it currently occupies will have a Microsoft product in it. Does this mean that you should find a cave and shiver in a corner until a clear victor appears? No, there will never be a winner. Just like the C/C++ conflict between Borland, Symantec, Microsoft, Watcom, and others that started years ago and still rages on today, there will never be a RAD tool champion. You have got to accept that there will always be good tools available, and like it or not you have to make a choice between them. But if you don't count the false start from Visual Basic, Delphi was first, and it is a solid product available today, with the Windows 95 version just around the corner.

Delphi-like products that I think you will see are:

- Visual C++. Not the Visual C++ that we know today, which incidentally I feel is a misleading name because of Visual Basic, but a true visual environment that uses C++ code as a language for implementation, but a Delphi or Visual Basic type visual environment. Microsoft will not be limited to this product though, *every* C++ vendor will jump on it, providing us with seemingly endless compatibilities and choices, but mostly just confusing us. Will this never end?

- A new and improved Visual Basic that can compete with Delphi. This would mean that the code would have to be truly compiled and that controls would be linked right in with the executable rather than being separate modules. The inevitability of this will make many Visual Basic users sit tight and wait rather than switch to Delphi.

What you won't see are any Pascal based Delphi-like products. Borland was brave when they made this decision to base Delphi on Pascal, and I loudly applaud them for it as do millions of other Pascal users. The fact remains that people have attitudes that prevent them from using anything but C/C++, and the manufacturers know it. So if you want to program in Pascal (and why wouldn't you?), you will be stuck with Delphi. Don't worry about this too much because it means that there will be only one product for you to choose, and what a fine choice it is!

My third and final prediction is a bit gloomy. If you are presently a good programmer, you undoubtedly have spent many years practicing and perfecting your craft. Because of its simplicity and power, Delphi will produce a glut of new programmers who can create products just as good as you can, without all the anguish and torment you went through. It is quite possible that through bad technical understanding of management, that one of these new programmers will get a job for which you are more qualified simply because they wrote X number of successful applications in less amount of time than it took you to write the same number. Rather than feeling contempt for the newcomer, which I admit will be hard to do, you should take comfort in the knowledge that you have amassed years of techniques and methods that cannot be replaced by any product, even one as good as Delphi. The better companies will time after time choose a person with your skills rather than the new programmer; and because you probably want to work for this sort of company, you have little to worry about.

If you are a newcomer to the world of programming and are letting Delphi be your guide, you have chosen the best and most exciting time possible. With Delphi, you already have your foot in the door to a successful programming career. However, there is one gotcha to be aware of: Delphi is just one product, and like I mentioned previously, it won't be King of the Hill forever. If you are serious about being a professional programmer, you must not wear Delphi blinders, and instead, you should take time out occasionally to explore the latest offerings available.

Introduction to the Visual Component Library

The VCL is truly the heart and soul of Delphi. Without it, Delphi would just be Borland Pascal 8.0, offering little advantage over its predecessor. Because the VCL is obviously so important, let's spend a few moments looking into what it is and how it is integrated with Delphi.

Earlier, I mentioned that VCL stands for Visual Component Library. This is the definition I see used the most, which is why I adopted it for this book; but on occasion you may find it referred to as the Visual *Class* Library, even in Borland's own documentation. I think that this definition is more in the spirit of what the VCL really is, except maybe for the unfortunate use of the word "visual." You see, beyond providing components that you can add to forms, the VCL also provides classes for more code-oriented things, such as maintaining lists of things with **TList**, managing printed output with **TPrinter**, and encapsulating the Windows Clipboard with **TClipboard**. These things are just icing on an already superb cake. However, let's not dwell on this because we are really interested in components.

When you add a component to a form, two things happen. First, you see the component on the form; and second, the class declaration of the form contained in the respective unit gains a new member variable of the same type as the component just added. It is through the use of this variable that you can access the component's properties and call its methods.

As you work with a component on a form, it may eventually become necessary to respond to some of the events that a component can generate. Component events trigger code in the forms unit to be executed based upon what sort of event occurred. For example, you might give a push button an event that causes a list of files to appear whenever the button was clicked on by the mouse.

You may be wondering how a component is initialized because there is no indication in the unit's code of doing so. The secret to understanding this is in knowing that the form becomes part of the unit because of the **{$R *.DFM}** contained in it, and therefore the form has knowledge of what the unit contains and vice versa. When the form is created by a call to **CreateForm**, the components it contains are created as well, without regard to the code contained in the unit. The form then uses its knowledge of the unit to assign the appropriate component member variable the proper value.

Two Distinct Kinds of Components

The primary way that a computer relays information to its user is by showing something on its display, whether it be text or graphics. In this age of Graphical User Interfaces, or GUIs, the display has transformed from its previous role as an output only device, and now is widely used as an *input* device. No, I am not talking about touch screens or light pens, but rather the mouse cursor. Although it really can't be considered a *device*, it can be considered a *virtual device* because it visually reflects the physical location of your mouse; and indeed, we often think of the mouse cursor and the mouse as being one and the same.

Most Delphi components take advantage of this visual input/output scenario and display on your screen images that you can watch, like a gas gauge, and sometimes images that you can interact with, like a button. Appropriately, these are known as *visual components*, reflecting the fact that they can be seen at run time. Of course, the traditional method of input, namely the keyboard, has not been forgotten and is still used for text entry in components such as edit boxes, as well as shortcuts for things like buttons and menus. All these have a visual presence on the screen, and therefore also qualify as visual components.

User interaction, although important, is only a small part of what a component is capable of doing. Sometimes it is necessary for a program to interact with the inner-workings of the computer, such as serial ports, timers, and database files, none of which would really qualify for a run time visual interface. Components that encapsulate these sorts of things are known as *nonvisual* components. At design time, a nonvisual component is depicted on a form as a little bitmap that indicates the component's function. In addition, properties can be set through the use of the Object Inspector, relieving the programmer from having to do it in the code and making future changes more accessible and convenient.

Bearing these major differences between visual and nonvisual components in mind, it is only fair to treat them as separate entities. I have divided the remainder of this book into two sections. The first deals with nonvisual components because they are the simplest to create and understand; thus paving the way to the second and somewhat more complex section, visual components, that show how to provide a gateway between the computer and the user.

CHAPTER 2

CREATING A SIMPLE NONVISUAL COMPONENT

In this chapter, you will become acquainted with the fundamental concepts behind programming nonvisual components. In first half of the chapter, we will focus on the basics:

- The component hierarchy
- Discussion of **TComponent**
- Creating a generic component
- Streamlining the component creation process with the Component Expert

In the second half of the chapter, we will create our first useful component that will serve to explore the following:

- Tackling a real-world problem
- Creating hidden windows to process messages
- Creating properties and event handlers

The Component Hierarchy

All the components that come with Delphi are ultimately derived from **TComponent**. This provides them with a level of compatibility that ensures they will behave as you and the Delphi environment expect them to. It therefore stands to reason that any component you create should also be derived from **TComponent** or one of its descendants.

The basic component hierarchy is a much like a family tree because it shows the relationships that components have to one another. It is this similarity that provides an explanation on how words like "ancestor" or "parent," "descendant" or "child," and "sibling" have evolved in object-oriented programming. The difference between the component hierarchy and all other objects in Object Pascal and a real family tree stems from the fact that there can be only *one* parent for a given child, although parents can have multiple children. In real life, a child is a combination of its parents' characteristics, so it is only natural to assume that with one parent, a child component would inherit *all* of its one parent's functionality. Much like real children grow and attain new skills that make them different from their parents, child components can add to and replace parts of the functionality that they have inherited from their parent.

Components descended from **TComponent** inherit a relatively large amount of predefined functionality in the form of properties and methods. At this stage, it becomes vital to give this some detailed attention to provide an understanding of how things work at the lowest level of component operation.

TComponent Dissected

TComponent is derived from **TPersistent**, which in turn is derived from **TObject**, the base class of Object Pascal that all classes are descendants of. It is **TPersistent**'s job to write and read the published properties of a component to and from a *form file*, which is simply a file with a **.DFM** extension that Delphi creates whenever you save a form. This is necessary to ensure that any form and the components it contains are reloaded with all the same property settings as when they were saved. Needless to say, **TPersistent** is crucial to the whole Delphi concept. Despite this, however, we will accept it as a "black box" that does what it does, and we will only explore it in the context of **TComponent**—how it can be used to store and retrieve *unpublished* properties. We will take a similar stand with **TObject** and discuss it only as far as it relates to **TComponent.**

Before we get into the thick of things, one item must be mentioned. In the following member descriptions, you will encounter the words "form" and "component" used interchangeably when talking about the same thing. This is because *forms are components*. **TForm** is inherited from **TComponent** just like every other component, so the same rules apply to it. Most often, forms will be referred to as components when we're talking about owned components, because the owner is usually a form.

TComponent Properties

ComponentCount

```
property ComponentCount:Integer;
```

This property is accessible only at run time and is read-only. Reading the value of **ComponentCount** returns the number of components owned by the component. **TPanel** and **TGroupBox** are examples of components that can own components.

ComponentIndex

```
property ComponentIndex:Integer;
```

This property is accessible only at run time and is read-only. Reading the value of **ComponentIndex** returns the index of the component in the **Components** array property, which is maintained by the component's owner.

Components

```
property Components[Index:Integer]:TComponent;
```

This property is accessible only at run time and is read-only. Reading the value of the array property **Components** with a given index will return the corresponding child **TComponent** class. The maximum index can be obtained by reading the **ComponentCount** property and subtracting one to account for the zero-based **Components** array.

ComponentState

```
property ComponentState:TComponentState;
```

This property is accessible only at run time and is read-only. Reading the value of **ComponentState** returns a value of type **TComponentState** that reflects any special mode that the component is in or any special action that it may be doing. This is better understood by looking at declaration of **TComponentState**:

```
TComponentState = set of (csLoading, csReading, csWriting,
  csDestroying, csDesigning);
```

Each member of the set (more on sets in Chapter 3) has a particular meaning when it is set:

Member	Meaning
csLoading	The component is in the process of being loaded.
csReading	The property values for the component are being read from a stream.
csWriting	The property values for the component are being written to a stream.
csDestroying	The component is about to be destroyed.
csDesigning	The component is on a form currently being designed with the Delphi IDE.

Of these members, the one that you will probably use most frequently is **csDesigning**. It is most useful during the design phase of your project if you want to prevent certain things from occurring. For example, in Chapter 3 we develop a serial communications component that has several properties that dictate which port to use and what its settings are. At run time, the port is opened, and changing any of the settings causes a change in the appropriate communications hardware, which is a good thing. But it would not be a good thing if this was to happen while we were designing a form. To remedy this minor problem, the **ComponentState** is checked to see if the **csDesigning** flag is set, and if it is, the hardware settings remain untouched despite any modifications to the properties that may be made.

DesignInfo

```
property DesignInfo:Longint;
```

DesiginInfo is used only by the form designer, so don't mess with it!

Name

```
property Name:TComponentName;   {TComponentName: string[63];}
```

This property may be accessed at both design time and run time. **Name** is a string that has the name of the component stored in it, which was set during the design phase of your project. By default, Delphi labels components with the type name less the "T" (**TCheckBox** becomes simply **CheckBox**) and sticks an index on the end: CheckBox1, CheckBox2, CheckBox3, etc. It is of little value to know the name of a component, except maybe if you are creating an array of components and you want to parse the name to find a particular index contained in it. If this is your intention, a much better way would be to use the **Tag** property of the component because it returns a **LongInt** and therefore does not require any parsing.

Owner

```
property Owner: TComponent;
```

This property may be accessed only during run time and is read-only. Reading the value of **Owner** returns the **TComponent** class for the owner of the component.

Tag

```
property Tag: Longint;
```

This property may be accessed at both design time and run time and can be written to or read from. The **Tag** property is not used by Delphi in any way. It is provided solely for the use of the programmer to store information that may be relevant to the component or how it is used in the program. A common use is to create an array of components. For example, you may have six push buttons that perform similar but slightly different functions—maybe pushing each one displays a different farm animal. By setting the **OnClick** event for each button to point at the same function, the value of the tag field can be used to determine which animal to show. This becomes particularly appealing if you consider that the animal can be changed by modifying the **Tag** property at design time without having to wade through source code.

TComponent Methods

ChangeName

```
procedure ChangeName(const NewName: TComponentName);
```

This procedure allows you to alter the internal name of the component. See the description of the **Name** property for more information.

Create

```
constructor Create(AOwner: TComponent); virtual;
```

The **Create** constructor is the first step toward bringing a component to life. It allocates memory for the component and sets all the properties to their default values. Normally, **Create** is called automatically for you during the loading of a form, but it is possible to call it yourself and add a component to a form at run time. For such an important method, there is really little else to say, except that its **AOwner** parameter is the class that owns it.

DefineProperties

```
procedure DefineProperties(Filer: TFiler); virtual;
```

TComponent inherits this member from **TPersistent**. Normally, only published properties are saved and loaded to and from a form file, but by overriding **DefineProperties**, it becomes possible to do the same for unpublished data. The primary reason for doing this is that some property types, such as arrays, cannot be declared as **published**. A secondary reason for doing this is to hide properties that can be visually manipulated and therefore do not require any additional method of doing so. A good example of this is the timer component whose left and top properties are changed by simply moving it around on the screen. Because the component is nonvisual and hence invisible at run time, its exact placement isn't critical, so there is no need to publish its left and top properties, which would be useful only if an exact position was required.

Once **DefineProperties** has been overridden, it is necessary to indicate what data to include. This is where the **Filer** parameter, which is a class of type **TFiler**, comes into play. **Filer** provides a method called **DefineProperty** that allows unpublished data to be included with published properties:

```
procedure DefineProperty(const Name: string; ReadData: TReaderProc;
  WriteData: TWriterProc;  HasData: Boolean);
```

The **Name** parameter is required to identify the property in the form file and is often the same as the property itself. The **ReadData** and **WriteData** parameters identify which member functions of **TComponent** to call, depending on whether data is being read from a form file or written to one. Read operations use the following function template:

```
TReaderProc = procedure(Reader: TReader) of object;
```

As you may notice, this procedure itself has a parameter, **Reader,** that is of type **TReader**, which provides methods such as **ReadInteger**, **ReadFloat**, and **ReadBoolean** that permit the data to be read from a form file. Write operations use a similar function template:

```
TWriterProc = procedure(Writer: TWriter) of object;
```

The only difference here is that the parameter **Writer** is of type **TWriter**, and as you might expect, it provides methods like **WriteInteger**, **WriteFloat**, and **WriteBoolean** that are used to write data to a form file.

Don't feel bad if you are confused at this stage—it all seems difficult because of the many different classes working in unison to provide what on the surface appears to be a simple operation. In Chapter 9, we will shed more light on the subject and provide an example of how it is used.

Destroy

```
destructor Destroy; virtual;
```

Destroy, the opposite of **Create**, is normally called automatically whenever a form is closed. Unlike **Create**, you should never call this method yourself; instead, you should call **Free** to remove the component at run time.

DestroyComponents

```
procedure DestroyComponents;
```

Calling this method will result in all the components owned by this component to be destroyed. Typically, this is called automatically whenever the component is about to be destroyed, ensuring that everything has been cleaned up.

Destroying

```
procedure Destroying
```

This method does two things. First, it sets the **csDestroying** flag of the **ComponentState** property, and second it calls **Destroying** for each owned component. You will rarely, if ever, need to call this method.

FindComponent

```
function FindComponent(const AName: string): TComponent;
```

This method simply performs a case-insensitive search through the list of all owned components and returns the one whose **Name** property matches the **AName** parameter.

Free

```
procedure Free;
```

Free is used to dispose of the component at run time by calling the **Destroy** destructor. Before it does this however, it ensures that the instance of the object is non-nil. Because of this level of protection, it is usually better to call **Free** instead of calling **Destroy** directly.

HasParent

```
function HasParent: Boolean; virtual;
```

This method returns true if the component's parent is responsible for writing and reading the component to and from the form file.

InsertComponent

```
procedure InsertComponent(AComponent: TComponent);
```

This method adds the component indicated by the **AComponent** parameter to the **Components** array. It is important to ensure that any component added this way has a **Name** property unique from all other components already in the array. The easiest way to accomplish this is to forgo naming the component. Once a component has been added, its destruction will occur automatically whenever its owner is destroyed, removing the need to do so manually.

Loaded

```
procedure Loaded; virtual;
```

After a component's published properties have been retrieved from a form file, this method is called. Overriding it provides a convenient location to do any initialization that requires property values.

Notification

```
procedure Notification(AComponent: TComponent; Operation:
  TOperation); virtual;
```

This method is called whenever an owned component is about to have one of the operations defined by **TOperation** performed on it. Currently, **TOperation** only contains two members, **opInsert** and **opRemove**. By overriding **Notification**, it is possible for the owner to make adjustments, typically to the screen, to compensate for the new addition or deletion. For example, the space between tools in a toolbar can be made smaller to accommodate the addition of a new tool.

ReadState

```
procedure ReadState(Reader: TReader); virtual;
```

This method is called whenever the component has to retrieve properties and data from the **Reader** object, which typically is associated with a form file.

RemoveComponent

```
procedure RemoveComponent(AComponent: TComponent);
```

RemoveComponent is the opposite of **InsertComponent**. Rather than specifying a component that is to be added to the list of owned components, the **AComponent** parameter indicates a component that is to be deleted from the list. Any removed component will obviously no longer be automatically destroyed when its owner is destroyed, so it is necessary to do so manually by calling its **Free** method.

SetDesigning

```
procedure SetDesigning(Value: Boolean);
```

This method is called with the **Value** parameter set to **True** to indicate that the component is currently being manipulated with the form editor, and as a result the **csDesigning** flag of the **ComponentState** member is also set. When **Value** is **False**, the opposite occurs; **csDesigning** is cleared, and the component is aware that it is alive at run time. Any call to **SetDesigning** has the effect of calling the **SetDesigning** members of all owned components to ensure that their **csDesigning** flag is also set. There should never be an occasion when it is necessary to call this member yourself because it is already part of the functionality of **TComponent** and is done for you automatically.

SetName

```
procedure SetName(const NewName: TComponentName); virtual;
```

This member is called whenever the **Name** property is changed, calling **ChangeName** to actually set the name of the component to **NewName**. Rarely, if ever, will you have to override **SetName**.

ValidateRename

```
procedure ValidateRename(AComponent: TComponent; const CurName,
  NewName: string); virtual;
```

This method is called by **SetName**, and its purpose is to verify that a component can successfully be renamed from its current name, **CurName**, to something else, **NewName**. It performs two tests to do this: First, it checks to see if the **AComponent** parameter is **nil**, which a valid component cannot be. Second, the list of currently owned components is searched to see if the new name is already in use by another component—all owned components must have unique names. If either of these tests fail, an **EComponentError** exception is raised. You should hardly ever encounter a situation where this **ValidateRename** will need to be called directly, because it is done for you whenever **SetName** is called as a result of setting the **Name** property.

WriteComponents

```
procedure WriteComponents(Writer: TWriter); virtual;
```

The purpose of **WriteComponents** is to allow contained components to be written to a form file by calling each component's **WriteState** method. Generally, only windowed components are permitted to have owned components, so the code for actually iterating through the owned component list is not implemented in **TComponent**. The full functionality of **WriteComponents** first appears with the **TWinControl** descendant, which overrides this normally do-nothing method.

WriteState

```
procedure WriteState(Writer: TWriter); virtual;
```

This method is called whenever the component has to send properties and data to the **Writer** object, which typically is associated with a form file.

If you took the time to read the descriptions for each of the properties and methods, you probably noticed that most of them—especially the methods—will never need to be used because the functionality that they provide (or allow you to override) is already implemented to such an extent that there would be little, if any, improvement in doing so. I can't really criticize Borland for leaving so many "unneeded" things available to the programmer because you never know—one day you might need them. If you worked with Borland Pascal 7.0 and OWL, you might have discovered this the hard way, like I did. One of the last major applications I wrote used OWL exclusively; unfortunately, during the course of the project, many problems were discovered that would have been easy to fix had everything been open-ended. For example, the printer unit that provided objects that allowed painless printing had a lazy Cancel button. You could click on it as much as you wanted, but the command to cancel would not take effect until the next band. I didn't want to write all the code over, and I didn't want users complaining about this, so I did the only reasonable thing I could think of: I modified the source code. This worked, but it was ugly. I had a similar experience trying to dispatch dynamic methods. The code for doing this was contained in the **OWINDOWS.PAS** unit, but it was private, so I was unable to call it. The solution? I copied that chunk of code and put it in my own unit—again, not the preferred answer, but the quickest one. The moral of the story is don't knock too much flexibility even if you have to wade through piles of information trying to find what you are looking for.

I could give you pages of information on how components work from the lowest to the highest level, but you probably wouldn't learn anything.

No one ever learns anything if they don't find it interesting. I want to teach you, not bore you, so let's get to work on something fun and leave the other stuff in the manuals where it belongs.

Your First Component

The time has come for me to describe the techniques that you will use to create your very first component. They are equally applicable to the last component you ever write, so pay attention closely.

Parentage and Naming Your Component

The first step in component creation is to decide from which preexisting component class it should be derived. This generally requires looking at all the components in the component hierarchy and finding the one that most closely meets your needs. For nonvisual components, **TComponent** is usually the class of choice, and it is the one that we will use here.

It is also necessary to choose a name for your component. This is normally an easy procedure that involves providing some sort of descriptive text as to the function your component performs. For this example, the name will be **TSimple**, indicating the component's nature. The "T" in front of "Simple" is not mandatory, but it is a convention used to indicate a type declaration. It is possible to do away with it and still have functioning code, but it is not really a good idea because the Delphi environment makes the assumption that it will be there, and for the purpose of easy reading, the first character of every component type is deleted when displaying their names in various places. For example, if you run your mouse cursor slowly along the component palette, component names such as MainMenu, PopupMenu, and Label will appear, even though they are known internally as TMainMenu, TPopupMenu, and TLabel.

With the ancestor and name decided, we can start to write some code to begin implementation of the component:

```
unit Simple;
interface
```

```
uses Classes;
type
  TSimple=class(TComponent)
  end;
implementation
end.
```

The first thing you may notice in the preceding code is the **unit** keyword located at the top. This is used to indicate that the file will be a *unit*, which is simply a module of code that can be linked into a program or a library, instead of a program. This modularity itself makes a unit highly reusable, which is fortunate because Delphi requires that all components be placed into units. It is usually a good idea to name the unit the same as the component itself, but foregoing the "T" prefix.

The **interface** portion of the preceding unit indicates what types, variables, functions, and so on are available to other units and program files. The **uses** keyword tells the compiler what units will be needed to successfully compile the unit. In this case, we are using the **Classes** unit, which provides the declaration for **TComponent** as well as all its functionality. The type declaration for **TSimple** is also indicated in the **interface** part. Notice that it is a direct descendant of **TComponent** and that nothing has been overridden.

Finally, we change scope from **interface** to **implementation**. The **implementation** section is where all the actual coding is to occur, but right now it is simply terminated with **end.** to indicate the end of the unit.

Registering the Component

At this point, although the component class has been declared, it is somewhat less than useful because there is no mechanism to tell Delphi that is a component. The process for doing this is known as *registering* the component; it involves creating an exported procedure called **Register**:

```
unit Simple;
interface
uses Classes;
```

```
type
  TSimple=class(TComponent)
  end;
procedure Register;
implementation

procedure Register;
begin
  RegisterComponents('Additional', [TSimple]);
end;
end.
```

Here we see an altered version of our component code. In the **interface** part you will notice the forward declaration of the **Register** procedure, whose full declaration occurs in the **implementation** part. The contents of **Register** contains a call to **RegisterComponents** that does the actual registering of the component. The first parameter specifies the component group that **TSimple** is to become part of. It can be any of the predefined groups such as "Standard," "Additional," "Data Access," and so forth, or if you don't feel any of these groups is descriptive of your component, you can name it something else; and when you add the component to the library, a new group of the same name will be created for you. For now, we'll stick with "Additional," but feel free to experiment with other names.

The second parameter of **RegisterComponents** is an open array that accepts component types. Because it is an open array, you can specify multiple types in it to register more than one component at a time, all of which will be put in the same group. If you want different groups for different components, you will need to call **RegisterComponents** more than once.

Finishing Touches

Now, there are piles of complex things left over that must be done to get the component up and running. Just kidding; the component is done! All that remains is to add it to the component library. To do this, you will need the code for **SIMPLE.PAS**, which if you have gone through the installation procedure of the disk included with this book, can be found in the **\DC\CHAP02** directory of your hard drive. Once you have located the code, fire up Delphi, if it isn't running already, and select **Options, Install Components, Add**, and **Browse**. A dialog box will open that will allow you to locate **\DC\CHAP02\SIMPLE.PAS**. Once you have located it, click OK, and the dialog box will disappear. Finally to complete the installation process, click OK in the Install Components dialog box. Your hard drive will churn for what may seem like an eternity, but eventually, it will stop. When it does, click on the **Additional** component group tab, and you should see a new component added to the end of the list. Congratulations, you have created and installed your first working component!

I can sense that you are feeling somewhat skeptical as to whether this really worked. The best way to put your concerns to rest is to create a new project by selecting **File** and then **New Project** from the menu. If your Delphi configuration displays the form gallery, select the blank project icon and click **OK**. Now, from the "additional" component group, select **Simple** and then click somewhere on the blank form you just created. The image of the component should now be on the form. Ensure that the Object Inspector is visible and that the properties window is up. If the Simple component is not selected (surrounded with eight black handles), do so by clicking on it. The Object Inspector should now be displaying two properties for the component: Name and Tag. Go ahead and change any property to any value that you want, and move the component anywhere you want. Now save the project, close it, and reopen it. Any of the properties that you changed should still be changed, and the position of the component should be where you left it.

The Component Expert

Remember back in high school when you were taught algebra and the teacher not only showed you the equations that you had to remember, but also how they were derived? Rarely was it necessary to go into this detail to use the equations, but he was making an attempt to show you how things go together and hopefully to excite you about the beauty of mathematics. I have to admit it; I pulled the same thing on you. I showed you step by step how to create a component when there's an automated way of doing it. It wasn't my intention to deceive you, but rather to excite you about the underlying simplicity of the component creation process.

It is the job of the Component Expert to perform all the steps that we just went through in just one step. To activate the Component Expert, select **Component**, then **New**. A dialog box like the one shown in Figure 2.1 will appear. Notice that there is a space for the class name, the ancestor type, and the palette page.

To create TSimple using the Component Expert, type in **TSimple2** for the class name. We will call it this to differentiate this component from the original **TSimple**. Next select **TComponent** for the ancestor type, and finally choose **Additional** for the palette page. As soon as you click OK, a new unit will be created that contains everything that we put into the original and more. The only thing left to do is to save the unit as **SIMPLE2**. Don't worry about changing the unit name; this will be done for you automatically as part of the save.

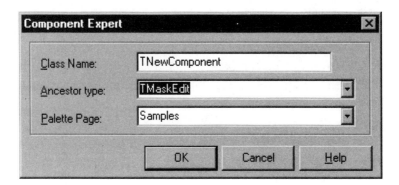

Figure 2.1 The Component Expert.

I just mentioned that the new unit contains more than our original did. The extra stuff includes additional units in the uses statement and private, protected, public, and published sections in the class declaration. None of these are needed for a component of this simplicity, but most components are admittedly not this simple, and some extras will be needed. Don't worry about any of this bulking up the resultant code, however, because if a unit is not used, the code for it isn't linked into the executable. Similarly, the private, protected, public, and published sections don't add any code unless there is something in them.

One limitation of the Component Expert is that it is only capable of automatically generating code for one component per unit. If you want to have more than this, you will have to either manually enter the required code or copy it from somewhere else.

Component Bitmaps

Both of the components that we just created are visually depicted by a bitmap of a blue square, yellow circle, and a red triangle. This may be fine for a test component, but something more descriptive is usually desirable for professional-quality components. This entails designing a custom bitmap. Fortunately, Delphi comes with a program called Image Editor that not only allows you to create and edit bitmaps, but also icons and cursors.

In actuality, the Image Editor is really just a scaled-down version of a conventional resource editor, like Resource Workshop. The only difference between the file produced by a resource editor and a component resource file produced by Image Editor is the extension; the latter has a **DCR** extension (short for dynamic component resource) instead of the standard **RES** extension of the former. This being the case, it should come as no surprise that a **DCR** file can contain bitmaps for any number of components—identical to how a resource file can also contain multiple bitmap images.

The name of the **DCR** file has to be the same as the component file itself. For example, because our component file is called **SIMPLE.PAS**, it follows that the DCR file must be called **SIMPLE.DCR**. When using the Image Editor to create a DCR file, it is important to make sure that the name you call the image is the same as the name of the component, *and that it is in uppercase letters*. Failure to use uppercase letters will result in the bitmap not being displayed on the Component Palette, and cause you much frustration as you try to figure out what is going on. In our case, this would mean that TSimple would be called TSimple in the DCR file. Note that the **DCR** file does not actually ever become part of the component file. This is because the bitmap image of the component is only needed at design time. If the bitmap were part of the component, unnecessary overhead would be added to the final **EXE** file produced.

The size of a component bitmap can range from 5x5 pixels up to 24x24 pixels. It makes no difference to Delphi, because the bitmap ends up centered in the component button for which it is destined. The only restriction placed on component bitmaps is that the lower-left pixel is reserved to indicate the *transparent* color of the bitmap. The transparent color is used to allow the face of the button to show through the bitmap because the button appears different when it is up than when it is down. Of course, the color chosen for the transparent color will disappear, so don't use a color that you want to have visible in the bitmap. Figure 2.2 shows the bitmap for TSimple. The file for the component bitmap is in the **\DC\CHAP02** directory, but its name is **SIMPLE.XXX**. To make it display in the component palette, rename it **SIMPLE.DCR**, and then select **Options, Install Components**, and click **OK** to recompile the component library.

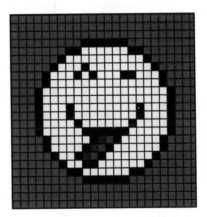

Figure 2.2 Component bitmap for TSimple.

Facing the Real World

Even though we have just spent quite a bit of time programming our first component, it is really useless. It can't do anything of any value other than show you the basics. The time has come to move beyond this stage and to start thinking about how components can be used in the real world. Most often, this involves identifying your problem and then identifying the solution.

The Problem Defined

Because you are reading this book, I will make the reasonable assumption that you are a Windows user. As you probably know, almost every aspect of Windows is customizable. For example, you can change the default color scheme, the sounds made by different events, the thickness of window borders, and the spacing between icons to name a few. Ask yourself this question: Have I ever written an application that assumed that these never changed during the course of a Windows session? Probably, the answer is yes—I know I have. Although you may be able to get away with it for some programs that you write, most programs, especially those aimed at "normal" users should respond to these sorts of changes, or you will just confuse them.

The problem can now be stated: How do we provide a means of responding to global changes in the Windows environment?

Searching for a Solution

All Windows programs have what are known as *message loops* for processing and dispatching incoming messages. One such message is called **WM_WININICHANGE**; it is sent to each running program whenever an entry in the **WIN.INI** file changes. The **WIN.INI** file contains most of the global settings that affect how Windows looks and feels, so responding to this message will provide the means of keeping our application up to date.

Even though Delphi programs have a message loop that can call a message handler identified by the **OnMessage** property of the **Application** instance, it is not always the most convenient to way to respond to an incoming message, especially if you want the code to be reusable with other projects. Sure, you could use the Form Expert and create a template that includes the required code for each project you write, but what if you want to process several such messages, but not all for the same program? You would have to have a different template for each combination! I don't know about you, but I have better things to do than create a cartload of templates. Besides, if you were to use different templates, you would be stuck with your initial choice, and you wouldn't be able to change anything later.

Suppose we create a component that processes incoming messages while looking specifically for **WM_WININICHANGE**? It then simply becomes a matter of dropping it into our program to get the functionality it provides. The same could be done for any number of message handlers. There is a downside to doing things this way, however. Each message handler component would essentially contain identical code, subjecting the program it is dropped into to bloat. Of course, the way to conquer this is to have only one component that manages all the message handlers you might need and to have flags that enable or disable specific handlers. Even if you later decided that you needed to handle a different message, you would be able to do so without affecting your application adversely.

While on the subject of bloat, let me say that if you think something may be too slow, stop thinking because it is. We are currently facing a trend where software is getting slower, and the requirements for running it are going up, with no end in sight. Anything that you can do to fight this will be dollars in your pocket instead of your competitor's. You have to be especially careful with Delphi, because although you may think that it is your best friend that allows you to program gee-whiz applications very quickly, it is also working against you with every form you add, every component you drop in, and every unit you link with. Remember, this is not your code that you are adding, it is someone else's. Someone who also wanted to get their product out as soon as possible, even if it meant making compromises to do so. Try not to get caught in this trap yourself. If it is too slow, rewrite the code; the world can wait a few more weeks for a better product, but it won't take notice of one that is unusable.

Turning back to the subject at hand, to process the incoming messages, we first need a way to receive them. As mentioned, the **OnMessage** property can accept a function to relay the messages to, so let's do this to intercept the messages. But what if some other piece of code does the same thing? Either our code or that code will get the messages, but not both. Suppose we were to read the **OnMessage** property, which is just a pointer to a function, save it, and then point it at our function. Whenever the function got called, we could do our stuff and then use the saved pointer to call the old **OnMessage** function. Again, this is no good because there is no guarantee that we would have the opportunity to do this after the other piece of code set **OnMessage** to point to its function. We may be first, and the other code, which probably has no knowledge that someone else might want to process messages, would simply set **OnMessage** after we did. Unfortunately, we are left with no options for using **OnMessage** directly, so what if we were to use it *indirectly*?

OnMessage, which is called whenever the application gets a message, is only part of what the message loop does. It also distributes the messages to the appropriate windows that belong to the application. In the case of the **WM_WININICHANGE** this distribution includes all top-level windows. It follows that if we were to create a hidden top-level window, we would be able to get the notification and act on it. All we have to do now is to create a hidden top-level window.

Creating Hidden Windows

It would not be very wise to use a form as a window because of the associated overhead involved. It is also not a particularly exciting task to create a window the old-fashioned way—the way that C programmers still do it. Happily, the engineers at Borland ran into this problem themselves, so they created the **AllocateHWnd** function that does just what we want, and it is easy to use:

```
function AllocateHWnd(Method: TWndMethod): HWND;
```

The only parameter to worry about is **Method**, a member function of a component class, as indicated by the **TWndMethod** declaration:

```
TWndMethod = procedure(var Message: TMessage) of object;
```

The return value of **AllocateHWnd** is the handle of the window that it creates, and for the purpose of later destroying the window, you should save it somewhere, ideally in the **private** part of your class declaration. When it comes time to destroy the window, use the **DeallocateHWnd** function:

```
procedure DeallocateHWnd(Wnd: HWND);
```

Notice that it is also easy to use; you only need to pass the window handle obtained from the original call to **AllocateHWnd** to do the job.

With this knowledge, now it is a good time to start laying down some code.

The TWinIni Component

```
unit Winini;

interface

uses
  SysUtils, WinTypes, WinProcs, Messages, Classes, Graphics, Controls,
  Forms, Dialogs;

type
  TWinIni = class(TComponent)
  private
    FWindowHandle:HWnd;
    procedure WndProc(var Msg:TMessage);
  public
    constructor Create(AOwner:TComponent);override;
    destructor Destroy;override;
  end;

procedure Register;

implementation

procedure TWinIni.WndProc(var Msg:TMessage);
begin
end;

constructor TWinIni.Create(AOwner:TComponent);
begin
```

```
    inherited Create(AOwner);
    FWindowHandle:=AllocateHWnd(WndProc);
end;


destructor TWinIni.Destroy;
begin
    DeallocatehWnd(FWindowHandle);
    inherited Destroy;
end;


procedure Register;
begin
    RegisterComponents('Additional', [TWinIni]);
end;
end.
```

In this code, the calls for **AllocateHWnd** and **DeallocateHWnd** are located in the **Create** constructor and the **Destroy** destructor, respectively. This has the effect of creating the hidden window whenever an instance of component class **TWinIni** is created and destroying it when the class is destroyed. The parameter of **AllocateHWnd** is the method **WndProc**, and therefore it is this procedure that receives all the messages associated with the window. The return value of **AllocateHWnd** is assigned to **FWindowHandle**, a private variable of type **HWnd**, so that it can be used later for destroying the window in the call to **DeallocateHWnd**.

Currently, **WndProc** is empty, and to differentiate between the **WM_WININICHANGE** message and all others, some logic is needed:

```
procedure TWinIni.WndProc(var Msg:TMessage);
begin
    with Msg do
    begin
        if Msg=WM_WININICHANGE then
        begin
        {The processing of the WM_WININICHANGE message will go here}
```

```
    end
    else
        Result:=DefWindowProc(FWindowHandle,Msg,wParam,lParam);
    end;

  end;
```

The **Msg** parameter of **WndProc** is of type **TMessage**. This type contains various fields that relate information about the exact nature of the message:

```
TMessage=record
  Msg:Word;
  case Integer of
      0:(
        WParam:Word;
        LParam:Longint;
        Result:Longint);
      1:(
        WParamLo:Byte;
        WParamHi:Byte;
        LParamLo: Word;
        LParamHi: Word;
        ResultLo: Word;
        ResultHi: Word);
  end;
```

It is the **Msg** field that will contain the **WM_WININICHANGED** message whenever the window receives notification that **WIN.INI** has changed, which is exactly what the preceding function looks for. It also does something else: if the **Msg** field is not **WM_WININICHANGED**, the function **DefWindowProc** is called. It is this function's job to perform any default processing that the window may need. Notice that the return value is assigned to **Result**, not to be confused with the built-in variable that functions allow you to assign your return value to, which wouldn't even make sense because **MsgProc** is a procedure and can't have a return type but a field of the **Msg** parameter.

Now that we can discriminate between our message and all others, we must somehow relay this information out of the component. This involves creating an event.

Creating Events

Events occur daily in our lives and can be described as something that makes you take notice, such as rain beginning to fall or a traffic light changing colors. In Delphi, events are similar because they make your program take notice of something that a component is doing, such as being clicked on or, as in our case, providing notification whenever the **WIN.INI** file changes. An event is said to have occurred when a component's code calls code that is not its own, usually a member function of the form or other component that owns it. To allow it to be called, a function template is needed:

```
TEvent=procedure of object;
```

This is about as much of a no-frills template as you can get because it has no parameters. Stuck on its end is **of object**, something that I have used here previously, but you might not be familiar with. Its purpose is to indicate to the compiler that the template identifies a member function of a class (so why call it "of object"?), to ensure that the proper code is generated when it comes time to call that function. If a variable of the template is created, it can be assigned any matching function. Consider the following:

```
type
  TEvent=procedure of object;

  TSomeClass=class
    procedure CallMe;
  end;
```

```
procedure TSomeClass.CallMe;
begin
  writeln('I have been called!');
end;

var
  SomeClass:TSomeClass;
  Event:TEvent;

begin
  SomeClass:=TSomeClass.Create;

  Event:=SomeClass.CallMe;
  Event;

  SomeClass.Free;
end.
```

The line that reads

```
Event:=SomeClass.CallMe;
```

is where the member function **CallMe** is assigned to **Event,** which is of the function template type **TEvent.** Note that **CallMe** and **TEvent** are identical in that they have the same number of parameters: none. If this were not the case, the preceding example would not compile.

The line that follows consists of only the **Event** variable and this might confuse you. If it is a variable, how can it stand alone on a line? Remember, it is of type **TEvent,** a function template. The compiler is smart enough to realize that a variable of such a type that is not being used in an expression is indeed a function—what else could it be? In a class, event variables are normally accessed through properties:

```
type
  TEvent=procedure of object;


  TFirstClass=class
```

```
    procedure CallMe;
  end;


  TSecondClass=class
  private
    FEvent:TEvent;
  property
    Event:TEvent read FEvent write FEvent;
  end;


procedure TFirstClass.CallMe;
begin
  writeln('I have been called!');
end;


var
  FirstClass:TFirstClass;
  SecondClass:TSecondClass;


begin
  FirstClass:=TFirstClass.Create;
  SecondClass:=TSecondClass.Create;

  SecondClass.Event:=FirstClass.CallMe;
  SecondClass.Event;

  SecondClass.Free;
  FirstClass.Free;
end.
```

The line that reads

```
SecondClass.Event:=FirstClass.CallMe;
```

assigns the **CallMe** method to the **Event** member of **SecondClass**; this is very similar to what was done in the first example. But the next line,

```
SecondClass.Event;
```

does not need to be typecast in order to compile correctly.

By making the event a property, we are also making it a candidate to be part of the **published** section of a component. This is required if you want to use the Object Inspector to create event handlers for you on the fly by simply double-clicking on the blank place by the event's name. This can now be applied to our **TWinIni** component:

```
unit Winini;

interface

uses
  SysUtils, WinTypes, WinProcs, Messages, Classes, Graphics, Controls,
  Forms, Dialogs;

type
  TWinIni = class(TComponent)
  private
    FWindowHandle:HWnd;
    FOnWinIniChange:TNotifyEvent;
    procedure WndProc(var Msg:TMessage);
  public
    constructor Create(AOwner:TComponent);override;
    destructor Destroy;override;
  published
    property OnWinIniChange:TNotifyEvent read FOnWinIniChange
      write FOnWinIniChange;
  end;

procedure Register;

implementation

procedure TWinIni.WndProc(var Msg:TMessage);
```

```
begin
  with Msg do
  begin
    if (Msg=WM_WININICHANGE) and Assigned(FOnWinIniChange) then
      OnWinIniChange(Self)
    else
      Result:=DefWindowProc(FWindowHandle,Msg,wParam,lParam);
  end;
end;


constructor TWinIni.Create(AOwner:TComponent);
begin
  inherited Create(AOwner);
  FWindowHandle:=AllocateHWnd(WndProc);
  FOnWinIniChange:=nil;
end;


destructor TWinIni.Destroy;
begin
  DeallocatehWnd(FWindowHandle);
  inherited Destroy;
end;


procedure Register;
begin
  RegisterComponents('Additional', [TWinIni]);
end;


end.
```

The function template for the event is the predefined **TNotifyEvent**, which supplies only one parameter, **ASender**, that is used to identify the component responsible for generating the event. Even though this parameter can be left out, it wouldn't be a good idea to do so because each event does not necessarily have its own event handler; several can just one. In situations such as these, **ASender** becomes the *only* way to identify the originator of the event.

During the **Create** constructor, the event variable, **FOnWinIniChange** is assigned to **nil**. This, in combination with the **Assigned** function located in **WndProc**, ensures that a call to an invalid address will not occur if the event has not been assigned. **FOnWinIniChange** is set to a valid address during the time that the owner of the component, usually a form, is being loaded.

If you were to add the component as it stands to the component palette, create a new form, drop on the component, and create a handler for the **OnWinIniChange** event, you would find that the handler would be called every time something in the **WIN.INI** file changed, as expected, but you wouldn't know *what* had changed. Fortunately, whenever the **WM_WININICHANGE** message is sent, one of its parameters, **LParam** (see the declaration for **TMessage** a few pages back), points to a string that contains the name of the section that changed. Obviously, by including this information with the event, we can make things easier on the programmer who eventually has to respond to it. The format of the returned string is a standard null-terminated one, which is compatible with type **PChar**. The VCL diverges from using type **PChar** in favor of the standard **String** type, so to maintain consistency, it is important to translate the string using the **StrPas** function before returning it. Also, this extra parameter means that a different function template must be used:

```
TOnWinIniChange=procedure(AOwner:TComponent;SectionName:String)
  of object;
```

The final source code for **WININI.PAS** is shown here:

Listing 2.1 WININI.PAS

```
unit Winini;

interface

uses
  SysUtils, WinTypes, WinProcs, Messages, Classes, Graphics, Controls,
  Forms, Dialogs;

type
  TOnWinIniChange=procedure(AOwner:TObject;SectionName:String)
    of object;
```

```
TWinIni = class(TComponent)
private
  FWindowHandle:HWnd;
  FOnWinIniChange:TOnWinIniChange;
  procedure WndProc(var Msg:TMessage);
public
  constructor Create(AOwner:TComponent);override;
  destructor Destroy;override;
published
  property OnWinIniChange:TOnWinIniChange read FOnWinIniChange
    write FOnWinIniChange;
end;

procedure Register;

implementation

procedure TWinIni.WndProc(var Msg:TMessage);
begin
  with Msg do
  begin
    if (Msg=WM_WININICHANGE) and Assigned(FOnWinIniChange) then
      OnWinIniChange(Self,StrPas(PChar(LParam)))
    else
      Result:=DefWindowProc(FWindowHandle,Msg,wParam,lParam);
  end;
end;

constructor TWinIni.Create(AOwner:TComponent);
begin
  inherited Create(AOwner);
  FWindowHandle:=AllocateHWnd(WndProc);
  FOnWinIniChange:=nil;
end;

destructor TWinIni.Destroy;
begin
```

```
    DeallocatehWnd(FWindowHandle);
    inherited Destroy;
end;

procedure Register;
begin
    RegisterComponents('Additional', [TWinIni]);
end;

end.
```

All that remains to be added is a bitmap, as shown in Figure 2.3, to crown the component. For those of you who are wondering about its meaning, it shows **WIN.INI** above a pile of coins, or "change," putting it together we get "**WIN.INI** change," descriptive of the component's purpose, even if it is a bit confusing.

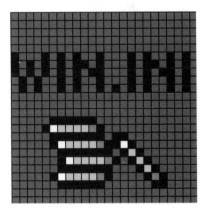

Figure 2.3 Component bitmap for TWinIni.

After any component has been created, it is always a good idea to test it to make sure that it behaves how you expect. For this purpose, here is a short program, **WCProj** (**WIN.INI** Change Project) that consists of **WCPROJ.DPR** and **WCMAIN.PAS**. The source can be found in the **\DC\CHAP02** directory if you want to try it out. Things to try in order to get the component to respond are changing the wallpaper, the desktop color, mouse settings and so forth.

Listing 2.2 WCMain.PAS

```
unit WCMain;

interface

uses
  SysUtils, WinTypes, WinProcs, Messages, Classes, Graphics, Controls,
  Forms, Dialogs, Winini, StdCtrls;

type
  TForm1 = class(TForm)
    Memo1: TMemo;
    Label1: TLabel;
    Button1: TButton;
    WinIni1: TWinIni;
    procedure WinIni1WinIniChange(AOwner: TObject; SectionName:
String);
    procedure Button1Click(Sender: TObject);
  private
    { Private declarations }
  public
    { Public declarations }
  end;

var
  Form1: TForm1;

implementation

{$R *.DFM}

procedure TForm1.WinIni1WinIniChange(AOwner: TObject;
  SectionName: String);
begin
  Memo1.Lines.Add(SectionName);
end;


procedure TForm1.Button1Click(Sender: TObject);
```

```
begin
  Close;
end;

end.
```

CHAPTER 3

SERIAL COMMUNICATIONS WITH DELPHI

The ability to communicate with one another is crucial to our everyday existence. Historically, such communication was done person to person, through smoke signals, via the Pony Express, over the phone and so forth. Within the past few decades, however, technology has been able to provide the means that allows us to talk to each other with our personal computers. This sort of interconnection generally occurs in two forms: networks and telecommunications, although it is not uncommon to find a mixture of the two. The popularity of both cannot be ignored; virtually every office is networked in one way or another, and a good portion of computer owners have modems installed inside their machines. The reason behind the latter can be attributed to on-line services, and especially, the Internet, whose drug-like influence has many of us sitting behind a monitor for hours at a time instead of doing real work (like writing a book).

The goal of this chapter is to create a component that will allow effortless communications via your computer's serial port. During the course of doing this, we will explore the following topics:

- Basics of serial communication
- Using the Windows API
- Working with threads
- Creating properties
- Keeping components harmless during design time
- Importance of setting properties in the create statement

Fundamentals of Serial Communications

For some, the very thought of serial communications stirs up visions of hot-shot programmers banging in countless lines of assembly code, staying up long hours trying to get things to work properly. This misconception, although partially true, most likely stems from the hardware nature of serial ports and is further compounded by their erratic, interrupt-driven personalities. When it gets right down to it though, they really are not as scary as they may seem, and you don't have to be a hardware whiz to use them. You see, they only do two things: send and receive data.

Sending and Receiving Serial Data

Giving a serial port data to send is as simple as writing the data byte by byte to one of its I/O addresses. However, you simply can't shove *all* your data into it and say "do your stuff," because serial ports transmit it at a much slower rate than you can give it. So to get around this, the port sets a flag in another of its I/O addresses to let you know that it is "full" and you should stop sending it data until it asks for some more. This "asking" can occur in two ways: The flag that indicates that the port is full will be cleared, which if you sit in a loop waiting for this to happen will let you know that it is safe to send some more data. But while you are waiting for permission to give some more data, wouldn't it be better to do something other than freezing the machine and annoying the user? Of course it would, which brings us to the second way that the port asks for more data: It triggers an interrupt. Whenever an interrupt occurs, the current flow of execution is *interrupted*, and a table of addresses is used to determine what code to call in response to it. If you were to modify this table, you could have the interrupt call *your* code instead, which would send more data to the port. When you were done doing this, you could simply call the old address from the table to finish the interrupt and return the flow of execution to the exact point where it left off. This process would then repeat over and over until all your data was sent, with the user none the wiser that this was happening.

Receiving data is even easier. Again, you could wait for a flag to be set indicating that data is present in the port, or you could respond to an interrupt that indicates the same thing. The advantage to responding to the interrupt is the same as before: the user does not have to wait for a transfer to be complete before continuing to work. The only functional difference is that the interrupt is triggered whenever the port's receive buffer fills up with data, instead of when it becomes empty.

Handshaking

Great, you now know how to send data from your computer to another computer or device. But what if it isn't listening? What if the data is garbled? What if you are sending it too fast? Excellent questions, all of them. So, let's provide some equally excellent answers, but first, a story.

Suppose that you just bought one of the most technologically advanced, serially controlled widgets on the market, or SCW for short. You bring it home, unwrap it, plug it into your computer, and then write some code to make it do its thing. When you're finished, you gather the family, start your program and... nothing! The family leaves, and you are left feeling a bit silly.

While writing the code, you noticed in the manual that accompanied the SCW, that it only accepts serial data and doesn't respond serially in any way. This opens a can of worms for you because you don't know which, if any, of the following are to blame:

- Incorrectly formatted data being sent
- Wrong baud rate
- Plugged into the wrong port
- A defective SCW
- Cable mites

You work on it for a while, trying to think of every possibility, but to no avail. Finally, you bring your SCW back to the store and have them test it. Ah, it seems that the SCW was at fault, and they give you a new—and improved—unit. This one responds to every command by echoing it back and sending a success or failure flag. With a few modifications to your program, you get the SCW to work, and your family is suitably impressed.

The purpose of this story is to illustrate the importance of handshaking. Without it, you clearly do not know where you stand. For this reason, you will be hard pressed to find any device that does not support it (except maybe for those old SCWs). Also, don't forget that the device does not have to be a peripheral, it may be your computer as well. This means that if you are writing a pair of programs, one for one computer that sends data, and the other for the computer whose primary purpose is to use that data, it would be foolish if you did not implement some sort of handshaking.

Handshaking may, as we just saw, be entirely software based. That is, you send something, and you get something in return. But it may also be hardware based. The standard serial port is capable of setting and reading the state of lines dedicated entirely for this purpose. When you connect two devices (again, they may be computers) together that support hardware handshaking, each one asserts its DTR (Data Terminal Read) line to indicate that it is present. The line goes to the DSR (Data Set Ready) line of the *opposite* computer, which can read the state of it to determine if an actual connection has been made. As great as this may sound, it has some serious drawbacks. For instance, even if you know that you are properly connected to your device of choice, it doesn't necessarily mean that all, or even any, of the points listed earlier have been vanquished. So your best bet to determine if you are properly connected is through the use of software handshaking, and leave the DTR and DSR lines to the terminals of old, where they actually were important.

Data Verification

OK, you're finally sending data, but is it being received exactly how you sent it? Probably, but not necessarily. It is of utmost importance to verify that the data you sent was received properly. Again, there is a hardware way and a software way to do this.

The hardware method can be spelled out in one word: *parity*. Parity is a method of checking the "correctness" of each byte as it is received, by examining the state of an extra bit that was tacked on to it. This bit indicates the count of set bits in the data byte. There are two types of parity detection methods: even and odd. If even parity is selected, the parity bit will be set if the count of set bits in the data byte is even, but will be clear when the count of set bits is odd. Odd parity, on the other hand, results in the parity bit being set if the count of set bits in the data byte is odd; otherwise it will be clear. If parity detection is set up to use one of these two methods, an error state can be detected when the bit count does not reflect the transmitted parity. The usefulness of this is limited though, because it is not guaranteed that a bad byte will have an unmatched parity bit. What if, for example, you send a 01110011b with an odd parity bit, and a 01110000 is received—slightly garbled, maybe because of line noise. The parity is still detected as odd, and the byte is allowed to pass undetected. Because of the relatively high odds that errors will go by unhindered and that the extra bit does decrease throughput, parity detection is largely ignored in real-world products in favor of the software alternatives.

Before we get to those alternatives, there are three remaining parity states to talk about, although they are not strictly for the purpose of error detection. These states are *none*, *mark*, and *space*. No parity simply means that the parity bit will not be included at the end of the data, and therefore, parity detection cannot occur. Mark parity does tack on the extra bit, but it is always set— really not much good for anything. Space parity is similar, but instead of the bit being always set, it is always clear.

Software error detection comes in many flavors. The simplest of which is to have the device you are communicating with echo back whatever you send it. All you then have to do is compare the data you sent to the data you received, and if they match, you can be certain that a successful transfer occurred. If the sent data does not match the echoed data, there are two possibilities as to what went wrong. The first is that something happened to the data on the way there. The second is that the data was received properly, but something happened to the echoed data. The worst possible case would be that the data was sent incorrectly and also returned incorrectly. If Murphy had a hand in this, it may turn out that the echoed data matches the transmitted data! All things considered though, this is admittedly a rare situation, and you should not be put off by it.

The method of echoing everything back is acceptable only if the flow of communication is primarily one way—that is, one device does the talking, and the other device does the listening. If the second device also sends back a good deal of data, you will find that things slow to a crawl as the two devices echo back what the other has sent. The solution here is not to echo back anything, but instead send your data in packets, along with a unique number whose value depends on the contents of the packet. That is, if the packet changes, the number also changes. Therefore, to determine if a received packet was good or bad, the receptor would perform the same process of calculating the number for the data it received and compare it to the number that was sent. If the numbers match, the data is good; otherwise, it is bad and will have to be retransmitted.

There are many ways to calculate the "magic" number for a data packet. The simplest is to add up the values of each byte of the packet that you want to send. This is known as a *checksum*, and for most purposes works well. But for more reliability, you might want to consider using a *cyclic redundancy check* (CRC) value. In addition to doing what the checksum does, it also ensures that the order and amount of data is correct. For example, with the checksum method, it is possible that if a data byte with a value of zero disappears, or even appears, in your data stream, you would not know about it, but the CRC value would reflect this instantly.

As briefly mentioned, it may be necessary to resend a data packet if the checksum or CRC values don't match. This obviously means that the receptor has to confirm whether a packet was received properly. Also, because you might have sent several additional packets before getting a response, it is necessary to have a unique identifier for each packet you send—sequentially numbering them works well. Finally, unless you can rebuild a packet on-the-fly with little overhead, always keep it in memory until you get confirmation of its successful reception; otherwise, you may be stuck with an error that you can't deal with.

Flow Control

Quick, run to your bathroom and flush the toilet. The bowl will empty, start to fill with water, and finally stop when it reaches its "full" level, waiting for the next flush. If you can understand this, congratulations; you're an expert on serial communications flow control!

Suppose that you have established a successful link with some device, and you are sending data to it. If you do this long enough, chances are that eventually it won't have anywhere to put the data, and a condition known as *overflowing the buffer* will occur. You don't want this to happen—not ever. So, what you have to do is wait for it to process the data and consequently clear out its buffer a bit, before sending more. Unless your computer is equipped with psychic powers, there is no way for it to know that the device's buffer has filled up in the first place. Thus, the burden of responsibility falls upon the device receiving the data to let you know when it can't accept any more data. This is the premise of flow control. Again, there is a hardware method and a software method to successfully implement it.

The hardware way of doing things relies on the availability of two lines, RTS (Request To Send) and CTS (Clear To Send). Whenever the device you want to talk to is in a position to accept data, it asserts its RTS line, which is connected directly to your CTS line. By checking the state of CTS, you know that you should begin transmitting data. If, however, the RTS line should ever become unasserted, it is imperative that transmission stop immediately. Because it is not always possible to stop transmitting at any given instance (a character may be on its way when the CTS line drops), it is always wise to make the device's RTS line drop *before* the buffer completely fills up— assuming that you have that kind of control over the device. Ten or so bytes ahead of time is a good rule of thumb. Of course, flow control is normally a two-way type of deal. Your RTS line can also be connected to the device's CTS line, informing it when to send and when not to send data.

Remember the DTR and DSR lines back in the "Handshaking" section? It is possible that if they are not being used for their intended purpose that they can be used for flow control in a manner identical to the RTS/CTS method. The only reason that you might want to do this is for backup purposes in mission-critical applications; otherwise, RTS/CTS will do just fine.

There is nothing wrong with using hardware-based flow control. In fact, it is probably the most reliable way of achieving it. So why is software-based flow control used much more frequently? Simplicity. You see, the thing about the RS232 port is its lack of standardization. The very term "RS232 standard" continues to bring chuckles from the more "mature" members of our crowd. Things have settled down somewhat, but still, why take the risk that you will have a chance encounter with an older device that doesn't behave like you expect it to, when you can implement flow control entirely in software?

The most common form of software-based flow control is XON/XOFF. If you are sending data to a device and it reaches a point that it can't accept any more, it sends an XOFF character, usually ASCII 13h. By receiving this character and interpreting its value, you know that you should stop sending data. When the amount of data in the devices buffer lowers to some preset acceptable level, it sends an XON character, usually ASCII 11h, informing you that data transmission may resume. Again, this works both ways: You can also send XON/XOFF characters.

There are several weak links in using XON/XOFF flow control, however. If you are sending text-based data, you never have to worry about wanting to transmit the XON/XOFF character. But if you are transmitting binary data, it is quite probable that these characters will be among the ones you want to send for reasons other than flow control. Also, the transmission of a solitary character can easily get lost or garbled, making you unaware that you should stop transmitting. What are you to do?

If you are communicating in data secure packets, which is a very good thing to do as explained earlier, you can make one of the packets contain a command to turn transmission on and off. This assures you that the commands will actually be received and interpreted correctly. One thing you have to watch out for, however, is that packets are typically a little larger, and thus take longer to transmit than single characters. Also, be aware that they might have to be resent if received incorrectly. This means that the command to turn off flow control should be sent somewhat earlier than XON/XOFF or RTS/CTS flow control methods to avoid overflowing the receive buffer.

The Windows Approach

As simple as transmitting and receiving characters serially can be, you would almost never want to do so manually under Windows because it handles all this for you. In addition, it provides an easy-to-use subset of the Windows API to read, write, and manipulate the port settings, as well as perfrom other small details that would be easy to overlook if your were to write your own communication driver. We will rely heavily upon this subset for the development of our component, so it is essential that we explore it in depth before proceeding. This will ensure that you have a complete understanding of what is involved once we get there. Learning everything you can about a subject before diving in is not just good programming sense, it's good common sense as well.

The Windows COMM API

With Windows 3.x, *all* communications-related activities are accomplished via the COMM API. For better or worse, this is not the case with Windows 95, which has adopted Windows NT's approach. With both Windows 95 and NT, the communication port is no longer opened with a call to **OpenComm**, but instead with a call to **CreateFile**, allowing the port to be manipulated with the same functions used for reading from and writing to files. Of course, the port is not really a file, so the COMM API still exists for doing communication-only activities that could not otherwise be accomplished. In the following list of functions, I have included the non-COMM API functions because they are core in using the communication ports.

CreateFile

The first thing that needs to be done before you can do any serial communications in Windows is to open the port with a call to **CreateFile**:

```
function CreateFile(lpFileName:PChar;dwDesiredAccess,

dwShareMode:Integer;lpSecurityAttributes:PSecurityAttributes;
  dwCreationDisposition,dwFlagsAndAttributes:DWORD;
  hTemplateFile: THandle): THandle;
```

While it appears exceedingly complex, this function is rather simple to use. **lpFileName** specifies the name of the file to open. For a communication port, it takes the form of "COM1," "COM2," and so on. **dwDesiredAccess** dictates if the port can be written to and read from by using one or both of the **GENERIC_READ** and **GENERIC_WRITE** flags. The **dwShareMode** parameter tells Windows if the open file can be shared with other applications. For a communication port, this value must be zero, indicating that the file cannot be shared. The **lpSecurityAtributes** parameter is only valid under

Windows NT. For compatibility reasons and convenience, this value is almost always **NIL**. **dwCreationDisposition** informs Windows how the file is to be created or opened. Because a communication file either exists or it doesn't, the only value that makes sense here is **OPEN_EXISTING**. If this functionality is not desired, the value of zero may be used.

The **dwFlagsAndAttributes** parameter is used to specify attributes for disk files, and for the most part has no real value when used with communication files. There is, however, one notable exception. When the value passed to it is **FILE_FLAG_OVERLAPPED**, the programmer gains the ability to perform an *overlapped I/O*, which means that writes and reads can be performed at the same time. Although this feature is generally used sparingly when working with a normal file, it is highly useful in the context of communication ports, which routinely send and receive data at the same time.

The final parameter is **hTemplateFile**, which is ignored for communication ports, and as such is passed a value of zero.

The return value of **CreateFile** provides a handle to a successfully opened port; or if the port does not exist or it isn't able to be opened, **INVALID_HANDLE_VALUE** is returned. If the latter is the case, the **GetLastError** function may be used to retrieve extended error information, providing insight into the exact problem.

CloseComm

After you have obtained a handle from **CreateFile**, you will eventually have to close the port. This can be done with a call to **CloseHandle**:

```
function CloseHandle(hObject:THandle):BOOL;
```

Here, **hObject** is the handle obtained from **CreateFile**. If the return value is **True**, which it will always be unless you pass a bad handle, success is indicated. A value of **False** indicates an error whose meaning can be determined using **GetLastError**

SetupComm

Opening the port is just one of the many requirements needed to use it properly. Some consideration must be given to the incoming data itself, specifically the quantity that you expect to receive or transmit at any given time and the amount of internal buffer space needed for it. For example, many communication protocols use consistently sized packets, such as blocks of 1K. In this instance, a read and write buffer size of 2 to 3K would work well. It should be noted that although your serial hardware might not have any problems keeping up with a fast onslaught of data, the software you write may. Buffer sizes should be adjusted accordingly.

Setting the size of the read and write buffers involves calling the **SetupComm** function:

```
function SetupComm(hFile:THandle;dwInQueue,dwOutQueue:DWORD):BOOL;
```

Here, **hFile** is the handle returned from **CreateFile**; **dwInQueue** is the amount of buffer space you want to give to the read buffer; and **dwOutQueue** is the amount of storage that the write buffer receives. Should the function fail, **False** will be returned.

There is no rule etched in stone that says you have to call **SetupComm** at all. It is quite possible to forgo calling it and have default-sized buffers allocated for you. Given the ability to have one small wish granted, I would do away with the manual setting of buffer sizes and opt instead to have the read and write buffers dynamically grow and shrink depending on what the flow of data is like. For example, if only a character or two trickles in on occasion, there is no need to have a buffer size of 64K—5 bytes would be generous. It would be quite convenient if Windows would recognize such a trend and adjust itself accordingly.

SetCommTimeouts and GetCommTimeouts

One of the sadder things that often occurs in the realm of communications is that we don't always receive the number of bytes we expect. The reasons for such occurrences vary. Perhaps the device being communicated with stops working, or maybe a bit of noise gets into the line and effectively nullifies a byte or two. Regardless of the cause, the result is the same—not enough data.

One functions that we will talk about later, **ReadFile**, reads a fixed amount of data from the input buffer. Although it is certainly possible to read only what is in the buffer itself, often a programmer will find that it is convenient to read the amount of data that is *expected* to be in the buffer. If the amount of data is there, fine; **ReadFile** returns immediately. But if it's not there, one of two things happens depending on how the programmer coded things. The first choice is that **ReadFile** sits there, waiting for the data to arrive, and in the meantime not letting anything else happen in the current thread. For those not quite on firm ground with threads, I should note that every program you run contains at least one thread—the main thread. It is also possible to have secondary threads that run parallel to the main thread. In the case of a waiting **ReadFile**, only the thread that it is in is suspended; the rest go about their normal business. If the suspended thread happens to be the main thread, you're in trouble because this locks up the user interface. The second choice is that **ReadFile** returns instantly, generating an event when it's done, but still allowing other things to go on their merry way. The event can either be polled for (not recommended), or it can wake up a thread (highly recommended). Regardless of how **ReadFile** is used, it may eventually become apparent that no more data is going to be received. Not now; not ever. In the first scenario, this is a real problem because it suspends the current thread forever. Thread suspension also occurs in the case where an event awakens a sleeping thread. The only real winner here is the polled method; but we have to discard that too because polling when you don't absolutely have to is a weenie thing to do.

So what are we to do? The answer lies in asking how do we know that nothing is happening? Time. As time goes on, no data is being received. The more time that passes, the more certain you can be that nothing is going to be received. Therefore, if we terminate **ReadFile** based upon time, we can detect when not enough data has been received. This situation is known as a *timeout*.

The function for incorporating timeouts is **SetCommTimeouts**:

```
function SetCommTimeouts(hFile:THandle;
  const lpCommTimeouts: TCommTimeouts):Bool;
```

hFile is the handle of the communication port. The **lpCommTimeouts** parameter is of type **TCommTimeouts**:

```
TCommTimeouts = record
  ReadIntervalTimeout:DWORD;
```

```
ReadTotalTimeoutMultiplier:DWORD;
ReadTotalTimeoutConstant:DWORD;
WriteTotalTimeoutMultiplier:DWORD;
WriteTotalTimeoutConstant:DWORD;
end;
```

Table 3.1 describes what each field does.

Table 3.1

Field	Description
ReadIntervalTimeout	Specifies the amount of time, in milliseconds, that is allowed to pass between the receipt of two consecutive bytes. If this time is exceeded, ReadFile will return with an error.
ReadTotalTimeoutMultiplier	This field is multiplied with the **nNumberOfBytesToRead** parameter of **ReadFile**. The result is then added to the **ReadTotalTime outConstant** field. The final value, in milliseconds, is used to indicate how long the read operation should take. For example, at 9600 baud, each character takes 1.04 milliseconds to transmit. Because we can't deal with fractions, we'll settle for the higher integer value of two milliseconds and assign it to **ReadTotalTimeoutMultiplier**. To compensate for initial internal delays, we will set **ReadTotalTime outConstant** to a value of 1000 milliseconds, or one second.

(continued)

Field	Description
ReadTotalTimeoutMultiplier (continued)	Now, whenever we do a read, it is certain that **ReadFile** will wait at least one second and an additional two milliseconds for each byte. For example, if we are waiting for 300 bytes to be received, **ReadFile** will hang around for 300 x 2 + 1,000 = 1,600 milliseconds before deciding to fail.
ReadTotalTimeoutConstant	This field specifies how milliseconds **ReadFile** is to wait before returning an error regardless of how many characters are expected. It is used in conjunction with **ReadTotalTimeoutMultiplier**.
WriteTotalTimeoutMultiplier	This field's function is identical to that of **ReadTotalTimeoutMultipler**, except it applies to the **WriteFiled** rather than **ReadFile**.
WriteTotalTimeoutConstant	This field's function is identical to that of **ReadTotalTimeoutConstant**, except it applies to the **WriteFiled** rather than the **ReadFile**.

The sister function to **SetCommTimeouts** is **GetCommTimeouts**:

```
function GetCommTimeouts(hFile:THandle;
  var lpCommTimeouts: TCommTimeouts):BOOL
```

hFile is the same as before, as is **lpCommTimeouts**. Instead of accepting a **TCommTimeouts** structure, the one pointed to is filled with the current settings. This function is useful if you don't want to set every field—read in the current **TCommTimeouts**, set the fields you want, and write the result back out with **SetCommTimeouts**.

BuildCommDCB, SetCommState, and GetCommState

For a communication port to behave the way you expect it to, it is mandatory to set the state of the port to indicate settings such as stop bits, baud rate, and parity. These settings are just a few of the many contained in the **TDCB** (Device Control Block) structure that must be initialized before the port can be used:

```
TDCB = record
  DCBLength:DWord;
  BaudRate:DWord;
  Flags:LongInt;
  wReserved:Word;
  XOnLim:Word;
  XOffLim:Word;
  ByteSize:Byte;
  Parity:Byte;
  StopBits:Byte;
  XOnChar:Char;
  XOffChar:Char;
  ErrorChar:Char;
  EOFChar:Char;
  EvtChar:Char;
  wReserved1:Word;
end;
```

As you can see, there are many fields that you probably won't ever care to set yourself if you just want to read and write data. For this reason, it is often useful to use the **BuildCommDCB** function to quickly fill in the **TDCB** fields for you:

```
function BuildCommDCB(lpDef:PChar;var lpDCB:TDCB):BOOL;
```

The **lpDef** parameter accepts a null-terminated string whose format is identical to that of the MS-DOS **mode** command:

```
MODE COMm[:] [BAUD=b] [PARITY=p] [DATA=d] [STOP=s] [RETRY=r]
```

So, an **lpDef** string of "COM3:9600,n,8,1" would initialize the contents of the **DCB** parameter in such a way that it would represent serial port three at a baud rate of 9600, no parity, eight data bits, and one stop bit. If the string is properly formatted, a value of **True** will be returned; otherwise, **False** will be returned. Of course, after you have the initialized **DCB** variable, you have to do something with it if you want these changes to take effect. This entails calling the **SetCommState** function:

```
function SetCommState(hFile:THandle;const lpDCB:TDCB):BOOL;
```

For this function, the handle returned from **CreateFile** and the newly constructed **DCB** variable that you obtained from **BuildCommDCB** are passed. If successful, **True** will be returned, and the new settings will immediately take effect. If **False** is returned, either the handle value is invalid, or the **lpDCB** parameter contains invalid information.

Although **BuildCommDCB** is great for quick and dirty test programs, it leaves something to be desired for everything else because it is only capable of simple port configurations. Also, because it requires a string, a program that offers port settings as a user option would have to build it piece by piece. Although this wouldn't be a difficult task, it would be a needless one because of the possibility of creating the **TDCB** structure yourself. Like I said before, there are probably fields in it that you will never want to change from their default values. The solution here is to read all the values, and then just change the ones that concern you. This is made easy with the **GetCommState** function:

```
function GetCommState(hFile:THandle;var lpDCB:TDCB):BOOL;
```

Here, **hFile** is the handle obtained from the call to **CreateFile**, and **lpDCB** is a variable of type **TDCB** that contains all the information that we are interested in changing. If the function is successful, the return value is **True**; otherwise, it is **False**.

After you have the values, the act of modifying them is simple and goes something like this:

```
var
  hComm:THandle;
  DCB:TDCB;

begin
  hComm:=OpenComm('COM2',2048,2048);
  hComm:=CreateFile('COM2',GENERIC_READ or GENERIC_WRITE,0,nil,
    OPEN_EXISTING,0,0);
  GetCommState(hComm,DCB);
  DCB.BaudRate:=CBR_9600;
  DCB.ByteSize:=8;
  DCB.Parity:=NOPARITY;
  DCB.StopBits:=ONESTOPBIT;
  SetCommState(hComm,DCB);
  CloseHandle(hComm);
end.
```

This small segment of code opens comm port two; reads in the current **DCB** record; changes some fields to achieve the desired 9600,n,8,1; and then transfers the modified **DCB** record to the port itself by calling **SetCommState**.

We have only touched on the bare minimum of what **TDCB** has to offer. For most applications, this is adequate; but sometimes you will want to use the more advanced features that it has to offer. So without further adieu, here is the run-down of what each field of the **TDCB** structure is used for:

DCBLength

This field specifies the length of the **TDCB** structure. Its primary purpose is to ensure that the proper structure is being passed to a function.

BaudRate

This field is used to specify the baud rate at which you want the port to transmit and receive data. Although you *can* use the rate in a numerical form—for example 4800—it is recommended that you use one of the predefined constants for this purpose:

CBR_110	CBR_2400	CBR_19200	CBR_256000
CBR_300	CBR_4800	CBR_38400	
CBR_600	CBR_9600	CBR_56000	
CBR_1200	CBR_14400	CBR_128000	

Flags

The **Flags** field contains many bit (that is, on/off) flags that are used to enable or disable features of the port:

Flag Name	Bit	Description
fBinary	0	This bit is not supported by Win32 and should always be set to one.
fParity	1	When set, parity checking is enabled. If a parity error occurs, it results in the next call to **GetCommError** returning with the **CE_RXPARITY** flag set.
fOutXCtsFlow	2	When this flag is set, no data will be transmitted unless the CTS line is set. This, in effect, automatically implements RTS/CTS flow control.
fOutXDsrFlow	3	When this flag is set, no data will be transmitted unless the DSR line, which is an input, is set. This, in effect, automatically implements DTR/DSR flow control.
fDtrControl	4,5	These two bits specify how the DTR line is to be used by the communication port. It can be one of three different values. The first, **DTR_CONTROL_DISABLE** places the line in its unasserted state. Conversely, **DTR_CONTROL_ENABLE** places the line in its asserted state. Finally, **DTR_CONTROL_HANDSHAKE** implements flow control with the DTR and DSR lines.

fDsrSensitivity		6 *64*	If this bit is set, any received bytes will be ignored *unless* the DSR line is high.
fTXContinueOnXOff		7 *128*	If XON/XOFF flow control enabled, this bit determines whether the transmission of bytes is permitted while waiting for an XON to be sent. If set, transmission is not hindered. However, if the bit is clear, transmission is halted until the count of bytes in the input buffer drops below **XOnLim**.
fOutX	*256*	8	When set, XON/XOFF flow control is enabled for data transmission. Whenever the XOFF character is received, data transmission halts until the XON character is received.
fInX	*512*	9	When set, XON/XOFF flow control is enabled for data reception. Whenever the number of characters in the receive buffer exceeds the value of the **XOffLim** field, the XOFF character is sent, indicating that data transmission should stop until the XON character is transmitted, which happens when the count of characters in the buffer falls below **XOnLim**.
fErrorChar	*1024*	10	If set, any characters received that have a parity error will be replaced with the character specified by the **ErrorChar** field.
fNull	*2048*	11	If set, received NULL characters will be discarded.
fRtsControl		12,13	These two bits specify how the RTS line is used by the communication port.
	4096,		

(continued)

Flag Name	Bit	Description
fRtsControl (*Continued*)		It can be one of three different values. The first, **RTS_CONTROL_DIS-ABLE** places the line in its unasserted state. Conversely, **RTS_CONTROL_ENABLE** places the line in its asserted state. The third possibility, **RTS_CONTROL_HAND-SHAKE,** implements flow control with the RTS and CTS lines. Finally, **RTS_CONTROL_TOGGLE** implements handshaking. That is, while there is data to be sent, the RTS line will be asserted.
fAbortOnError	14	If this flag is set, it causes any read or write operation that results in an error to be terminated immediately. For example, if while reading bytes over the serial port, a parity error occurs, the read operation will be canceled and an error code will be returned. This error condition will persist until **ClearCommError** is called.

XonLim

This field contains the number of bytes that data in the receive buffer must fall below before the XON character is sent, resuming data reception.

XoffLim

When the number of bytes contained in the receive buffer exceeds the value contained in this field, the XOFF character is sent to indicate that data transmission should halt until the XON character is sent.

ByteSize

The **ByteSize** field is used to indicate how many bits are in one byte of transmitted or received data and can be a value from four to eight.

Parity

Parity is used to ensure that data is being sent correctly and can be one of the following constants:

Constant	Meaning
NOPARITY	No parity
EVENPARITY	Even parity
ODDPARITY	Odd parity
MARKPARITY	Mark parity
SPACEPARITY	Space parity

StopBits

Stop bits are used to keep data in sync. Without them it becomes almost certain that the data you received would be garbled and meaningless because of slight timing variations from port to port. **StopBits** can be one of the following constant values:

Constant	Meaning
ONESTOPBIT	One stop bit per byte
ONE5STOPBITS	One and a half stop bits per byte
TWOSTOPBITS	Two stop bits per byte

XonChar

This field is specifies a character, normally 11h, that is used to indicate an **XON** condition, for both receiving and transmitting data.

XoffChar

This field is specifies a character, normally 13h, that is used to indicate an **XOFF** condition, for both receiving and transmitting data.

ErrorChar

If a character with a parity error is received, it will be replaced with the character contained in this field, but only if the **fErrorChar** flag of the **Flags** field is set to one.

EofChar

This field does nothing under Win32.

EvtChar

Whenever the character in this field is received, the **EV_RXFLAG** bit of the comm event mask will be set, but only if the event has been enabled with a call to **SetCommMask**. To determine the status of the **EV_RXFLAG** bit, use the **GetCommMask** function.

BuildCommDCBAndTimeouts

BuildCommDCBAndTimeouts is a strange hybrid of **BuildCommDCB** and **SetCommTimeouts**:

```
function BuildCommDCBAndTimeouts(lpDef:PChar;var lpDCB:TDCB;
  var lpCommTimeouts:TCommTimeouts):BOOL;
```

Strange as it may be, it has a gee-whiz factor that makes it more appealing than using the two functions separately. It accepts the standard **lpDef** string that we talked about in **BuildCommDCB**, but it allows an extra substring, "TO=xxx". As you can guess, "TO" stands for timeout. The "xxx" part can be either "ON," which applies the settings of the **lpCommTimeouts** parameter, or "OFF," which disables all timeouts. Should the "TO=xxx" substring not be used, the **lpCommTimeouts** parameter is ignored, and current timeout settings are used.

TransmitCommChar, WriteFile, and ReadFile

Once the port has been opened and properly configured, you can start writing to it and reading from it. The simplest way to send a single character is to use the **TransmitCommChar** function:

```
function TransmitCommChar(hFile:THandle;cChar:CHAR):BOOL;
```

hFile is the handle of the port, obtained from the original call to **CreateFile**, and **cChar** is the character that you want to transmit. If transmission was successful, the function will return **True;** otherwise, it will return **False**. One important factor to be aware of if you use **TransmitCommChar** is that it if you call it once to transmit a character, you must wait for the character to actually be transmitted before you can successfully call it again or an error condition will be returned. However, because this error tells you whether you have sent the character, it is possible to repeatedly call the function until it returns zero before proceeding to the next character.

If your intention is to send more than one character at a time, the function of choice is **WriteFile**:

```
function WriteFile(hFile:THandle;const Buffer;
  nNumberOfBytesToWrite:DWORD;var lpNumberOfBytesWritten:DWORD;
  lpOverlapped:POverlapped):BOOL;
```

Again, **hFile** is the handle of the port. **Buffer** is a pointer to the block of data that you want to transmit, and **nNumberOfBytesToWrite** is the number of characters contained in that block. The **lpNumberOfBytesWritten** parameter is filled with the count of bytes actually transmitted when the function returns. The final parameter, **lpOverlapped**, is a pointer to a **TOverlapped** structure that when present, permits the asynchronous use of the serial port. What this means is that bytes may be written without having to wait for the operation to be completed. We will go deeper into this topic later on when we talk about threads. If the function is successful, the return value will be **True**; however, if an error occurs, **False** will be returned.

Reading data from the port requires the use of the **ReadFile** function:

```
function ReadFile(hFile:THandle;var Buffer;nNumberOfBytesToRead:DWORD;
  var lpNumberOfBytesRead:DWORD;lpOverlapped:POverlapped):BOOL;
```

hFile is the port handle. **Buffer** identifies a pointer to a memory block to hold the data. **nNumberOfBytesToRead** is how many bytes of data you want to read from the receive buffer.

lpNumberOfBytesRead is filled with a number indicating how many bytes have actually been read. The **lpOverlapped** parameter, when not **nil**, allows the reception of data to occur in the background. This will also be discussed in the section on threads. Finally, a **True** return value indicates success; whereas a **False** return value indicates failure.

PurgeComm

Suppose that an application is communicating with a serial printer, and there are several thousand bytes of data in the transmit buffer. Suddenly the user aborts the print job. He expects the printer to stop what it is doing, and maybe even do a form feed to eject the page. At this moment in time, all of the data in the buffer becomes worthless and the need to continue transmitting it vanishes. Also, it is only friendly to eject the page immediately instead of continuing to print on it. The user is lucky because the programmer of the application was wise enough to flush the data from the buffer before issuing the form feed command, providing near instantaneous response. This thoughtful programmer accomplished this feat by using the **PurgeComm** function:

```
function PurgeComm(hFile:THandle;dwFlags:DWORD):BOOL;
```

hFile is the port handle, and **dwFlags** specifies whether the transmit buffer or the receive buffer is to be flushed and/or aborts any subsequent ones. **dwFlags** can be any combination of the following values:

Value	Description
PURGE_TX_ABORT	Aborts all pending write operations. Obviously, this operation only makes sense when using the port in an asynchronous fashion, where multiple writes can be stacked on top of one another.
PURGE_RX_ABORT	Aborts all pending read operations. Like **PURGE_TX_ABORT**, this operation only applies when multiple are reads stacked on top of one another.
PURGE_TX_CLEAR	Flushes the contents of the output buffer.
PURGE_RX_CLEAR	Flushes the contents of the input buffer.

Success is indicated by a return value of **True**. A **False** value is returned if **hFile** is not a proper handle or **dwFlags** is not one or more of the above values.

ClearCommError

This is perhaps one of the most important functions in the communication API subset. Its purpose is to notify you of any errors that occur on a port, and failing to call it after an error has occurred will place your program in a situation where nothing can be transmitted or received.

```
function ClearCommError(hFile:THandle;var lpErrors:DWORD;
  lpStat:PComStat):BOOL;
```

hFile is the handle of the port that you want to check for errors. **lpErrors** is filled with a bit mask of the errors that are currently pending:

Constant	Bit	Description
CE_RXOVER	0	The receive buffer overflowed as a result of too much received data, or data is being received after the reception of the end of file character, **EofChar**.
CE_OVERRUN	1	The comm driver failed to remove a character from the currently full UARTs (universal asynchronous receiver/transmitter) relatively small buffer while it was in the process of receiving an additional character, resulting in data loss.
CE_RXPARITY	2	A parity error occurred. Unfortunately, it is not possible to determine the exact byte responsible for the error.
CE_FRAME	3	A frame error occurred. This happens whenever the stop bit of a byte is not detected. There is no mechanism to determine the exact byte that caused this error; however, this error is typically caused by mismatched baud rates.

(continued)

Constant	Bit	Description
CE_BREAK	4	The receive line has detected a break condition. This occurs when the cable physically "breaks" or becomes disconnected. However, it is also possible for a transmitting device to simulate this condition by holding the transmit line low. Typically, this is done to initialize a device or set it to a known state.
CE_TXFULL	5	The transmit buffer was full when an attempt was made to add an additional character.
CE_PTO	6	Parallel device timeout.
CE_IOE	7	Parallel device I/O error.
CE_DNS	8	Parallel device not selected.
CE_OOP	9	Parallel device out of paper.
CE_MODE	10	Requested mode of operation for the port is not supported by the hardware, or the port handle is invalid.

lpStat is a structure of type **TComStat** and declared as **var** to allow information to be set and passed back. The **TComStat** record itself contains three fields that can be used to extract additional information about the state of the port:

```
TComStat = record
  Flags: DWord;
  cbInQue: DWord;
  cbOutQue: DWord;
end;
```

The **Flags** field contains bit flags that provide information about the status of transmission:

Flag Name	Bit	Description
fCtsHold	0	If set, transmission is waiting for the CTS line to become asserted before sending more data.
fDsrHold	1	If set, transmission is waiting for the DSR line to become asserted before sending more data.
fRlsdHold	2	If set, transmission is waiting for the RLSD line to become asserted before sending more data.
fXoffHold	3	If set, transmission is waiting for the XON character to be received before sending more data.
fXoffSent	4	Set whenever an XOFF character was sent, but cleared as soon as the matching XON is sent.
fEof	5	Set when the end of file character, **EofChar**, has been received.
fTxim	6	If set, a character is waiting to be transmitted. If clear, the transmit buffer is empty.

The field **cbInQueue** contains a value that indicates how many characters are in the receive buffer. Before attempting to read anything out of the buffer, it is a good idea to make sure that there is something to read and that it is long enough for what you are expecting.

cbOutQueue contains the number of characters that are in the transmit buffer. Before making additions to the transmit buffer, it is always smart to make sure that there is room for it. There is one small problem worthy of mentioning here. If you are performing asynchronous I/O, multiple calls to **WriteFile** do not update this value as you might expect. Suppose, for instance, that you make two calls to **WriteFile**. With the first call you write five bytes, and with the second you write three. You might be inclined to think that **cbOutQueue** would contain and eight at this point, indicating the number of bytes waiting to be transmitted. Unfortunately, it just does not work this way. What will happen is this: **cbOutQueue** will start with the value of five and work its way down to zero, corresponding to the first write. After this happens, it will then work its way down from three to zero, corresponding to the second write. This "feature" makes it a royal pain to know at any given moment how many bytes are waiting to be transmitted.

SetCommBreak and ClearCommBreak

Often to get a device to a known state, it is necessary to send what is known as a *break condition* over the transmit line. This is totally unique compared to anything else that you can do with the transmit line and easy to detect by the receptor. In addition, it simulates a physical disconnection, so the advantage of having the device reset itself when this happens is obvious.

To set a break condition, the **SetCommBreak** function is called:

```
function SetCommBreak(hFile:THandle):BOOL;
```

The only parameter to worry about is **hFile**, the handle of the port; and if it is valid, **True** will be returned to indicate success. The break condition need not last very long; a duration of the baud rate times ten, yielding a result in milliseconds, will suffice for most applications. To complete the break condition, call **ClearCommBreak**:

```
function ClearCommBreak(hFile:THandle):BOOL;
```

Again, the only parameter is **hFile**, and the return value will be **True** if it is a valid handle.

SetCommMask, GetCommMask and WaitCommEvent

A typical communication session can produce many events that you may need to know about. For example, whenever a character has been received, or when a break condition occurs. For this purpose, it is desirable to have a way to know when such an event takes place. The first step in doing so is to call **SetCommMask** to inform the comm driver what events you are interested in receiving:

```
function SetCommMask(hFile:THandle;dwEvtMask:DWORD):BOOL;
```

hFile is the handle for the port, and **dwEvtMask** is a double word that can have certain bits set, representative of the events you want to be informed of. These bits are identified by constants, whose meanings are shown here:

Constant	Bit	Description
EV_RXCHAR	0	If set, an event will be generated whenever a character is received.
EV_RXFLAG	1	If set, an event will be generated when the **EvtChar** character is received.
EV_TXEMPTY	2	If set, an event will be generated when the transmit buffer becomes empty.
EV_CTS	3	If set, an event will be generated whenever the CTS line changes state.
EV_DSR	4	If set, an event will be generated whenever the DSR line changes state.
EV_RLSD	5	If set, an event will be generated whenever the RLSD line changes state.
EV_BREAK	6	If set, an event will be generated when a break condition is detected.
EV_ERR	7	If set, an event will be generated whenever a frame error, overrun error, or parity error occurs.
EV_RING	8	If set, an event will be generated whenever your connected modem gets a call.
EV_PERR	9	If set, an event will be generated whenever a printer error occurs.

SetCommMask returns **True** if the function succeeds, or **False** if it fails.

On occasion, it is also useful to know what the particular event mask configuration of a given port is. This can be determined by calling **GetCommMask**:

```
function GetCommMask(hFile:THandle;var lpEvtMask:DWORD):BOOL;
```

The **hFile** parameter is the same as before, but this time the **lpEvtMask** parameter returns with a value that specifies which events are "armed."

Once the appropriate events have been configured, you have to know whether they occur. This is done via the **WaitCommEvent** function:

```
function WaitCommEvent(hFile:THandle;var lpEvtMask:DWORD;
  lpOverlapped:POverlapped):BOOL;
```

This function accepts the handle to the open communication port as **hFile** and returns a bit mask containing the events that have occurred in **lpEvtMask**. The **lpOverlapped** parameter may either be **nil,** or it may point to a valid **TOverlapped** structure. If **lpOverlapped** is **nil** or **CreateFile** was called without **FILE_FLAG_OVERLAPPED**, **WaitCommEvent** does just what its name implies—it waits. While it is doing so, your application waits as well, except for any independent threads that are running concurrently. This can be a big problem if your application doesn't use threads. So, what if you put **WaitCommEvent** in a thread of its own? Now we are getting somewhere. It is entirely possible to start a new thread of execution and then call **WaitCommEvent**. While it is waiting for an event to occur, very little CPU resources are being consumed, and the main flow of execution is not interrupted. We'll go into this topic in further detail when we talk about threads.

GetCommModemStatus

While **WaitCommEvent** can notify you when the **CTS**, **DSR**, or **RLSD** lines change state, it doesn't tell you what the new state is. Happily, this information is provided with the **GetCommModemStatus** function:

```
function GetCommModemStatus(hFile:THandle;var lpModemStat:DWORD):BOOL;
```

Here, **hFile** is the handle of the communication port returned from **CreateFile**. When the function returns, **lpModemStat,** a double word, has bits that are set or reset depending on the state of the hardware itself. These bits are identified by constants:

Constant	Value	Description
MS_CTS_ON	10h	Set when the **CTS** line is asserted.
MS_DSR_ON	20h	Set when the **DSR** line is asserted.
MS_RING_ON	40h	Set when an incoming call is detected.
MS_RLSD_ON	80h	Set when the **RLSD** line is asserted.

Should **GetCommModemStatus** fail for any reason, **False** will be returned.

GetCommProperties

One of the worst things that a programmer can do is assume that a communication port supports everything he wants it to. Such blind faith often spells trouble in the real world. For this reason, **GetCommProperties** exists:

```
function GetCommProperties(hFile:THandle;
  var lpCommProp:TCommProp): BOOL;
```

The sole purpose of this function is to inform the programmer what settings are available for any given port. It does this by accepting a handle to an open port, **hFile**, and filling the **lpCommProp**, of type **TCommProp**, structure with the resulting information. **TCommProp** is fairly complex, as you can see:

```
TCommProp=record
  wPacketLength:Word;
  wPacketVersion:Word;
  dwServiceMask:DWORD;
  dwReserved1:DWORD;
  dwMaxTxQueue:DWORD;
  dwMaxRxQueue:DWORD;
  dwMaxBaud:DWORD;
  dwProvSubType:DWORD;
  dwProvCapabilities:DWORD;
  dwSettableParams:DWORD;
  dwSettableBaud:DWORD;
  wSettableData:Word;
  wSettableStopParity:Word;
```

```
dwCurrentTxQueue:DWORD;
dwCurrentRxQueue:DWORD;
dwProvSpec1:DWORD;
dwProvSpec2:DWORD;
wcProvChar:array[0..0] of WCHAR;
end;
```

To better understand what each member of this record does, let's look at each a bit closer.

wPacketLength

When **GetCommProperties** returns, this field is filled with the length of the **TCommProp** structure.

wPacketVersion

This field indicates the version number of the **TCommProp** structure. This ensures that as **TCommProp** evolves, older structures will still be usable by **GetCommProperties**.

dwServiceMask

This field is a bitmask of services provided by the communication port. Currently, the only service defined is **SP_SERIALCOMM**, indicating a serial device.

dwReserved1

This field is reserved for internal use by Windows.

dwMaxTxQueue

This specifies the maximum size of the transmit buffer. If this value is filled with a zero, the driver does not impose a limit on what the size may be.

dwMaxRxQueue

This specifies the maximum size of the receive buffer. If this value is filled with a zero, the driver does not impose a limit on what the size may be.

dwMaxBaud

This specifies the maximum baud rate of the port. It may be one of the following constant values:

BAUD_075	BAUD_1800	BAUD_7200	BAUD_56K
BAUD_110	BAUD_600	BAUD_9600	BAUD_57600
BAUD_134_5	BAUD_1200	BAUD_14400	BAUD_115200
BAUD_150	BAUD_2400	BAUD_19200	BAUD_128K
BAUD_300	BAUD_4800	BAUD_38400	BAUD_USER

Should **BAUD_USER** be returned, it does not mean that the maximum achievable baud rate is infinite, but rather that the baud rate is not limited to the values indicated by the constants. For example, a baud rate of 432 would be possible.

dwProvSubType

Identifies the device that provides the communication, indicated by the following constants:

Constant	Description
PST_FAX	FAX device
PST_LAT	LAT protocol
PST_MODEM	Modem
PST_NETWORK_BRIDGE	Unspecified network bridge
PST_PARALLELPORT	Parallel port
PST_RS232	RS-232
PST_RS422	RS-422
PST_RS423	RS-423
PST_RS449	RS-449
PST_SCANNER	Scanner device
PST_TCPIP_TELNET	TCP/IP protocol
PST_UNSPECIFIED	Unspecified device
PST_X25	X.25 standards

dwProvSubType

This bitmask field is filled with the capabilities offered by the port and can be a combination of any these constants:

Constant	Description
PCF_16BITMODE	Port supports a special 16 bit mode.
PCF_DTRDSR	The DTR and DSR lines are available.
PCF_INTTIMEOUTS	Interval timeouts are supported for read operations.
PCF_PARITY_CHECK	Parity checking is supported.
PCF_RLSD	The RLSD line is available.
PCF_RTSCTS	The RTS and CTS lines are available.
PCF_SETXCHAR	The XON and XOFF control characters are externally setable.
PCF_SPECIALCHARS	Special character support is provided.
PCF_TOTALTIMEOUTS	Elapsed timeouts are supported.
PCF_XONXOFF	Port supports XON / XOFF flow control.

dwSettableParams

The various bits of this field each represent a physical property of the port. If the bit is set, the property can be set through software. The bits are represented by constant values:

Constant	Description
SP_BAUD	Baud rate
SP_DATABITS	Number of data bits
SP_HANDSHAKING	Handshaking
SP_PARITY	Type of parity
SP_PARITY_CHECK	Parity error checking
SP_RLSD	RLSD line
SP_STOPBITS	Number of stop bits

dwSettableBaud

The various bits of this field each represent a certain allowable baud rate. Should the bit be set, the baud rate is supported. For a list of the corresponding constants, see the **dwMaxBaud** description.

wSettableData

This field specifies the number of data bits supported by the port. Any combination of the following constants can be present:

Constant	Description
DATABITS_5	5 data bits
DATABITS_6	6 data bits
DATABITS_7	7 data bits
DATABITS_8	8 data bits
DATABITS_16	16 data bits
DATABITS_16X	Special 16 data bits

wSettableStopParity

This member is a bitmask that returns with the allowable stop bits and parities indicated through the setting of individual bits, represented by these constants:

Constant	Description
STOPBITS_10	1 stop bit
STOPBITS_15	1.5 stop bits
STOPBITS_20	2 stop bits
PARITY_NONE	No parity
PARITY_ODD	Odd parity
PARITY_EVEN	Even parity
PARITY_MARK	Mark Parity
PARITY_SPACE	Space Parity

dwCurrentTxQueue

This is a double word that is filled with the size of the current transmit buffer.

dwCurrentRxQueue

This is a double word that is filled with the size of the current receive buffer.

dwProvSpec1, dwProvSpec2, and wcProvChar

These values are vendor specific.

EscapeCommFunction

Last but not least on our exploration of the communications API subset is **EscapeCommFunction:**

```
function EscapeCommFunction(hFile:THandle;dwFunc:DWORD):BOOL;
```

This function allows you to do many of the things that the other functions won't let you do, such as manually set the state of the RTS line or determine how many serial ports are available on any given system. The **hFile** parameter is the handle to the port, and **dwFunc** represents the function that you want to call, indicated by one of the following constants:

Constant	Description
CLRDTR	Clears the DTR line
CLRRTS	Clears the RTS line
SETDTR	Sets the DTR line
SETRTS	Sets the RTS line
SETXOFF	Simulates the reception of an XOFF character, effectively halting transmission
SETXON	Simulates the reception of an XON character, resuming transmission
SETBREAK	Identical to the **SetCommBreak** API function
CLEARBREAK	Identical to the **ClearCommBreak** API function

The return value of **EscapeCommFunction** is dependent on the actual function being called, but will return 8000h to indicate an error. You may be wondering why 8000h is used instead of the normal negative value. As an integer,

8000h is indeed equivalent to -1, but this function returns a *long integer* where the two are not equivalent, making it necessary to check if the value is equal to 8000h.

Defining the Requirements

Wow, it took a while, but we're finally at the stage where we can begin laying down what we want the communication component to do. When you have a certain application in mind for which a component would be ideal, it is often tempting to design the component around the application. Don't do this! The whole point of using a component in the first place is that you want it to be reusable later on, and therefore making it dependent on or limited by a certain application should be avoided. Even if you don't intend on reusing the component for your own use, making it properly from the start increases your chances of selling it to other people. Obviously, it is easy to take this idea too far and end up with a "Swiss Army" component, whose complexity outweighs its usefulness; therefore some discretion is required when determining an optimal balance between the two.

In keeping with this "complete but simple" idea, our component will provide only the following essential capabilities:

- Setting of baud rate, stop bits, buffer sizes, and so on
- Reading and writing data
- Basic flow control
- Event notifications

This will provide a good starting point for any more advanced communication component that you may want to design. The best approach to take, if this is what you have in mind, is to create a descendant from our component and put the extra functionality in it, instead of putting it all in the original. This way, you ensure that if you ever require a communication component without all the fancy stuff, you have it; and in the process, you don't mess up what is already working.

Now, with our goal clearly established, lets begin to code.

The Code to Success

The road to achieving a functional component has a bit of a incline to it when first starting out. You already know that you must decide on a parent and a name for your component, but there is also a great deal of grunt work to do before reaching the point where you are actually coding the *purpose* of the component. This involves creating all the properties, publishing them, providing event handlers, and so forth. Because our **TWinIni** component touched on these, I'll simply present the final code, **\DC\CHAP03\COMM.PAS**, and then fill you in on what we haven't looked at before as well as any notables concerning the communication aspect of the component itself.

Listing 3.1 Comm.PAS

```
unit Comm;

interface

uses
  SysUtils, Windows, Messages, Classes, Graphics, Controls, Forms,
  Dialogs;

type

TPort=(tptNone,tptOne,tptTwo,tptThree,tptFour,tptFive,tptSix,
        tptSeven,tptEight);

TBaudRate=(tbr110,tbr300,tbr600,tbr1200,tbr2400,tbr4800,tbr9600,

tbr14400,tbr19200,tbr38400,tbr56000,tbr128000,
            tbr256000);
  TParity=(tpNone,tpOdd,tpEven,tpMark,tpSpace);
  TDataBits=(tdbFour,tdbFive,tdbSix,tdbSeven,tdbEight);
  TStopBits=(tsbOne,tsbOnePointFive,tsbTwo);
  TFlowControl=(tfcNone,tfcXONXOFF,tfcCTSRTS,tfcDSRDTR);
  TEvent=(tceBreak,tceCts,tceDsr,tceErr,tceRing,tceRlsd,
            tceRxChar,tceRxFlag,tceTxEmpty);
```

```
TEvents=set of TEvent;
TError=(tcrFrame,tcrOverrun,tcrRxParity);
TErrors=set of TError;

TNotifyEventEvent=procedure(const Sender:TObject;
  const Events:TEvents;const Errors:TErrors) of object;
TNotifyReceiveEvent=procedure(const Sender:TObject;
  const RxBytes:Word) of object;
TNotifyTransmitEvent=procedure(const Sender:TObject;
  const TxBytes:Word) of object;

const
  DCB_fBinary=$0001;
  DCB_fParity=$0002;
  DCB_fOutxCtsFlow=$0004;
  DCB_fOutxDsrFlow=$0008;
  DCB_fDtrControl=$0010;
  DCB_fDsrSensitivity=$0012;
  DCB_fTxContinueOnXOff=$0014;
  DCB_fOutX=$0018;
  DCB_fInX=$0020;
  DCB_fErrorChar=$0021;
  DCB_fNull=$0022;
  DCB_fRtsControl=$0024;
  DCB_fAbortOnError=$0030;

  PortDefault=tptNone;
  ReadBufferSizeDefault=2048;
  WriteBufferSizeDefault=2048;
  BaudRateDefault=tbr9600;
  ParityDefault=tpNone;
  DataBitsDefault=tdbEight;
  StopBitsDefault=tsbOne;
  EventMaskDefault=[];
  XOnCharDefault=$11;
  XOffCharDefault=$13;
  ResumeDefault=1024;
```

```
    PauseDefault=2048;
    EventCharDefault=0;
    ParityErrorDetectDefault=False;
    ParityReplacementDefault=False;
    ParityCharDefault=0;
    NullStripDefault=False;
    ReadFullDefault=1024;
    FlowControlDefault=tfcNone;

    COMM_INIT=WM_USER+0;
    COMM_RX=WM_USER+1;
    COMM_TX=WM_USER+2;
    COMM_EVENT=WM_USER+3;

type
    PBufferNode=^TBufferNode;
    TBufferNode=record
      Next:PBufferNode;
      BufferSize:DWord;
      Buffer:PChar;
    end;

    TComm = class(TComponent)
    private
      CriticalSection:TRTLCriticalSection;
      hComm:THandle;
      hWindow:hWnd;
      hReadThread:THandle;
      ReadOverlapped:TOverlapped;
      ReadOffset:DWord;
      ReadBuffer:PChar;
      hWriteThread:THandle;
      WriteOverlapped:TOverlapped;
      hCommThread:THandle;
      CommOverlapped:TOverlapped;
      FirstWriteBuffer:PBufferNode;
      LastWriteBuffer:PBufferNode;
```

```
FirstReadBuffer:PBufferNode;
LastReadBuffer:PBufferNode;

FPort:TPort;
FBaudRate:TBaudRate;
FParity:TParity;
FDataBits:TDataBits;
FStopBits:TStopBits;
FReadBufferSize:DWord;
FWriteBufferSize:DWord;
FEventMask:TEvents;
FXONChar:Byte;
FXOFFChar:Byte;
FResume:Word;
FPause:Word;
FEventChar:Byte;
FParityErrorDetect:Boolean;
FParityReplacement:Boolean;
FParityChar:Byte;
FNullStrip:Boolean;
FReadFull:DWord;
FFlowControl:TFlowControl;
FOnEvent:TNotifyEventEvent;
FOnReceive:TNotifyReceiveEvent;
FOnTransmit:TNotifyTransmitEvent;
FRxBytes:DWord;
FTxBytes:DWord;

procedure SetDCB;
procedure SetBuffers(OldReadBufferSize:DWord);
procedure DoTx;
procedure DoRx;
procedure DoEvent(EventFlags:DWord);
procedure WndProc(var Msg:TMessage);
procedure ClosePort;
procedure KillWriteBuffers;
procedure KillReadBuffers;
```

```
    procedure SetPort(APort:TPort);
    procedure SetBaudRate(ABaudRate:TBaudRate);
    procedure SetParity(AParity:TParity);
    procedure SetDataBits(ADataBits:TDataBits);
    procedure SetStopBits(AStopBits:TStopBits);
    procedure SetReadBufferSize(AReadBufferSize:DWord);
    procedure SetWriteBufferSize(AWriteBufferSize:DWord);
    procedure SetEventMask(AEventMask:TEvents);
    procedure SetXONChar(AXONChar:Byte);
    procedure SetXOFFChar(AXOFFChar:Byte);
    procedure SetResume(AResume:Word);
    procedure SetPause(APause:Word);
    procedure SetEventChar(AEventChar:Byte);
    procedure SetParityErrorDetect(AParityErrorDetect:Boolean);
    procedure SetParityReplacement(AParityReplacement:Boolean);
    procedure SetParityChar(AParityChar:Byte);
    procedure SetNullStrip(ANullStrip:Boolean);
    procedure SetReadFull(AReadFull:DWord);
    procedure SetFlowControl(AFlowControl:TFlowControl);
    procedure FlushRx(DummyRxBytes:DWord);
    procedure FlushTx(DummyTxBytes:DWord);
  public
    constructor Create(AOwner:TComponent);override;
    destructor Destroy;override;
    procedure Write(Data:PChar;Count:DWord);
    function Read(Data:PChar;Count:DWord):DWord;
    procedure SetBreak;
    procedure ClearBreak;
    function IsOpen:Boolean;
    property RxBytes:DWord read FRxBytes write FlushRx;
    property TxBytes:DWord read FTxBytes write FlushTx;
  published
    property Port:TPort read FPort write SetPort
      default PortDefault;
    property BaudRate:TBaudRate read FBaudRate write SetBaudRate
      default BaudRateDefault;
```

```
property Parity:TParity read FParity write SetParity
   default ParityDefault;
property DataBits:TDataBits read FDataBits write SetDataBits
   default DataBitsDefault;
property StopBits:TStopBits read FStopBits write SetStopBits
   default StopBitsDefault;
property ReadBufferSize:DWord read FReadBufferSize
   write SetReadBufferSize default ReadBufferSizeDefault;
property WriteBufferSize:DWord read FWriteBufferSize
   write SetWriteBufferSize default WriteBufferSizeDefault;
property EventMask:TEvents read FEventMask write SetEventMask
   default EventMaskDefault;
property XONChar:Byte read FXONChar write SetXONChar
   default XONCharDefault;
property XOFFChar:Byte read FXOFFChar write SetXOFFChar
   default XOFFCharDefault;
property Resume:Word read FResume write SetResume
   default ResumeDefault;
property Pause:Word read FPause write SetPause
   default PauseDefault;
property EventChar:Byte read FEventChar write SetEventChar
   default EventCharDefault;
property ParityErrorDetect:Boolean read FParityErrorDetect
   write SetParityErrorDetect default ParityErrorDetectDefault;
property ParityReplacement:Boolean read FParityReplacement
   write SetParityReplacement default ParityReplacementDefault;
property ParityChar:Byte read FParityChar write SetParityChar
   default ParityCharDefault;
property NullStrip:Boolean read FNullStrip write SetNullStrip
   default NullStripDefault;
property ReadFull:DWord read FReadFull write SetReadFull
   default ReadFullDefault;
property FlowControl:TFlowControl read FFlowControl
   write SetFlowControl default FlowControlDefault;
property OnEvent:TNotifyEventEvent read FOnEvent
   write FOnEvent;
```

```
    property OnReceive:TNotifyReceiveEvent read FOnReceive
      write FOnReceive;
    property OnTransmit:TNotifyTransmitEvent read FOnTransmit
      write FOnTransmit;
  end;

procedure Register;

implementation

function ReadThread(Comm:TComm):DWord;stdcall;
var
  BytesRead:DWord;
begin
  with Comm do
  begin
    repeat
      ReadFile(hComm,ReadBuffer^,FReadFull,BytesRead,
        @ReadOverlapped);
      GetOverlappedResult(hComm,ReadOverlapped,BytesRead,True);
      if hComm=INVALID_HANDLE_VALUE then ExitThread(0);
      if BytesRead<>0 then
      begin
        EnterCriticalSection(CriticalSection);
        inc(FRxBytes,BytesRead);
        if FirstReadBuffer=nil then
        begin
          new(FirstReadBuffer);
          LastReadBuffer:=FirstReadBuffer;
        end
        else
        begin
          new(LastReadBuffer^.Next);
          LastReadBuffer:=LastReadBuffer^.Next;
        end;
        LastReadBuffer^.Next:=nil;
```

```
        GetMem(LastReadBuffer^.Buffer,BytesRead);
        LastReadBuffer^.BufferSize:=BytesRead;

Move(ReadBuffer^,LastReadBuffer^.Buffer^,BytesRead);
        PostMessage(hWindow,COMM_RX,0,BytesRead);
        LeaveCriticalSection(CriticalSection);
        SuspendThread(hReadThread);
      end;
    until False;
  end;
end;

function WriteThread(Comm:TComm):DWord;stdcall;
var
  BytesWritten:DWord;
  TempBuffer:PBufferNode;
begin
  with Comm do
  begin
    repeat

GetOverlappedResult(hComm,WriteOverlapped,BytesWritten,
        True);
      if hComm=INVALID_HANDLE_VALUE then ExitThread(0);
      EnterCriticalSection(CriticalSection);
      if FirstWriteBuffer<>nil then
      begin
        dec(FTxBytes,BytesWritten);
        FreeMem(FirstWriteBuffer^.Buffer,
          FirstWriteBuffer^.BufferSize);
        TempBuffer:=FirstWriteBuffer^.Next;
        Dispose(FirstWriteBuffer);
        FirstWriteBuffer:=TempBuffer;
        if FirstWriteBuffer=nil then LastWriteBuffer:=nil;
        PostMessage(hWindow,COMM_TX,0,BytesWritten);
      end;
```

```
      LeaveCriticalSection(CriticalSection);
      SuspendThread(hWriteThread);
    until False;
  end;
end;


function CommThread(Comm:TComm):DWord;stdcall;
var
  Events:DWord;
begin
  with Comm do
  begin
    repeat
      WaitCommEvent(hComm,Events,@CommOverlapped);
      WaitForSingleObject(CommOverlapped.hEvent,INFINITE);
      if hComm=INVALID_HANDLE_VALUE then ExitThread(0);
      if Events<>0 then
      begin
        PostMessage(hWindow,COMM_EVENT,0,Events);
        SuspendThread(hCommThread);
      end;
    until False;
  end;
end;


procedure TComm.SetDCB;
var
  DCB:TDCB;
  CommTimeouts:TCommTimeouts;
begin
  if hComm=INVALID_HANDLE_VALUE then exit;

  GetCommState(hComm,DCB);

  case FBaudRate of
    tbr110:DCB.BaudRate:=110;
```

```
  tbr300:DCB.BaudRate:=300;
  tbr600:DCB.BaudRate:=600;
  tbr1200:DCB.BaudRate:=1200;
  tbr2400:DCB.BaudRate:=2400;
  tbr4800:DCB.BaudRate:=4800;
  tbr9600:DCB.BaudRate:=9600;
  tbr14400:DCB.BaudRate:=14400;
  tbr19200:DCB.BaudRate:=19200;
  tbr38400:DCB.BaudRate:=38400;
  tbr56000:DCB.BaudRate:=56000;
  tbr128000:DCB.BaudRate:=128000;
  tbr256000:DCB.BaudRate:=256000;
end;

CommTimeouts.ReadIntervalTimeout:=100000 div DCB.BaudRate;
CommTimeouts.ReadTotalTimeoutMultiplier:=1000 div
  DCB.BaudRate+1;
CommTimeouts.ReadTotalTimeoutConstant:=100;
CommTimeouts.WriteTotalTimeoutMultiplier:=1000 div
  DCB.BaudRate+1;
CommTimeouts.WriteTotalTimeoutConstant:=100;
SetCommTimeouts(hComm,CommTimeouts);

case FParity of
  tpNone:DCB.Parity:=NOPARITY;
  tpOdd:DCB.Parity:=ODDPARITY;
  tpEven:DCB.Parity:=EVENPARITY;
  tpMark:DCB.Parity:=MARKPARITY;
  tpSpace:DCB.Parity:=SPACEPARITY;
end;

case FDataBits of
  tdbFour:DCB.ByteSize:=4;
  tdbFive:DCB.ByteSize:=5;
  tdbSix:DCB.ByteSize:=6;
  tdbSeven:DCB.ByteSize:=7;
```

```
    tdbEight:DCB.ByteSize:=8;
  end;

  case StopBits of
    tsbOne:DCB.StopBits:=ONESTOPBIT;
    tsbOnePointFive:DCB.StopBits:=ONE5STOPBITS;
    tsbTwo:DCB.StopBits:=TWOSTOPBITS;
  end;

  case FFlowControl of
    tfcXONXOFF:DCB.Flags:=DCB.Flags or dcb_fOutX or dcb_fInX;
    tfcCTSRTS:DCB.Flags:=DCB.Flags or dcb_fOutXCtsFlow or
      (dcb_fRtsControl*RTS_CONTROL_HANDSHAKE);
    tfcDSRDTR:DCB.Flags:=DCB.Flags or dcb_fOutXDsrFlow or
      (dcb_fDtrControl*DTR_CONTROL_HANDSHAKE);
  end;

  DCB.EvtChar:=Char(FEventChar);
  DCB.XOnChar:=Char(FXONChar);
  DCB.XOffChar:=Char(FXOFFChar);
  DCB.XONLim:=FResume;
  DCB.XOFFLim:=FPause;

  if FParityErrorDetect then inc(DCB.Flags,dcb_fParity);
  if FParityReplacement then inc(DCB.Flags,dcb_fErrorChar);
  DCB.ErrorChar:=char(FParityChar);
  if FNullStrip then inc(DCB.Flags,dcb_fNull);

  SetCommState(hComm,DCB);
end;

procedure TComm.SetBuffers(OldReadBufferSize:DWord);
begin
  if hComm=INVALID_HANDLE_VALUE then exit;
  SetupComm(hComm,FReadBufferSize,FWriteBufferSize);
  if OldReadBufferSize<>FReadBufferSize then
  begin
```

```
      FreeMem(ReadBuffer,OldReadBufferSize);
      GetMem(ReadBuffer,FReadBufferSize);
    end;
  end;

procedure TComm.DoTx;
begin
  if Assigned(FOnTransmit) then FOnTransmit(Self,FTxBytes);
  ResumeThread(hWriteThread);
end;

procedure TComm.DoRx;
begin
  if Assigned(FOnReceive) then FOnReceive(Self,FRxBytes);
  ResumeThread(hReadThread);
end;

procedure TComm.DoEvent(EventFlags:DWord);
var
  Events:TEvents;
  ErrorCode:DWord;
  Errors:TErrors;
begin
  Events:=[];
  if EventFlags and EV_BREAK<>0 then Events:=Events+[tceBreak];
  if EventFlags and EV_CTS<>0 then Events:=Events+[tceCts];
  if EventFlags and EV_DSR<>0 then Events:=Events+[tceDsr];
  if EventFlags and EV_ERR<>0 then
  begin
    Events:=Events+[tceErr];
    Errors:=[];
    ClearCommError(hComm,ErrorCode,nil);
    if ErrorCode and CE_FRAME<>0 then Errors:=Errors+[tcrFrame];
    if ErrorCode and CE_OVERRUN<>0 then Errors:=Errors+
      [tcrOverrun];
    if ErrorCode and CE_RXPARITY<>0 then Errors:=Errors+
```

```
          [tcrRxParity];
    end;
    if EventFlags and EV_RING<>0 then Events:=Events+[tceRing];
    if EventFlags and EV_RLSD<>0 then Events:=Events+[tceRlsd];
    if EventFlags and EV_RXCHAR<>0 then Events:=Events+[tceRxChar];
    if EventFlags and EV_RXFLAG<>0 then Events:=Events+[tceRxFlag];
    if EventFlags and EV_TXEMPTY<>0 then Events:=Events+
      [tceTxEmpty];
    if Assigned(FOnEvent) then FOnEvent(Self,Events,Errors);
    ResumeThread(hCommThread);
  end;

procedure TComm.WndProc(var Msg:TMessage);
var
  Events:TEvents;
begin
  with Msg do
  begin
    case Msg of
      COMM_INIT:SetPort(FPort);
      COMM_TX:DoTx;
      COMM_RX:DoRx;
      COMM_EVENT:DoEvent(LParam);
    else
      Result:=DefWindowProc(hWindow,Msg,wParam,lParam);
    end;
  end;
end;

procedure TComm.ClosePort;
begin
  if hComm=INVALID_HANDLE_VALUE then exit;

  CloseHandle(hComm);

  hComm:=INVALID_HANDLE_VALUE;
```

```
    ResumeThread(hReadThread);
    ResumeThread(hWriteThread);
    ResumeThread(hCommThread);

    SetEvent(ReadOverlapped.hEvent);
    SetEvent(WriteOverlapped.hEvent);
    SetEvent(CommOverlapped.hEvent);

    WaitForSingleObject(hReadThread,INFINITE);
    WaitForSingleObject(hWriteThread,INFINITE);
    WaitForSingleObject(hCommThread,INFINITE);

    CloseHandle(hReadThread);
    CloseHandle(hWriteThread);
    CloseHandle(hCommThread);

    CloseHandle(ReadOverlapped.hEvent);
    CloseHandle(WriteOverlapped.hEvent);
    CloseHandle(CommOverlapped.hEvent);

    FreeMem(ReadBuffer,FReadBufferSize);
    ReadBuffer:=nil;

  KillWriteBuffers;
  KillReadBuffers;
end;

procedure TComm.KillWriteBuffers;
var
  TempBuffer:PBufferNode;
begin
  while FirstWriteBuffer<>nil do
  begin
    FreeMem(FirstWriteBuffer^.Buffer,
      FirstWriteBuffer^.BufferSize);
    TempBuffer:=FirstWriteBuffer^.Next;
    Dispose(FirstWriteBuffer);
```

```
      FirstWriteBuffer:=TempBuffer;
    end;
  FirstWriteBuffer:=nil;
  LastWriteBuffer:=nil;
end;

procedure TComm.KillReadBuffers;
var
  TempBuffer:PBufferNode;
begin
  while FirstReadBuffer<>nil do
  begin

FreeMem(FirstReadBuffer^.Buffer,FirstReadBuffer^.BufferSize);
    TempBuffer:=FirstReadBuffer^.Next;
    Dispose(FirstReadBuffer);
    FirstReadBuffer:=TempBuffer;
  end;
  FirstReadBuffer:=nil;
  LastReadBuffer:=nil;
end;

procedure TComm.SetPort(APort:TPort);
var
  CommStr:String;
  TempID:DWord;
begin
  FPort:=APort;

  if (csLoading in ComponentState) or (csDesigning in
    ComponentState) then exit;

  ClosePort;

  if FPort=tptNone then exit;

  CommStr:='COM'+IntToStr(Ord(FPort));
  hComm:=CreateFile(PChar(CommStr),
```

```
                    GENERIC_READ or GENERIC_WRITE,
                    0,
                    nil,
                    OPEN_EXISTING,
                    FILE_FLAG_OVERLAPPED,
                    0);
   if hComm=INVALID_HANDLE_VALUE then exit;

ReadOverlapped.hEvent:=CreateEvent(nil,False,False,nil);
   WriteOverlapped.hEvent:=CreateEvent(nil,False,False,nil);

CommOverlapped.hEvent:=CreateEvent(nil,False,False,nil);

hCommThread:=CreateThread(nil,0,@CommThread,Self,0,TempID);

hReadThread:=CreateThread(nil,0,@ReadThread,Self,0,TempID);

hWriteThread:=CreateThread(nil,0,@WriteThread,Self,0,TempID);

   SetBuffers(0);
   SetDCB;
   SetEventMask(FEventMask);
end;

procedure TComm.SetBaudRate(ABaudRate:TBaudRate);
begin
   FBaudRate:=ABaudRate;
   SetDCB;
end;

procedure TComm.SetParity(AParity:TParity);
begin
   FParity:=AParity;
   SetDCB;
end;

procedure TComm.SetDataBits(ADataBits:TDataBits);
begin
```

```
    FDataBits:=ADataBits;
    SetDCB;
  end;

procedure TComm.SetStopBits(AStopBits:TStopBits);
begin
  FStopBits:=AStopBits;
  SetDCB;
end;

procedure TComm.SetReadBufferSize(AReadBufferSize:DWord);
var
  OldReadBufferSize:DWord;
begin
  OldReadBufferSize:=FReadBufferSize;
  FReadBufferSize:=AReadBufferSize;
  SetBuffers(OldReadBufferSize);
end;

procedure TComm.SetWriteBufferSize(AWriteBufferSize:DWord);
begin
  FWriteBufferSize:=AWriteBufferSize;
  SetBuffers(FReadBufferSize);
end;

procedure TComm.SetEventMask(AEventMask:TEvents);
var
  Mask:DWord;
begin
  FEventMask:=AEventMask;
  if hComm=INVALID_HANDLE_VALUE then exit;
  Mask:=0;
  if tceBreak in AEventMask then inc(Mask,EV_BREAK);
  if tceCts in AEventMask then inc(Mask,EV_CTS);
  if tceDsr in AEventMask then inc(Mask,EV_DSR);
  if tceErr in AEventMask then inc(Mask,EV_ERR);
  if tceRing in AEventMask then inc(Mask,EV_RING);
  if tceRlsd in AEventMask then inc(Mask,EV_RLSD);
```

```
    if tceRxChar in AEventMask then inc(Mask,EV_RXCHAR);
    if tceRxFlag in AEventMask then inc(Mask,EV_RXFLAG);
    if tceTxEmpty in AEventMask then inc(Mask,EV_TXEMPTY);
    SetCommMask(hComm,Mask)
end;

procedure TComm.SetXONChar(AXONChar:Byte);
begin
  FXONChar:=AXONChar;
  SetDCB;
end;

procedure TComm.SetXOFFChar(AXOFFChar:Byte);
begin
  FXOFFChar:=AXOFFChar;
  SetDCB;
end;

procedure TComm.SetResume(AResume:Word);
begin
  FResume:=AResume;
  SetDCB;
end;

procedure TComm.SetPause(APause:Word);
begin
  FPause:=APause;
  SetDCB;
end;

procedure TComm.SetEventChar(AEventChar:Byte);
begin
  FEventChar:=AEventChar;
  SetDCB;
end;

procedure TComm.SetParityErrorDetect(
  AParityErrorDetect:Boolean);
```

```
begin
  FParityErrorDetect:=AParityErrorDetect;
  SetDCB;
end;

procedure TComm.SetParityReplacement(
  AParityReplacement:Boolean);
begin
  FParityReplacement:=AParityReplacement;
  SetDCB;
end;

procedure TComm.SetParityChar(AParityChar:Byte);
begin
  FParityChar:=AParityChar;
  SetDCB;
end;

procedure TComm.SetNullStrip(ANullStrip:Boolean);
begin
  FNullStrip:=ANullStrip;
  SetDCB;
end;

procedure TComm.SetReadFull(AReadFull:DWord);
begin
  FReadFull:=AReadFull;
  if hComm=INVALID_HANDLE_VALUE then exit;
  SetEvent(ReadOverlapped.hEvent);
end;

procedure TComm.SetFlowControl(AFlowControl:TFlowControl);
begin
  FFlowControl:=AFlowControl;
  SetDCB;
end;
```

```
procedure TComm.FlushRx(DummyRxBytes:DWord);
begin
  if hComm=INVALID_HANDLE_VALUE then exit;
  SuspendThread(hReadThread);
  PurgeComm(hComm,PURGE_RXABORT or PURGE_RXCLEAR);
  KillReadBuffers;
  FRxBytes:=0;
  ResumeThread(hReadThread);
end;

procedure TComm.FlushTx(DummyTxBytes:DWord);
begin
  if hComm=INVALID_HANDLE_VALUE then exit;
  SuspendThread(hWriteThread);
  PurgeComm(hComm,PURGE_RXABORT or PURGE_RXCLEAR);
  KillWriteBuffers;
  FTxBytes:=0;
  ResumeThread(hWriteThread);
end;

constructor TComm.Create(AOwner:TComponent);
begin
  inherited Create(AOwner);
  InitializeCriticalSection(CriticalSection);
  hComm:=INVALID_HANDLE_VALUE;
  FPort:=PortDefault;
  FBaudRate:=BaudRateDefault;
  FParity:=ParityDefault;
  FDataBits:=DataBitsDefault;
  FStopBits:=StopBitsDefault;
  FReadBufferSize:=ReadBufferSizeDefault;
  FWriteBufferSize:=WriteBufferSizeDefault;
  FEventMask:=EventMaskDefault;
  FXONChar:=XONCharDefault;
  FXOFFChar:=XOFFCharDefault;
  FResume:=ResumeDefault;
```

```
      FPause:=PauseDefault;
      FEventChar:=EventCharDefault;
      FParityErrorDetect:=ParityErrorDetectDefault;
      FParityReplacement:=ParityReplacementDefault;
      FParityChar:=ParityCharDefault;
      FNullStrip:=NullStripDefault;
      FReadFull:=ReadFullDefault;
      FFlowControl:=FlowControlDefault;
      FOnEvent:=nil;
      FOnReceive:=nil;
      FOnTransmit:=nil;

      FirstWriteBuffer:=nil;
      LastWriteBuffer:=nil;
      FirstReadBuffer:=nil;
      LastReadBuffer:=nil;

      ReadOffset:=0;
      FRxBytes:=0;
      FTxBytes:=0;

      hWindow:=AllocateHWnd(WndProc);
      PostMessage(hWindow,COMM_INIT,0,0);
    end;

    destructor TComm.Destroy;
    begin
      ClosePort;
      DeallocatehWnd(hWindow);
      DeleteCriticalSection(CriticalSection);
      inherited Destroy;
    end;

    procedure TComm.Write(Data:PChar;Count:DWord);
    var
      BytesWritten:DWord;
    begin
```

```
    if hComm=INVALID_HANDLE_VALUE then exit;
    SuspendThread(hWriteThread);
    if LastWriteBuffer=nil then
    begin
      new(LastWriteBuffer);
      FirstWriteBuffer:=LastWriteBuffer;
    end
    else
    begin
      new(LastWriteBuffer^.Next);
      LastWriteBuffer:=LastWriteBuffer^.Next;
    end;
    LastWriteBuffer^.Next:=nil;
    LastWriteBuffer^.BufferSize:=Count;
    GetMem(LastWriteBuffer^.Buffer,Count);
    Move(Data^,LastWriteBuffer^.Buffer^,Count);
    inc(FTxBytes,Count);
    ResumeThread(hWriteThread);

WriteFile(hComm,LastWriteBuffer^.Buffer^,Count,BytesWritten,
    @WriteOverlapped);
end;


function TComm.Read(Data:PChar;Count:DWord):DWord;
var
  BytesInBuffer:DWord;
  BytesRemaining:DWord;
  DataOffset:DWord;
  TempBuffer:PBufferNode;
  BytesRead:DWord;
begin
  Read:=0;
  if hComm=INVALID_HANDLE_VALUE then exit;
  if FirstReadBuffer=nil then exit;
  BytesRemaining:=Count;
  DataOffset:=0;
  BytesRead:=0;
```

```
  SuspendThread(hReadThread);
  repeat
    BytesInBuffer:=FirstReadBuffer^.BufferSize-ReadOffset;
    if BytesRemaining<BytesInBuffer then
    begin

Move(FirstReadBuffer^.Buffer[ReadOffset],Data[DataOffset],
      BytesRemaining);
      inc(BytesRead,BytesRemaining);
      inc(ReadOffset,BytesRemaining);
      dec(FRxBytes,BytesRemaining);
      BytesRemaining:=0;
    end
    else
    begin

Move(FirstReadBuffer^.Buffer[ReadOffset],Data[DataOffset],
      BytesInBuffer);
      dec(BytesRemaining,BytesInBuffer);
      dec(FRxBytes,BytesInBuffer);
      inc(DataOffset,BytesInBuffer);
      inc(BytesRead,BytesInBuffer);
      TempBuffer:=FirstReadBuffer^.Next;
      FreeMem(FirstReadBuffer^.Buffer,
        FirstReadBuffer^.BufferSize);
      Dispose(FirstReadBuffer);
      FirstReadBuffer:=TempBuffer;
      ReadOffset:=0;
    end;
  until (BytesRemaining=0) or (FirstReadBuffer=nil);
  ResumeThread(hReadThread);
  Read:=BytesRead;
end;

procedure TComm.SetBreak;
begin
  if hComm=INVALID_HANDLE_VALUE then exit;
```

```
    SetCommBreak(hComm);
end;

procedure TComm.ClearBreak;
begin
  if hComm=INVALID_HANDLE_VALUE then exit;
  ClearCommBreak(hComm);
end;

function TComm.IsOpen:Boolean;
begin
  IsOpen:=hComm<>INVALID_HANDLE_VALUE;
end;

procedure Register;
begin
  RegisterComponents('Additional', [TComm]);
end;

end.
```

I'll be the first to admit that there is a lot of code here—it's by far the largest component in this book! This is where the true beauty of creating a component reveals itself; the mountain of code is hidden when you go to use it, with the only hint that it is actually there being its bitmap during the design phase and the references to properties and events used throughout your application's code. And, if you forget what a property or event is named, you don't have to scour the source code looking for what you want; just take a peek at the Object Inspector and all will be revealed—well, almost, only a list of *published properties* is given, nonpublished properties still have to be hunted down manually. Now, you might be wondering why you wouldn't want to publish a property. The answer lies in understanding two things. First, some properties are read-only, meaning that they can never be assigned a value. There would be little point to publishing such a property, if you could, because the whole point of the published section is to allow the property's value to be written to and read from a form file, and to be set with the Object Inspector. Second, even if a property can be both read and written, sometimes it is used to perform an action that only makes sense at run time. For instance, consider a date property. It is reasonable to read from it—get the date, or write to it—set the date, but only at run time; publishing this property would be decidedly silly because you will never know at design time what the date will be!

Threads of Desire

While the concept of multithreaded applications has existed for quite some time, they were restricted to the nonconsumer-popular environments such as Windows NT and OS/2. The introduction of Windows 95 changed all this in the blink of an eye. Users of Windows 95-specific products no longer get frustrated when their system becomes nonresponsive during a lengthy operation—now they can simply do something else and allow the task to continue quietly in the background. Although it is possible to emulate this sort of thing in previous releases of Windows, it doesn't begin to approach the power of having it performed as a native function of the operating system.

Definition of a Thread

You probably already know what a thread is, or at least have a foggy notion of what it might be, but to clear up any possible confusion, let's take a moment to define it. Bluntly, a thread is the execution of instructions one after another. That's it; it's that simple. Reading this book can be considered a thread of sorts. You, the CPU, look at each word, the instruction, as it appears; interpret its meaning; and carry on to the next one. This concept is certainly not magical—all computers can do this. The real interesting part is when you have multiple threads running at the same time. If you go the library, you will see many people reading books. Each is a CPU executing a thread, all independent of one another. Likewise, if you have multiple processors in your computer, you can run multiple independent threads.

Most of us don't have multiple CPUs; however, we have one. Yet, we know that Windows 95 is capable of executing multiple concurrent threads. How can this be? Ponder this: As you sit reading this book, chances are you will not read it cover-to-cover in once sitting. You will probably stop reading to do something else, read the newspaper (another, different, thread), for example. When you finish with that, you might get back to this book. If you look at the little picture, you are doing two things independently: reading this book and reading the newspaper. But, if you look at the overall picture— "What did you do today?"; "I read a book and the newspaper."—it appears that you performed the two tasks at the same time. This procedure is known as *time-slicing*. A bit of time is given to one task to execute, and when the time is up, another task executes for a while, and so on. If the time slices are small enough, the illusion of concurrent operation results.

Creating Windows Threads

Every native Windows 95 application that you run is assigned its own thread of execution. Thus if one program gets bogged down with heavy-duty calculations, the others go about their business unhindered. Although this is good, it leaves the application that is performing the calculations unresponsive to user input. To prevent this from happening, many programmers create an independent thread for time consuming tasks. This is achieved by calling the Windows API function **CreateThread**:

```
function CreateThread(lpThreadAttributes:Pointer;dwStackSize:DWORD;
  lpStartAddress:TFNThreadStartRoutine;lpParameter:Pointer;
  dwCreationFlags:DWORD;var lpThreadId:DWORD):THandle;
```

Don't be put off by the overwhelming amount of parameters that confront you. We will now examine each in turn, and I'm sure you'll agree that they're not as intimidating as they initially appear to be.

The first parameter is **lpThreadAttributes**. It can either be a pointer to a **TSecurityAttributes** structure, allowing you to specify how the thread is shared and inherited by other processes, or it can be **nil**, the most common choice.

The second parameter, **dwStackSize**, determines how much memory is allocated for the threads stack. Should this parameter be zero, a default stack size will be used. A *stack*, as you may already know, is a block of memory used to store temporary data. Newcomers to threads are often surprised to learn that for each running thread, an independent stack is required. The reason for it is quite simple: Suppose that for a moment all threads used one global stack, and that we have two running threads, A and B. Further suppose that as thread A is running, it stores something on the stack; and just after it does that, it is preempted by thread B, which itself stores something on the stack. When thread B is itself preempted, the information it placed on the stack will still be there! When it comes time for thread A to retrieve what it believes to be the data it placed originally, it will be in for a shock because it will get thread B's data. Of course, thread B will be none too pleased about this situation either. Any operating system that attempted to incorporate such a single-stack multithreading scheme, would find itself crashed in nanoseconds after starting more than one thread.

The **lpStartAddress** parameter identifies the location in memory where the thread is to begin executing. Normally, this is a function declared as **std-call**:

```
function ThreadProc(Param:Pointer):DWord;stdcall;
```

The **lpParameter** parameter is used to supply user-defined information to the thread function. This is what the **Param** parameter of the preceding declaration for **ThreadProc** is all about. The same value passed to **lpParameter** will be mirrored to **Param**. Although it is declared as **Pointer**, it is by no means limited to being a pointer. Any 32-bit value will work equally well.

Finally, we come to the **lpThreadID** parameter, which is used primarily for thread enumeration and message posting. For most applications, the value is not needed and may be safely discarded. Note that even though the value is not needed, a variable must be passed because Delphi declares it as **var**. Although it is possible to redefine **CreateThread** so that it accepts a pointer instead, it is not advisable to do so. Under Windows 95, you could indeed do this and pass a **nil**, but if you were to try the same trick with Windows NT, you would be distressed at the enormous crash that results.

The return value of **CreateThread** is a handle to the newly created thread if the call succeeds, or zero if it fails. This handle is used for nearly every thread-oriented action you will care to perform, so hang on to it.

The **dwCreationFlags** parameter is used to specify whether the thread will be created *suspended*. A suspended thread uses no processor power and is a good way of creating a thread that does not have to execute immediately. To create a thread in the suspended state, use the constant

CREATE_SUSPENDED; otherwise, use zero. To wake up a suspended thread, call the **ResumeThread** function.

When the thread is up and running, the code contained in **ThreadProc** executes as if it were a normal function, with the sole exception that other code is executing at the same time. While the thread is doing its thing, you can do certain things to it. The most popular of which are suspending it, having it wait for an event of some sort, and terminating it.

Suspending a thread requires nothing more fancy than a call to **SuspendThread**:

```
function SuspendThread(hThread:THandle):DWORD;
```

Here, **hThread** is the handle that was returned by **CreateThread**. Waking the thread up is done via the **ResumeThread** function:

```
function ResumeThread(hThread:THandle):DWORD;
```

Again, **hThread** is the handle returned by **CreateThread** and identifies the thread that is to be resumed.

Using Event Objects

Configuring a thread to wait for an event of some sort is a very big topic, certainly not one that can be fully covered here. I can, however, briefly give you the scoop on events. An *event* is similar to a *switch*. Both have two states: on and off in the case of the switch, and signaled and nonsignaled for the event. An event is created with the **CreateEvent** function:

```
function CreateEvent(lpEventAttributes:PSecurityAttributes;
  bManualReset,bInitialState:BOOL;lpName:PChar):THandle;
```

You saw the **lpEventAttributes** parameter back in the description for **CreateThread**. Everything is the same for **CreateEvent**. **bManualReset** is used to specify if the thread will reset the event after it occurs itself, or if you must do it on your own. **bInitialState** determines if the event is created in the signaled (TRUE) or nonsignaled (FALSE) state. Finally, you may choose to name your event, by passing a string to the **lpName** parameter. You probably won't want to do this, and as such may pass a **nil** instead. The return value **CreateEvent** is the handle of the event; or if the function fails for some reason, it is zero.

An event may be set to the signaled state by calling **SetEvent**:

```
function SetEvent(hEvent:THandle):BOOL;
```

Or, it may be set to the nonsignaled by calling **ResetEvent**:

```
function ResetEvent(hEvent:THandle):BOOL;
```

Regardless of which call you make, the **hEvent** parameter is the handle of the event, returned from **CreateEvent**.

To wait for an event, one of the several API functions available must be called, **WaitForSingleObject**, for example. When such a function is called, one of two thing will happen. If the corresponding event is in the signaled state, the thread will continue to execute normally. If, however, the event is in the nonsignaled state, the thread will cease to execute, and very little processor power will be consumed while it waits for the event to become signaled.

The most desirable way of terminating a thread is to have the thread function call **ExitThread**. This can occur in one of two ways: First, the thread function can exit as if it were a normal function. This indirectly calls **ExitThread**. Second, **ExitThread** can be called directly inside of the thread function.

Files under Win32 can have events associated with them if **CreateFile** was called with **FILE_FLAG_OVERLAPPED** included in the **dwFlagsAndAttributes** parameter. By passing a valid **TOverlapped** structure to the **lpOverlapped** parameter of functions like **ReadFile** and **WriteFile**, asynchronous transfer is enabled, meaning that reads and writes can occur simultaneously. The **TOverlapped** structure contains a few fields that must first be set before such calls can be made:

```
TOverlapped=record
  Internal:DWORD;
  InternalHigh:DWORD;
  Offset:DWORD;
```

```
OffsetHigh:DWORD;
  hEvent:THandle;
end;
```

Internal and **InternalHigh** are reserved for use by the operating system, so it isn't necessary to initialize them. **Offset** is the position in the file where data is to be read from, in the case of **ReadFile,** or written to, in the case of **WriteFile.** Because communication files are not random access, this field has little meaning when used in conjunction with one, and is ignored. If you are working with very large files, in excess of 4G, you will have to use the **OffsetHigh** field as the most significant digit of **Offset.** The field that interests us is **hEvent.** Like any other event, it must be created by calling **CreateEvent.** Once done, the **TOverlapped** structure is initialized and ready to go.

When a valid **TOverlapped** structure is passed to **ReadFile** or **WriteFile,** they will return immediately, and the data will be transferred silently in the background. When the operation has been completed, the event identified by the **hEvent** field of the **TOverlapped** structure is signaled and can be trapped by using **WaitForSingleObject,** as discussed earlier.

Terminating the Thread

The least desirable method to kill a thread is by calling **TerminateThread.** Although this function will indeed stop the thread dead in its tracks, it has some undesirable side effects such as not deallocating the thread's stack, and not notifying any DLLs used by the thread that it is terminating.

Regardless of the method used to terminate a thread, it is important to always close the thread object itself by calling **CloseHandle.**

Threads and Delphi

The last stop in our discussion of threads deals with how they and Delphi get along together. Unfortunately, it isn't as smoothly as one might hope. Delphi has a built-in thread class, **TThread,** that does a little of you would ever want to do with a thread—but no more. It doesn't, for example, encapsulate many of the more exotic thread-related API calls as it could have. The primary sticking-out-like-a-sore-thumb omission is that it has no built-in support for events. For this reason, and a couple of others, it didn't really make too much sense to program **TComm** using **TThread**.

Perhaps the saddest part of this whole Delphi-thread fiasco is that Delphi wasn't really built to support multiple threads; at least not in the context of visual things. You cannot have a form that operates in a thread separate from the main thread. This means that while one form is busy doing something, all other forms are locked out until it finishes. Some Windows 3.1 tricks can be used to circumvent this, such as calling **PeekMessage** or Delphi's **Application.ProcessMessages** procedure on occasion, but it doesn't compare to having a form operate in its own thread.

The next visual thing that is hindered when using threads is the VCL. VCL calls can only be made if the **TThread** method **Synchronize** is called. **Synchronize** accepts a function as a parameter, and it is in this function where the VCL-related stuff must be done. At the point that the function is called, the primary thread is executing, not the secondary one where the call to **Synchronize** originated. Can we say "slow?" To make matters much worse, if you have several VCL calls to make, you have a choice. You can either put them all in one **Synchronize** function, or you can put each one in a separate function. Both choices are highly undesirable. The first one defeats the whole point of having a secondary thread because the VCL code ends up executing in the primary thread, and the second choice means you need a whole pile of **Synchronize** functions. So much for readability and ease of maintenance.

Enumerated Types, Sets, and Properties

If you were to gather a room of Pascal programmers and ask them to raise their hand if they know what an enumerated type or a set is, all of them would respond positively. However, probably half would be lying! I have never seen such standard and useful features ignored as much as these, and I couldn't even hazard a guess as to why this is. Although it might have been possible to avoid them in the past, as a component programmer, you must understand them fully if you want to be consistent with the "feel" of the VCL; and, of course, you do.

Enumerated Types

Enumerated types are really quite simple. All they are is a custom type that allows you to define what possible values a variable can have:

```
Type
   TTemperature=(Freezing,Cold,Cool,Comfortable,Warm,Hot);
```

```
Var
   Temperature:TTemperature;
```

In this example, **TTemperature** is an enumerated type. The thing that may slightly unbalance you at first is that its list of values does not contain numbers, but rather words, or *identifiers*. **Temperature**, a variable of type **TTemperature**, is now restricted in that it can only be assigned one of these identifiers—**Freezing**, **Cold**, **Cool**, **Comfortable**, **Warm**, or **Hot**—and the compiler will enforce this, generating an error if you attempt to use either a numerical value or some other identifier that is not a member of the type.

The only real problem with enumerated types is that once you use an identifier in one, you can't use it again for another:

```
Type
   TTemperature=(Freezing,Cold,Cool,Comfortable,Warm,Hot);
   TChili=(Tasteless,Mild,Medium,Hot,Volcanic);
```

The preceding code won't compile because **Hot** appears in both **Temperature** and **TChili**. This is really unfortunate because it means that otherwise descriptive identifiers have to have prefixes attached to them to work properly:

```
Type
   TTemperature=(ttFreezing,ttCold,ttCool,ttComfortable,ttWarm,
              ttHot);
   TChili=(tcTasteless,tcMild,tcMedium,tcHot,tcVolcanic);
```

Now, there won't be an error because the two "hots" have different identifiers, **ttHot** and **tcHot**.

The fact that you can't have duplicated identifiers is one of my pet peeves about Pascal. I contacted a source at Borland to express my dismay, and I was told that it is done this way to keep the compilation time fast. I, for one, would be willing to wait an extra second or so if it meant doing away with confusing prefixes. For now though, we have to live with it.

In the source code for the communication component, **TComm**, there are several enumerated types:

```
Type
  TPort=(tptNone,tptOne,tptTwo,tptThree,tptFour,tptFive,tptSix,
         tptSeven,tptEight);
  TBaudRate=(tbr110,tbr300,tbr600,tbr1200,tbr2400,tbr4800,
            tbr9600,tbr14400,tbr19200,tbr38400,tbr56000,
            tbr128000,tbr256000);
  TParity=(tpNone,tpOdd,tpEven,tpMark,tpSpace);
  TDataBits=(tdbFour,tdbFive,tdbSix,tdbSeven,tdbEight);
  TStopBits=(tsbOne,tsbOnePointFive,tsbTwo);
  TFlowControl=(tfcNone,tfcXONXOFF,tfcCTS,tfcDSR);
  TEvent=(tceBreak,tceCts,tceDsr,tceErr,tceRing,tceRlsd,
          tceRxChar,tceRxFlag,tceTxEmpty);
```

All these types are used to configure the serial port to make it behave how you want. To facilitate this, variables of each type are accessed as properties. For example, here is how **TPort** is used as a property:

```
const
  PortDefault=tptNone;

Type
  TComm = class(TComponent)
  private
    FPort:TPort;
    procedure SetPort(APort:TPort);
  published
    property Port:TPort read FPort write SetPort
      default PortDefault;
  end;
```

For clarity, I removed references to non-**TPort** code. Whenever the property **Port** is read, the variable **FPort** is accessed directly. When it is written to an access procedure, **SetPort** is called, which first sets **FPort** and then calls code to reflect the change. Like all properties, the allowable range of values is determined by their type. For example, a **Word** property can range from 0 to 65535. So it should come as no surprise that **Port** is restricted by the allowable values of **TPort**.

The main advantage of using enumerated types is evident at design time. The Object Inspector creates a list of all allowable identifiers that the property may be and visually allows you to pick one among them that fulfills your needs. For instance, when the properties of **TComm** are in the Object Inspector, clicking on the **Port** property reveals a list of the identifiers **tptNone** and **tptOne** through **tptEight**. Selecting the port you want is then as easy as clicking on the proper identifier.

Sets

On occasion, you will have properties that can be either true or false, such as the **NullStrip** property of **TComm**. However, you will often find that many such boolean properties are related closely to one another and grouping them logically would be beneficial, much like the **BorderIcons** property of **TForm** that allows you to specify whether the maximize, minimize, or system menu bitmaps are visible. This is also the case with the **EventMask** property, which permits you to set various flags that correspond directly to the flags of the **SetCommMask** function. There is no rule that says that they have to be grouped, but in addition to being logical, it will keep the list of properties in the Object Inspector short and manageable.

The way to go about this grouping is through the use of sets. A good analogy for a set is a bookshelf—let's call it a "book set." If a book is on the shelf, it is a member of the set. If you put another book on the shelf, it is also a member. Take any book off the shelf, and it ceases to be a member. Codified, the bookshelf would look like this:

```
Type
  TBooks=(MobyDick,TreasureIsland,WarAndPeace,RobinsonCrusoe,
         AliceInWonderland);
  TBookshelf=set of TBooks;
```

```
Var
  Bookshelf:TBookshelf;
```

The bookshelf, **Bookshelf**, is of type **TBookshelf**, which is a set of the books contained in the enumerated type **TBooks**. This means that **BookShelf** can have none, some, or all of the books from **TBooks** in it. Creating an empty book set goes like this:

```
Bookshelf=[];
```

The square brackets indicate a set, and the fact that they are empty means that the set is empty (has no books in it). Of course, it is also possible to have books in the shelf from the outset, either individually:

```
Bookshelf=[TreasureIsland,RobinsonCrusoe];
```

by ranges:

```
Bookshelf=[MobyDick..AliceInWonderland];
```

or a combination of both:

```
Bookshelf=[MobyDick..WarAndPeace,AliceInWonderland];
```

However, the power of sets comes from the fact that they are *dynamic*, or that you can add and remove members at run time:

```
Bookshelf:=Bookshelf+[MobyDick];
Bookshelf:=Bookshelf-[RobinsonCrusoe];
```

Although these two examples are done in "classic Pascal", Delphi allows for several optimizations to be made by using the procedures **Include** and **Exclude**:

```
Include(Bookshelf,MobyDick);
Exclude(Bookshelf,RobinsonCrusoe);
```

Testing if a member is present in a set requires the use of the **in** keyword:

```
if MobyDick in Bookshelf then
  writeln('A whale of a story!');
```

Going back to **TComm**, there are two sets that are used: **TEvents** and **TErrors**. **TEvents** is the type of the aforementioned **EventMask** published property, but it is also used as the type of the **Events** parameter of the **OnEvent** property event function to let the recipient know what event(s) was responsible for the calling it. The declaration for both the enumerated type and the set itself looks like this:

```
TEvent=(tceBreak,tceCts,tceDsr,tceErr,tceRing,tceRlsd,
        tceRxChar,tceRxFlag,tceTxEmpty);


TEvents=set of TEvent;
```

Design-Time Safety

Setting any one of the **TComm**'s properties during run time should reflect the change to the serial hardware itself. It would be entirely inappropriate if this was allowed to happen during design time, however, because not only would it be meaningless to do so, but it also would slow things down as ports were opened and closed and events responded to. It is therefore essential to put the component to "sleep" while in the design phase of a project.

As you may recall from Chapter 2, all descendants of **TComponent** have a **ComponentState** property that has the **csDesigning** member set while the component is engaged in a design-time session. By checking whether this member is set, it becomes possible to prevent the hardware from being accessed. The question that arises is where should the check be made? If you study the source code for **TCOMM**, you will notice that nearly every method verifies that the **hComm** value is something other than **INVALID_HANDLE_VALUE**, thereby blocking out any illegal actions that may occur if the corresponding port is not actually open. This fact can be used to our advantage because the only place that **hComm** has a chance of becoming valid is in the **SetPort** method. By having **SetPort** check for the **csDesigning** flag, and exiting if set, the component becomes dead during design time.

There is another related issue to consider. The first thing a component does during run time is to load all of its properties that differ from the default values. Attempting to predict or control the order that the properties are loaded is difficult, to say the least. Without this capability, **TComm** cannot initialize itself in the proper sequence—that is, setting **Port**, which in turn calls **SetPort**, prior to setting any other property. Because there are no guarantees, I have chosen to dispense with having true initialization occur during the loading of the component. Don't get me wrong, the properties *values* are set, but the actions associated with them are not performed.

To accomplish this task, **ComponentState** is additionally checked for the **csLoading** member during the call to **SetPort**. If **csLoading** is present, indicating that the component is being loaded, **SetPort** exits without opening a port. No port, no **hComm**; therefore preventing the setting of any other property from attempting to access it. When all properties have finally been loaded, the **Loaded** method is called. It is tempting to stick a call to **SetPort** here to wake up the port, thus assigning **hComm** to a valid value, and get the ball rolling, but there is a serious drawback if this is done.

Loaded is only called if, and only if, the component is being loaded along with a form. If you chose to create a component on-the-fly at run time, **Loaded** is simply not called. Although it is possible to call it yourself, it's not very practical, and chances are good that you will forget to do it entirely, producing some buggy, hair-pulling code as a result. Not wanting to be the cause of your baldness, let me present a satisfactory solution.

For reasons that we'll get into later, one of the things that happens in **Create** is that it makes an invisible window whose sole purpose is to accept posted messages and perform actions based upon them. A posted message has a high gee-whiz factor when compared to a sent message. When you send a message to a window, usually with the **SendMessage** function, it is processed immediately; it really amounts to nothing more than doing a call to a function. Compare this to posting a message, typically with **PostMessage**, to a window. When you do this, nothing immediately happens, and your program goes about its business. The message didn't just vanish, however. It's waiting for your program to enter its message loop, and once it gets there, the message is sent to the window.

So if we post a message to the window during **Create**, it will not arrive to the window until everything associated with create, including the loading of properties, has been accomplished. When it gets to the window, it is a simple matter to trap it and call **SetPort** to initialize the port.

Earlier, I mentioned the default values of properties. These are the same as the values you see in the Object Inspector whenever you add a new component to a form. They are connected to a property through the use of the **default** keyword:

```
property Port:TPort read FPort write SetPort default PortDefault;
```

This indicates that the **Port** property will have the initial value of **PortDefault** (which happens to be **tptNone**) whenever one of two things occurs:

- The component is added to a form.
- The component is created on-the-fly at run time.

The **default** keyword does not work without help, however. In addition, it is of utmost importance to set the initial default value of the property in the **Create** constructor. The reason for this is twofold: First, if the component is created automatically because a form is being loaded, only properties that are different from their default values will be set because the compiler assumes that the others have already set to their default values in **Create**. This means that all the other properties will be uninitialized! Second, if you create a component at run time, the **default** keyword is ignored entirely, and the only initialization that happens is that which is in the **Create** constructor.

TComm Notables

Theory of Operation

Unfortunately, it is impossible for me to go into the communications aspect of **TComm** in very great detail. There are so many things to explain that it could very well be the topic of its own book. I have little choice but to give you a short form description in lieu of a thorough discussion of the use of the component. Don't be put off by this though; the source code is here, and it can provide you with a much better understanding of how things really work than I could.

Like all components, **TComm** begins its life in the **Create** method. Here, the mandatory setting of default values is done; a window for messages, **hWindow**, is created; and the user message **COMM_INIT** is sent to it. After **Create** exits, all the properties values are loaded, and the **hWindow** window receives the **COMM_INIT** message, calling **SetPort** as a result.

SetPort is where all the important port initialization code is located. One of the first things it does is close any port that it may have previously opened by calling **ClosePort**. Next, it attempts to create a valid port handle, **hComm**, by calling **CreateFile** with a string in the form of COMx. If the call fails, **SetPort** aborts. If, however, all is well, three event objects (not to be confused with Delphi events) are created: one for indicating when a read operation has been completed; one for indicating when a write operation has been completed; and one for signaling when a communication event has occurred (again, not to be confused with Delphi events). After the events have been created, three threads are created, each corresponding to one of the above events.

It is the purpose of **ReadThread** to wait for the number of received bytes to equal the **ReadFull** property or a timeout to occur (provided that at least one byte has been received). When either happens, the received data is transferred to linked-list for storage; a **COMM_RX** message is posted to **hWindow**; and the thread puts itself to sleep by calling **SuspendThread**. When the window receives the message, it calls the **OnReceive** event handler, if present, and then wakes up **ReadThread** by calling **ResumeThread**.

When data is written to the port and has been fully transmitted, **WriteThread** wakes up from its normally dormant state. It deletes the node from the linked list that contains the data that it just finished transmitting (which is separate from the linked list that **ReadThread** uses); posts a **COMM_TX** message to **hWindow**; and then suspends itself. When the window receives the **COMM_TX** message, it calls the **OnTransmit** event handler, if it exists, and then resumes the thread.

The purpose of **CommThread** is to wait for incoming communication-related events. When it detects one of these, it posts a **COMM_EVENT** message to **hWindow** and puts itself to sleep. When **hWindow** receives the message, it builds a **TEvents** set based upon the current events, and if one of the events was **EV_ERR**, it also builds a **TErrors** set. After the set(s) have been constructed, the **OnEvent** event handler is called, allowing the programmer to respond to the event, and the **CommThread** is woken up by calling **ResumeThread**.

After **SetPort** exits, **TComm** is ready for reading and writing. Writing data to the port is done via the **Write** method:

```
procedure TComm.Write(Data:PChar;Count:DWord);
```

The **Data** parameter is a **PChar** style pointer to the block of data that you want to write, and **Count** identifies how many bytes of data are in the block. The type **PChar** was chosen for **Data** because it offers compatibility with strings, the most likely type of data to be transmitted, and because it can accept a pointer to any other type without the need for typecasting.

When **Write** is called, the data has to be transferred to an intermediate buffer—a node of a linked list—before it is written to the port. The reason for this is that the data has to stay in memory while it is being transferred to the ports buffer silently in the background. Because **Write** returns immediately, it would be very likely that the buffer being transferred would be overwritten with new data had this intermediate buffer scheme not been incorporated.

Reading data from the port is achieved by calling the **Read** method:

```
function TComm.Read(Data:PChar;Count:DWord):DWord;
```

The parameters are the similar to the **Write** method; **Data** points to a block of memory that is to have data from the port written to it, and **Count** is how many bytes of data you want to read. It is possible that how many bytes that you want to read and how many bytes you actually *can* read will be two entirely different values. This is why **Read** was declared as a function. Its return value is the number of bytes that were read.

Read also relies on an intermediate buffer. When data is received, waking up the **ReadThread** thread, it is placed into a buffer that is stored as a node of a linked list. When it comes time for the data to be retrieved for processing, the linked list is accessed.

In addition to **Read** and **Write**, a few supporting functions can be used to enhance your **TComm** experience. **SetBreak** sets a break condition on the transmit line. This can be cleared by calling **ClearBreak**. **IsOpen** returns a boolean value that is **True** if the port is physically open. This is handy for incorporating look-before-you-leap smarts into your project.

When it comes time to close the port, either because a new port number has been selected or the component is being destroyed, **ClosePort** is called. It closes the **hComm**, by calling **CloseHandle** and then sets **hComm** to **INVALID_HANDLE_VALUE**. It then goes about terminating all the threads. As you may recall, the best way to terminate a thread is to have it exit normally or by calling **ExitThread**. Unfortunately, this is easier than it sounds. Any of the threads can be in different modes when it comes time to do this. For example, one might be suspended while waiting for a message to be sent, and the other two might be waiting for an event to be generated.

To overcome the fact that a thread may be suspended, **ResumeThread** is called for each thread, ensuring that they all are active. To wake up threads waiting for events, a phony event is generated for each thread. When any one of the threads wakes up, the first thing that is done is to check **hComm** to see if it is equal to **INVALID_HANDLE_VALUE**. If it is equal, the thread has no need to continue, so it calls **ExitThread**. This is done for all three threads.

It is not easy to predict when or in what order the threads will be terminated, but **Close** must know this so that it can kill the thread handle itself. One of the neat things about threads is that a thread handle also represents an event object. During the lifetime of the thread, the event is nonsignaled; but as soon as the thread terminates, it becomes signaled. Like other event objects, it is possible to wait for the thread event to become signaled by calling **WaitForSingleObject**. When each call, one for each thread, has been cleared, the threads handles are closed by calling **CloseHandle**. To conclude the **Close** method, all the linked list structures are cleaned up.

Odds and Ends

I tried to make **TComm** both easy to use and just as powerful and full-featured as many commercial products available. However, for simplicity, I made a few sacrifices along the way. First, the manual setting of handshaking and flow control lines is not supported. If this is something you need, it is a simple matter to implement it yourself. Second, full error handling is not in place. For example, the possibility that the call to **AllocateHWnd** might fail is ignored. Although the chances of it happening are remote, for mission-critical applications, such error checking is mandatory.

Before moving on to the example, however, we must give the component a bitmap. This can be found in the **\DC\CHAP03** directory as **COMM.DCR**, and is also shown in Figure 3.1.

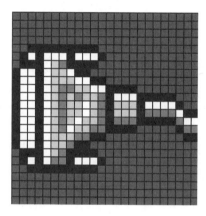

Figure 3.1 Palette bitmap for **TComm**.

TComm Example

The example I have chosen to demonstrate the features of **TComm** is a simple terminal program, shown in Figure 3.2. With it, it is possible to dial-up online services using "AT" modem commands, but of course, you can't upload or download anything. You can, however, configure important parameters such as the port number and baud rate through the use of a dialog box, as shown in Figure 3.3, that is available by first selecting the Configure menu item and then selecting Communication Settings. Also available under the Configure menu is Local Echo, which can be used to prevent your keystrokes from being viewed in the terminal window. This is especially helpful when using a modem because, by default, it echoes everything back to you, causing two of everything you type to appear in the window. Here now, is the code for **SimpTerm**, which consists of three source files, **SIMPTERM.DPR**, **MAIN.PAS**, and **COMMCFG.PAS**, and can also be found in the **\DC\CHAP03** directory.

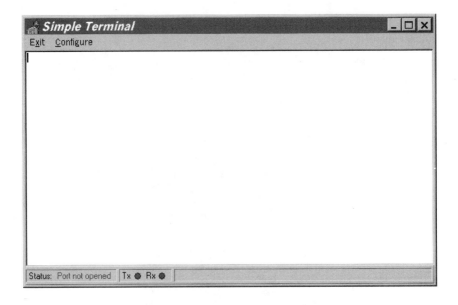

Figure 3.2 SimpTerm main window.

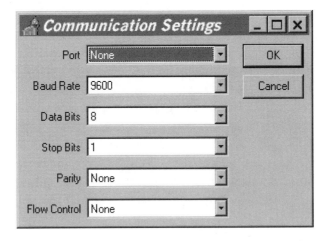

Figure 3.2 Communication configuration dialog box.

Listing 3.2 SimpTerm.PAS

```pascal
program Simpterm;

uses
  Forms,
  Main in 'MAIN.PAS' {Terminal},
  Commcfg in 'COMMCFG.PAS' {CommSettings};

{$R *.RES}

begin
  Application.CreateForm(TTerminal, Terminal);
  Application.CreateForm(TCommSettings, CommSettings);
  Application.Run;
end.
```

Listing 3.3 Main.PAS

```pascal
unit Main;

interface

uses
  SysUtils, WinTypes, WinProcs, Messages, Classes, Graphics,
  Controls,Forms, Dialogs, Menus, StdCtrls, Comm,CommCfg,
  ExtCtrls;

type
  TTerminal = class(TForm)
    Comm: TComm;
    MainMenu: TMainMenu;
    ExitProgram: TMenuItem;
    Configure: TMenuItem;
    CommunicationSettings: TMenuItem;
    LocalEcho: TMenuItem;
```

```
    Timer1: TTimer;
    TerminalMemo: TMemo;
    Panel1: TPanel;
    Bevel1: TBevel;
    Label4: TLabel;
    StatusText: TLabel;
    Bevel2: TBevel;
    Label2: TLabel;
    RxLED: TShape;
    Label3: TLabel;
    TxLED: TShape;
    Bevel3: TBevel;
    procedure ExitProgramClick(Sender: TObject);
    procedure CommReceive(const Sender: TObject; const RxBytes: Word);
    procedure TerminalMemoKeyPress(Sender: TObject; var Key: Char);
    procedure CommunicationSettingsClick(Sender: TObject);
    procedure LocalEchoClick(Sender: TObject);
    procedure ShowStatus;
    procedure FormCreate(Sender: TObject);
    procedure Timer1Timer(Sender: TObject);
  private
    RxCount:Byte;
    TxCount:Byte;
  end;

var
  Terminal: TTerminal;

implementation

{$R *.DFM}

procedure TTerminal.ExitProgramClick(Sender: TObject);
begin
  Close;
end;
```

```
procedure TTerminal.CommReceive(const Sender: TObject;
  const RxBytes: Word);
var
  i:Word;
  RxText:PChar;
  KeyPress:TKeyPressEvent;
begin
  RxLED.Brush.Color:=clLime;
  RxCount:=2;
  KeyPress:=TerminalMemo.OnKeyPress;
  TerminalMemo.OnKeyPress:=nil;
  GetMem(RxText,RxBytes);
  Comm.Read(RxText,RxBytes);
  for i:=0 to RxBytes-1 do
    SendMessage(TerminalMemo.Handle,WM_CHAR,Word(RxText[i]),0);
  FreeMem(RxText,RxBytes);
  TerminalMemo.OnKeyPress:=KeyPress;
end;


procedure TTerminal.TerminalMemoKeyPress(Sender: TObject;
  var Key: Char);
begin
  TxLED.Brush.Color:=clLime;
  TxCount:=2;
  Comm.Write(@Key,SizeOf(Key));
  if not LocalEcho.Checked then Key:=#0;
end;


procedure TTerminal.CommunicationSettingsClick(Sender: TObject);
begin
  with CommSettings do
  begin
    PortCombo.ItemIndex:=Ord(Comm.Port);
    BaudCombo.ItemIndex:=Ord(Comm.BaudRate);
    DataBitsCombo.ItemIndex:=Ord(Comm.Databits);
    StopBitsCombo.ItemIndex:=Ord(Comm.StopBits);
```

```
    ParityCombo.ItemIndex:=Ord(Comm.Parity);
    FlowCombo.ItemIndex:=Ord(Comm.FlowControl);
    if ShowModal=mrCancel then exit;
    Screen.Cursor:=crHourglass;
    Comm.Port:=TPort(PortCombo.ItemIndex);
    Comm.BaudRate:=TBaudRate(BaudCombo.ItemIndex);
    Comm.DataBits:=TDataBits(DataBitsCombo.ItemIndex);
    Comm.StopBits:=TStopBits(StopBitsCombo.ItemIndex);
    Comm.Parity:=TParity(ParityCombo.ItemIndex);
    Comm.FlowControl:=TFlowControl(FlowCombo.ItemIndex);
    Screen.Cursor:=crDefault;
    ShowStatus;
  end;
end;

procedure TTerminal.LocalEchoClick(Sender: TObject);
begin
  LocalEcho.Checked:=not LocalEcho.Checked;
end;

procedure TTerminal.ShowStatus;
begin
  if Comm.IsOpen then
  begin
    StatusText.Caption:='On-Line';
    StatusText.Font.Color:=clGreen;
  end
  else
  begin
    StatusText.Caption:='Port not opened';
    StatusText.Font.Color:=clRed;
  end;
end;

procedure TTerminal.FormCreate(Sender: TObject);
begin
  ShowStatus;
```

```
end;

procedure TTerminal.Timer1Timer(Sender: TObject);
begin
  if TxCount<>0 then
  begin
    dec(TxCount);
    if TxCount=0 then TxLED.Brush.Color:=clRed
  end;
    if RxCount<>0 then
  begin
    dec(RxCount);
    if RxCount=0 then RxLED.Brush.Color:=clRed
  end;

end;

end.
```

Listing 3.4 Commcfg.PAS

```
unit Commcfg;

interface

uses
  SysUtils, WinTypes, WinProcs, Messages, Classes, Graphics, Controls,
  Forms, Dialogs, StdCtrls,Comm;

type
  TCommSettings = class(TForm)
    PortLabel: TLabel;
    BaudLabel: TLabel;
    DataBitsLabel: TLabel;
    StopBitsLabel: TLabel;
    PartiyLabel: TLabel;
    FlowLabel: TLabel;
```

```
      PortCombo: TComboBox;
      BaudCombo: TComboBox;
      DataBitsCombo: TComboBox;
      StopBitsCombo: TComboBox;
      ParityCombo: TComboBox;
      FlowCombo: TComboBox;
      OK: TButton;
      Cancel: TButton;
      procedure FormCreate(Sender: TObject);
   end;

var
   CommSettings:TCommSettings;

implementation

{$R *.DFM}

procedure TCommSettings.FormCreate(Sender: TObject);
var
   i:Byte;
begin
   PortCombo.Items.Add('None');
   for i:=1 to 8 do
     PortCombo.Items.Add(IntToStr(i));

   BaudCombo.Items.Add('110');
   BaudCombo.Items.Add('300');
   BaudCombo.Items.Add('600');
   BaudCombo.Items.Add('1200');
   BaudCombo.Items.Add('2400');
   BaudCombo.Items.Add('4800');
   BaudCombo.Items.Add('9600');
   BaudCombo.Items.Add('14400');
   BaudCombo.Items.Add('19200');
   BaudCombo.Items.Add('38400');
   BaudCombo.Items.Add('56000');
   BaudCombo.Items.Add('128000');
```

```
BaudCombo.Items.Add('256000');

for i:=4 to 8 do
  DataBitsCombo.Items.Add(IntToStr(i));

StopBitsCombo.Items.Add('1');
StopBitsCombo.Items.Add('1.5');
StopBitsCombo.Items.Add('2');

ParityCombo.Items.Add('None');
ParityCombo.Items.Add('Odd');
ParityCombo.Items.Add('Even');
ParityCombo.Items.Add('Mark');
ParityCombo.Items.Add('Space');

FlowCombo.Items.Add('None');
FlowCombo.Items.Add('XON/XOFF');
FlowCombo.Items.Add('CTS/RTS');
FlowCombo.Items.Add('DSR/DTR');

end;

end.
```

The program is centered on a memo component, **TerminalMemo**, located in **MAIN.PAS**, that is responsible for both sending and receiving characters. A character is sent whenever a key is pressed, thanks to **TerminalMemo's OnKeyPress** event handler, which translates the key press to an ASCII value and then calls the **Write** method of **Comm** to do the actual transmission.

Processing incoming characters is handled in **Comm's OnReceive** event. First, a memory block, **RxText**, is allocated. Its size is dictated by the **RxChars** parameter to ensure that it is big enough to hold the received data. Next, the data is transferred from the receive buffer to **RxText**, via a call to **Comm's Read** method. Finally, a loop goes through the entire **RxText** buffer, sending the characters one by one to **TerminalMemo** by sending a **WM_CHAR** message to it. Sadly, this is the only way to append a single character to a memo component, and it also produces an undesirable (at least in this application) side-effect.

The problem is that whenever a **WM_CHAR** message is sent to **TerminalMemo**, it results in the **OnKeyPress** event handler being called. Because this handler responds to key presses by transmitting them, it is quite possible that an infinite-loop situation could develop. The solution I used, which is by no means the only one, was to first save the address of the **OnKeyPress** handler in the variable **KeyPress**, disable **OnKeyPress** by setting it to **nil**, execute the receive code, and then reenable **OnKeyPress** by restoring the saved value. Now whenever a **WM_CHAR** message is sent, the **OnKeyPress** event won't be called because the call address is invalid.

The code for the Communication Settings dialog box is located in **COMMCFG.PAS**. Whenever the dialog box is opened, each combo box is filled with values relevant to the property it is responsible for setting. Careful attention was paid to ensure that the order of the items in the combo boxes was consistent with the order that the items appear in their type declaration. For example, the type declaration for **TParity** contains the members **tpNone**, **tpOdd**, **tpEven**, **tpMark**, and **tpSpace**, in that order. Therefore, the **ParityCombo** combo box also receives them in that order:

```
ParityCombo.Items.Add('None');
ParityCombo.Items.Add('Odd');
ParityCombo.Items.Add('Even');
ParityCombo.Items.Add('Mark');
ParityCombo.Items.Add('Space');
```

The reason this is important is because it allows the properties to be set and retrieved in single lines of code. Making **ParityCombo** display the correct string requires using the **Ord** function to get the internal value of the enumerated type property, **Parity**, and then setting the **ItemIndex** property:

```
ParityCombo.ItemIndex:=Ord(Comm.Parity);
```

Retrieving the current setting of **ParityCombo** is just the opposite. The same property, **ItemIndex**, returns which string is visible and assigns it to **Parity**:

```
Comm.Parity:=TParity(ParityCombo.ItemIndex);
```

Note the need to typecast the value returned by **ItemIndex** to the same type of **Parity** itself.

CHAPTER · 4

CREATING DIALOG BOX COMPONENTS

Have you ever created a dialog box that you used in one place and later found that you needed it elsewhere? Chances are good that you have. Chances are equally good that the code for the dialog box was written in such a way that made it impossible to use the dialog box again without completely rewriting the code. Such incidents are generally—hopefully—learning experiences. That is, having been forced to rewrite the code for the first dialog box, you make sure to code future ones in a portable fashion.

Popular techniques for promoting portability are to place your dialog box in a Pascal unit or a Windows DLL, or to wrap an object around it. Of these techniques, the DLL method has the highest success rate because it is isolated from the rest of the application, preventing contamination from "short-cuts" that can be used with the other two. As a bonus, you are able to load in the DLL only when it is needed, saving precious memory.

Delphi takes the notion of wrapping an object around a dialog box to the extreme by permitting, but by no means forcing, them to be contained in nonvisual components. Need a certain dialog box for a form? No problem. Drop one on, and—presto!—it's there, and it's consistent with everywhere else it appears in your application.

We will spend this chapter looking at how you can put your dialog boxes into components, and by the time we're done, you will have learned about the following:

- What dialog boxes should be made into components
- Opening a dialog box component
- Setting the value of components in a dialog box

The Case of the Disappearing Dialog Boxes

If you have ever used a Delphi (including Delphi itself) or Visual Basic application, you have probably seen a dialog box or two. At least that's what you *think*. In reality, true dialog boxes are going the way of the dodo; more and more development environments, especially visual ones, are using normal windows that masquerade as dialog boxes. This makes some sense. First, the environment and its programmers do not have to support two distinctly different window models. Second, real dialog boxes are resources of the system. You know as well as I do that when resources go down, so does performance. On the other side of the coin, we could argue in favor of resources because they are inherently discardable—if you're not using a particular dialog box, the system may very well free it from memory and in the process create room for something else. An unused normal window is never discarded, and all the code for implementing it just sits there taking up space, except under special circumstances when the code segment that the window code is in is marked as discardable. However, chances are that there will be other code in the segment that will ever prevent this from happening. In the long run, however, window emulated dialog boxes have the most flexibility, which is the reason that both Delphi and Visual Basic use them.

How does this information affect you? For the most part, it doesn't, but it might help to clear up some preconceived notions you have as to the way dialog boxes work in Delphi. For example, you might have heard that you can't use a menu in a dialog box. This is no longer a limitation. Also, at one time setting the icon of a dialog box was a messy ordeal. Again, using a normal window solves this problem.

Casting Your Vote—The Dialog Box/Component Decision

I told you why embedding a dialog box into a component is desirable, but you may want to draw the line somewhere; not all dialog boxes need to be "componentized," especially when using Delphi because it strongly encourages a one-form-per-unit arrangement. Because this is the situation, the three strongest arguments for putting a dialog box into a component are code hiding, code protection, and reusability with other applications.

Code Hiding

After you finish creating a dialog box, coding it, and finally, debugging it, you will rarely have to go back to make changes. For this reason, it is advantageous to hide the dialog box completely inside a component. This reduces the complexity of your project because you're no longer working with code, but a symbolic representation of it.

Code Protection

If a dialog box is placed into a component, and then the original source code is "locked away," there is no way that someone can fiddle with it, perhaps creating bugs in the process. Also, you may not always want someone to have access to the source code to a dialog box; maybe, you're trying to sell it, or it contains information that not all members involved in your project should have access to. Either way, placing it into a component provides this level of protection, without sacrificing usability.

Reusability with Other Projects

If you work with many applications, it is quite likely that they share some of the same dialog boxes. The most obvious example would be the About dialog box that is typically, but not always, identical between different applications from the same company. The advantage to putting this into a component is apparent: Drop it on the form and be done with it, thereby reducing the amount of work that must be performed. Of course, this doesn't apply just to limited function dialog boxes like About dialog boxes, but to any dialog box that may be reused among projects.

Components versus Units

One question that may occur to you is why bother with dialog box components. Why not just place it in a unit and access it that way? You see, as human beings we are generally a lazy lot. We don't like to do anything we don't have to do, and we certainly don't enjoy remembering minuscule details if it can be avoided. Trying to remember the name of a particular unit falls under this category. The 8.3 restriction of DOS is mainly to blame for this because you can only fit a limited amount of description into eight characters. Time and again, I have found myself popping out to a DOS shell to use a text search program that allows me to examine *every* source file, looking for a known piece of text just to find the one file that I am interested in. Certainly, Windows 95 has abolished the need for such cryptic names, allowing file names up to 255 characters in length, but I quickly grow tired of typing in long names, or searching through a long list of names just for the one I want. To me, putting a dialog box into a component where you can visually pick what you want rather than a unit is justified by these reasons alone.

There is also the design-time aspect of components to consider. Do you want the dialog box to be centered on the screen or centered on a certain window? Is it to be modal, system modal, or modeless? Should a certain button be hidden because it does not make sense in the context of your application? The answers to all these questions can be decided at design time using the Object Inspector, provided, of course, that you code your dialog box component to support these types of decisions.

The About Box

No discussion of dialog box components would be worthy of the paper it is printed on unless it included the About box, perhaps the simplest of them all. An About box, as you already know, is a window that provides users details about the application that they are using, such as the name of the company that made it and its version number. Often, there will be other things including serial numbers, phone numbers, and sometimes a pretty picture to look at. We will now investigate the methods required to construct our own About box component from start to finish.

The Chicken or the Egg

The design of any dialog box component requires merging two features of Delphi: a *form* and a *component*. As a Delphi programmer, you already know that creating a form and its associated unit is as simple as selecting **File**, **New Form**. A couple of chapters back, I told you about the benefits of using the Component Expert to create a blank component template unit. The question that arises now is, how do you use these to create a dialog box component? If you use New Form first, you obviously can't proceed to use the Component Expert because it will create an additional unit. On the other hand, the same problem will occur if you use the Component Expert first because New Form will create an additional unit. The chicken or the egg... but not both.

One solution would be to create an expert of our own, but that is a topic for another book. This means that we have to decide whether it is more work to create a form and fill in component code or create a component and fill in the form code. No contest. Creating a form by any means other than New Form is a tedious proposition. Because tedium is the nemesis of Delphi, we will opt for creating the form automatically and filling in the component code manually.

Preparing the About Box

The first step involved in creating the About box form is to ensure that there is currently no project open in the Delphi environment. If there is, close it by selecting **File**, **Close**. This is necessary to make sure that the project does not get messed up because of the automatic code generation that would occur with the next step. Next, select **File**, **New Form**. At this point, a blank form should be on the screen, and the edit window should have a form template unit in it. Using the Object Inspector, set the name to **AboutBox**, the caption to About, the font to Arial 10, and the position to **poScreenCenter**.

We now have to "decorate" the form to make it look like the About box shown in Figure 4.1. As you can see, it contains mostly label components, but there is also an **OK** button located at the bottom, and an image component occupying the whole client area. After placing all the components, their names should be changed from their default values to something more appropriate. The names that I chose are also shown in Figure 4.1. After this has been done, the form is ready to be componentized.

Figure 4.1 About box form.

Making the About Box into a Component

The About box form that we just created is currently no different from any other Delphi form. If you wanted, you could still use it as part of your project without having to make any changes. In this light, it must be acknowledged that it is possible to create a dialog box component that can also function as a normal dialog box. The only real requirement is to ensure that the class declaration for the form is in the interface section of the unit it is declared in, so that other units may access it. Of course, you may not always want to provide that kind of two-way usage; the call is up to you. For our About box, however, we'll make it callable as either a component or a form, just to show how to go about it.

Wrapping a component around the About box is quite simple. First, the standard component code needs to be written. This involves selecting a parent, naming the component, and registering it—stuff you learned about back in Chapter 2. Next, a method needs to be added that, when called, will open the About box. For the sake of consistency with the rest of the VCL, we'll name this method **Execute**. The code contained in **Execute** is really nothing special; it's the same sort of thing you would see in any typical noncomponent Delphi project:

```
procedure TAboutBox.Execute;
var
   AboutForm:TAboutForm;
begin
   AboutForm:=TAboutForm.Create(Owner);
   AboutForm.ShowModal;
   AboutForm.Free;
end;
```

First, an instance of **TAboutForm** is created and initialized by the call to **Create**. Note that **Create**'s single parameter specifies the owner of the dialog box. For our About box, the owner is **Owner**, the form that houses the About component. Next, **ShowModal** is called to display the About form. **ShowModal** is similar to the standard **Show** function, which is normally called to display a window; however, **ShowModal** does not permit the owner form to be manipulated while the dialog box is visible. This means that the owner form is effectively disabled until the call to **ShowModal** returns, which typically occurs whenever the **OK** or **Cancel** button of the dialog form is clicked on. In our About box example, only an **OK** button exists; thus, by clicking on it, the About box is closed, and execution resumes on the line following **ShowModal**. The final operation of the **Execute** procedure is to free the form, by calling the **Free** member.

As an aside, **ShowModal** is a function, meaning that it returns a value. This value is dictated by the **ModalResult** member, which, if set to a value other than zero, immediately closes the form. This explains how the **ModalResult** property of buttons works. Whenever a button with a **ModalResult** property set to a value other than **mrNone** is clicked, the **ModalResult** member of the owner form is set to the same value, thereby closing the form and returning the appropriate value through the **ShowModal** call. Normally, you should check which value was returned from **ShowModal** to determine whether the information entered into the dialog box should be accepted or rejected; but for our About box, it doesn't really matter because no information is modified as a result of displaying it. For a dialog box component, it is difficult to do anything useful with the result of **ShowModal** while in the **Execute** method because generally, the appropriate action should be performed by the caller of **Execute**. This makes it necessary to pass the return value of **ShowModal** directly to the return value of **Execute**, which, of course, requires that **Execute** be made into a function, rather than a procedure, as used in the About box.

I intentionally omitted some code from the **Execute** method shown earlier. While the missing code isn't required for displaying the About box, it is needed if the contents and color of the labels are to be set properly, as well the background image. Here, is the complete **Execute** method:

```
procedure TAboutBox.Execute;
var
  AboutForm:TAboutForm;
begin
  AboutForm:=TAboutForm.Create(Owner);
  AboutForm.Product.Caption:=FProduct;
  AboutForm.Company.Caption:=FCompany;
  AboutForm.Copyright.Caption:=FCopyright;
  AboutForm.Version.Caption:=FVersion;
  AboutForm.SalesPhone.Caption:=FSalesPhone;
  AboutForm.TechSupportPhone.Caption:=FTechSupportPhone;
  AboutForm.Fax.Caption:=FFax;
  AboutForm.OnLineService.Caption:=FOnLineService;
```

```
ABoutForm.Product.Font.Color:=FTextColor;

ABoutForm.Company.Font.Color:=FTextColor;

ABoutForm.Copyright.Font.Color:=FTextColor;

ABoutForm.Version.Font.Color:=FTextColor;

ABoutForm.SalesPhone.Font.Color:=FTextColor;

ABoutForm.TechSupportPhone.Font.Color:=FTextColor;

ABoutForm.Fax.Font.Color:=FTextColor;

ABoutForm.OnLineService.Font.Color:=FTextColor;

ABoutForm.ByLabel.Font.Color:=FTextColor;

ABoutForm.VersionLabel.Font.Color:=FTextColor;

ABoutForm.SalesLabel.Font.Color:=FTextColor;

ABoutForm.TechLabel.Font.Color:=FTextColor;

ABoutForm.FaxLabel.Font.Color:=FTextColor;

ABoutForm.OnLineLabel.Font.Color:=FTextColor;

AboutForm.Image1.Picture.Assign(Background);

AboutForm.ShowModal;

AboutForm.Free;
end;
```

After the form has been created, its labels captions are assigned to the same values as the properties of the **TAboutBox** component. Next, the color of the labels and the background image are set. A word of caution is in order here. The background image is stored in the **FBackground** member of the component, which is of type **TPicture**. When the time comes to display the image on the About form, the **Picture** member (again of type **TPicture**) of the **Image1** property of **TAboutForm** is assigned **FBackground**. You might be inclined to think that this could be done like so:

```
AboutForm.Image1.Picture:=FBackground;
```

Sadly, this will give you nothing but grief if you attempt it because **Picture** property has already been allocated and initialized. Assigning it to something else will result in a memory leak when the **Image1** is freed because all the allocated memory for it will not be released; instead, the memory associated with **FBackground** will be. The proper way to assign one **Picture** property to another is to use the **Assign** method, as shown previously.

Wrapping Things Up

This just about concludes our discussion of **TAboutBox**. The palette bitmap for it is shown in Figure 4.2.

Figure 4.2 Palette bitmap for **TAboutBox**.

Finally, here is the final code, which can also be found in the **\DC\CHAP04** directory:

Listing 4.1 ABOUT.PAS

```
unit About;

interface

uses
  SysUtils, WinTypes, WinProcs, Messages, Classes, Graphics, Controls,
  Forms, Dialogs, StdCtrls, ExtCtrls;

const
  ProductDefault='Your Product';
  CompanyDefault='Your Company';
  CopyrightDefault='Your Copyright';
```

```
      VersionDefault='Your Version Number';
      SalesPhoneDefault='Your Sales Number';
      TechSupportPhoneDefault='Your Tech Support Number';
      FaxDefault='Your Fax Number';
      OnLineServiceDefault='Your On-line Account';
      TextColorDefault=clWindowText;

type
  TAboutForm = class(TForm)
     Product: TLabel;
     ByLabel: TLabel;
     Company: TLabel;
     Copyright: TLabel;
     Bevel1: TBevel;
     Bevel2: TBevel;
     VersionLabel: TLabel;
     Version: TLabel;
     SalesLabel: TLabel;
     SalesPhone: TLabel;
     TechLabel: TLabel;
     TechSupportPhone: TLabel;
     FaxLabel: TLabel;
     Fax: TLabel;
     OnLineLabel: TLabel;
     OnLineService: TLabel;
     Bevel3: TBevel;
     Button1: TButton;
     Image1: TImage;
  end;

  TAboutBox=class(TComponent)
  private
     FProduct:String;
     FCompany:String;
     FCopyright:String;
     FVersion:String;
```

```
    FSalesPhone:String;
    FTechSupportPhone:String;
    FFax:String;
    FOnLineService:String;
    FBackground:TPicture;
    FTextColor:TColor;
    procedure SetBackground(ABackground:TPicture);
  public
    constructor Create(AOwner:TComponent);override;
    destructor Destroy;
    procedure Execute;

  published
    property Product:String read FProduct write FProduct;
    property Company:String read FCompany write FCompany;
    property Copyright:String read FCopyright write FCopyright;
    property Version:String read FVersion write FVersion;
    property SalesPhone:String read FSalesPhone write FSalesPhone;
    property TechSupportPhone:String read FTechSupportPhone
      write FTechSupportPhone;
    property Fax:String read FFax write FFax;
    property OnLineService:String read FOnLineService
      write FOnLineService;
    property Background:TPicture read FBackground
      write SetBackground;
    property TextColor:TColor read FTextColor write FTextColor
      default TextColorDefault;
  end;

procedure Register;

implementation

{$R *.DFM}

procedure TAboutBox.Execute;
var
```

```
  AboutForm:TAboutForm;
begin
  AboutForm:=TAboutForm.Create(Owner);
  AboutForm.Product.Caption:=FProduct;
  AboutForm.Company.Caption:=FCompany;
  AboutForm.Copyright.Caption:=FCopyright;
  AboutForm.Version.Caption:=FVersion;
  AboutForm.SalesPhone.Caption:=FSalesPhone;
  AboutForm.TechSupportPhone.Caption:=FTechSupportPhone;
  AboutForm.Fax.Caption:=FFax;
  AboutForm.OnLineService.Caption:=FOnLineService;
  ABoutForm.Product.Font.Color:=FTextColor;
  ABoutForm.Company.Font.Color:=FTextColor;
  ABoutForm.Copyright.Font.Color:=FTextColor;
  ABoutForm.Version.Font.Color:=FTextColor;
  ABoutForm.SalesPhone.Font.Color:=FTextColor;
  ABoutForm.TechSupportPhone.Font.Color:=FTextColor;
  ABoutForm.Fax.Font.Color:=FTextColor;
  ABoutForm.OnLineService.Font.Color:=FTextColor;
  ABoutForm.ByLabel.Font.Color:=FTextColor;
  ABoutForm.VersionLabel.Font.Color:=FTextColor;
  ABoutForm.SalesLabel.Font.Color:=FTextColor;
  ABoutForm.TechLabel.Font.Color:=FTextColor;
  ABoutForm.FaxLabel.Font.Color:=FTextColor;
  ABoutForm.OnLineLabel.Font.Color:=FTextColor;
  AboutForm.Image1.Picture.Assign(Background);
  AboutForm.ShowModal;
  AboutForm.Free;
end;

procedure TAboutBox.SetBackground(ABackground:TPicture);
begin
  FBackground.Assign(ABackground);
end;

constructor TAboutBox.Create(AOwner:TComponent);
begin
```

```
  inherited Create(AOwner);
  FBackground:=TPicture.Create;
  FProduct:=ProductDefault;
  FCompany:=CompanyDefault;
  FCopyright:=CopyrightDefault;
  FVersion:=VersionDefault;
  FSalesPhone:=SalesPhoneDefault;
  FTechSupportPhone:=TechSupportPhoneDefault;
  FFax:=FaxDefault;
  FOnLineService:=OnLineServiceDefault;
  FTextColor:=TextColorDefault;
end;

destructor TAboutBox.Destroy;
begin
  FBackground.Free;
  inherited Destroy;
end;

procedure Register;
begin
  RegisterComponents('Additional', [TAboutBox]);
end;

end.
```

The Demo Program

To demonstrate the features of **TAboutBox**, I wrote a small program, shown in Figure 4.3 and Figure 4.4. The code for the example is shown here, but it can also be found in the **\DC\CHAP04** directory in case you're interested in fooling around with it.

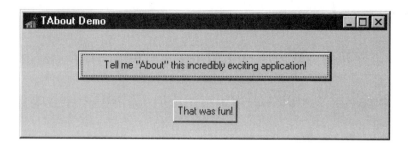

Figure 4.3 Main window of the demo program.

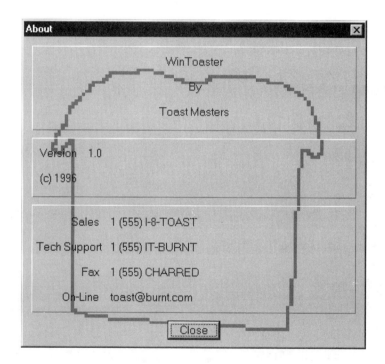

Figure 4.4 The About box.

Listing 4.2 AboutDemo.DPR

```
program AboutDemo;

uses
  Forms,
  AboutMain in 'AboutMain.pas' {Form1};

{$R *.RES}

begin
  Application.Initialize;
  Application.CreateForm(TForm1, Form1);
  Application.Run;
end.
```

Listing 4.3 AboutMain.PAS

```
unit AboutMain;

interface

uses
  Windows, Messages, SysUtils, Classes, Graphics, Controls, Forms,
Dialogs,
  StdCtrls, About;

type
  TForm1 = class(TForm)
    AboutBox1: TAboutBox;
    Button1: TButton;
    Button2: TButton;
    procedure Button1Click(Sender: TObject);
  private
    { Private declarations }
  public
    { Public declarations }
```

```
  end;

var
  Form1: TForm1;

implementation

{$R *.DFM}

procedure TForm1.Button1Click(Sender: TObject);
begin
  AboutBox1.Execute;
end;

end.
```

CHAPTER 5

CREATING A VISUAL COMPONENT

Until now, we have restricted our discussion of components to strictly nonvisual ones. However, most of the components you will want to create will need to be visual, meaning that you can see them on a form at run time. Therefore, the goal of this chapter is to ease you into the ideas behind visual components by discussing a real-world component, an *LED style gauge*. Throughout this chapter, you will become acquainted with the following:

- Types of visual components
- Adding graphics to a component
- Updating a component's graphics when a property changes
- Supporting multiple views of a component

Interactive versus Noninteractive Components

The two major styles of visual components are *interactive* and *noninteractive*. As its name suggests, an interactive component allows a user to manipulate it at run time. A prime example would be a button that can be clicked on. The sole purpose of a noninteractive component is to graphically convey information to the user, or just to spice up the form a bit to make it pleasant to look at. A good example of a noninteractive component would be the bevel component included with Delphi that gives a form a three-dimensional appearance.

All visual components are derived from **TControl**, regardless of whether they support user interaction. However, you will never want to derive your own component directly from **TControl** because there are two descendant classes, **TGraphicControl** and **TCustomControl**, that are more suited for this task. Specifically, **TGraphicControl** is used to create noninteractive components; whereas **TCustomControl** is used to create interactive ones. **TCustomControl** is not an immediate descendant of **TControl**; instead, it is descended from **TWinControl**, which in turn is descended from **TControl**. Note, however, that **TWinControl** is probably not something that you will ever want to use because it does not directly support the use of graphic commands; its primary reason for existing is to accommodate native Windows controls.

The major difference between **TGraphicControl** and **TCustomControl** is that components descended from **TGraphicControl** do not have a window of their own; any drawing that is done occurs directly on their owner's window. Components descended from **TCustomControl**, on the other hand, have one window for each instance of the component. Put another way, the fundamental difference between the two is performance: **TCustomControl** components eat memory and are somewhat slower than **TGraphicControl** components. Therefore, it is always to your advantage to use **TGraphicControl** whenever possible.

TGraphicControl

If simplicity is equivalent to elegance, then **TGraphicControl** is akin to Cinderella at the ball. This is because, aside from **Create** and **Destroy**, there is only one method that you will ever need to override to use this class, namely Paint. As a Delphi programmer, you are probably already familiar with the **Paint** method; but for those of you who aren't, the following discussion provides a brief description of what it is and how it is used.

Whenever a window needs to be drawn, either fully or partially, it is the responsibility of Windows to send a **WM_Paint** message to it. Although this is not complex to use, a VCL program simplifies this process dramatically by responding to the message itself, performing some basic initialization, and then calling the **Paint** method of the form (window) that needs to be repainted. If you have overridden **Paint**, your code will be called, giving you the opportunity to do some custom painting.

In addition to the **Paint** method, **TGraphicControl** provides one property that you will need to use extensively, **TCanvas.** In the days of Borland Pascal, it was necessary to call various GDI (Graphical Device Interface) functions directly to do any drawing that you might want to do. Delphi makes this practice obsolete by providing the **TCanvas** class, which wraps the majority of the GDI functions into one neatly packaged bundle. Despite the fact that it is just a wrapper, **TCanvas** adds a level of protection to the code you write by managing handles, such as device contexts and brush handles internally. This means that if you want to draw a rectangle and have it filled with a certain color, you no longer have to call the GDI's **CreateSolidBrush** function to create the brush, **SelectObject** to apply the brush to the device context, **Rectangle** to do the actual drawing, **SelectObject** once more to restore the old brush handle, and finally **DeleteObject** to destroy the brush. All you have to do is assign the **Brush** property of **TCanvas** to the *color* you want and call **Rectangle** to do the drawing. You don't have to worry about **HDC**'s or **HBrushes** because the VCL does the worrying for you. If you have ever written a Windows program the old way, you most likely recognize the advantage to this; no more will you be stung because you fail to release a device context or if you forget to restore the original brush handle.

In addition to the layer of protection that **TCanvas** offers, it also provides a consistent interface for all graphical objects in Delphi. This means that code you write to draw something on a form could be easily reused to draw it in a component, or to print it on a printer. Admittedly, this is similar to what Windows already allows, but the implementation in Delphi is more straightforward.

The LED Gauge Component

As mentioned, this chapter's example is an LED style gauge component. This type of component is often useful as an alternative to simply displaying a number on a form; it graphically displays the magnitude of a value relative to some maximum, and as such may provide more insight than a number alone would.

The specification for the component is as follows:

- The orientation can be either vertical or horizontal.
- The LED shape can be round, rectangular, or rounded rectangular.
- A User-definable number of LEDs.
- The LEDs are to be auto-sized and auto-spaced depending on the size of the component.
- The color of the LEDs can be solid, or a green, orange, and red stereo style arrangement.
- The orange and red "on" levels for the stereo style can be set as a percentage of full scale.

These criteria are similar to what you would expect to find in a commercial quality component; yet, I suspect that you will be amazed at the small amount of code required to make your own.

Component Creation

The parent of this component, which we will call **TLEDGauge**, is appropriately **TGraphicControl** because we have no need for user interaction. After creating the skeleton of the component with the Object Inspector, it is necessary to add properties to reflect the user-definable settings we want to provide. These properties are shown in Table 5.1.

Table 5.1 Properties of TLEDGauge

Property	Type	Description
Style	TStyle	If set to **stSolid**, the **Color** property will be used for LEDs that are on. If set to **stStereo**, the LEDs will be colored green, yellow, and red, depending on the magnitude of **Value**.
Mode	TMode	If set to **stBar**, all the LEDs below and including the one indicated by the **Value** property will light. If set to **stDot**, only the single LED corresponding to the **Value** property will light.
Shape	TShape	Determines the shape of the LEDs. It can be one of three values: **shRound**, **shRectangular**, **shRoundedRect**.
Count	TCount	Indicates how many LEDs will be used in the component, and can be a value from 1 to 50.
Color	TColor	If the **Style** property is set to **stSolid**, this property determines the "on" color of the LED.
Mirror	Boolean	If this property is set to **False**, vertical gauges have a value of zero at the bottom, and the maximum value at the top, whereas horizontal gauges have zero at the left and the maximum value at the right. Setting this property to **True** reverses this. That is, the zero for a vertical gauge is at the top, and for a horizontal gauge, it is at the left.

(Continued)

Property	Type	Description
OffColor	TColor	This property determines the color the LEDs will be when they are "off."
Maximum	LongInt	This property is the "full scale" value for the gauge. When the **Value** property is set to this number, all the LEDs will be light if in bar mode.
Yellow-Percent	TPercent	Specifies what percent of full scale has to be reached before green LEDs stop and yellow LEDs begin. Only works if **Style** is **stStereo** and can be a value from 0 to 100.
RedPercent	TPercent	Specifies what percent of full scale has to be reached before yellow LEDs stop and red LEDs begin. Only works if **Style** is **stStereo** and can be a value from 0 to 100.
Value	LongInt	This property is used in conjunction with **Maximum** to determine how many LEDs to light. For example, if **Maximum** is 100 and **Value** is 50, one-half of the available LEDs will light.

These properties can be set either at design time through the Object Inspector, or at run time by modifying them directly. Each property has its own function that is called when the property is set to a different value. This ensures that the proper visual change occurs.

Painting Efficiently

Originally, when I first wrote the component, I had each property call the **Refresh** method to redraw the entire gauge. This presented two major problems. First, **Refresh** works by erasing the entire component before it is redrawn in the **Paint** method. This produced an intolerable flickering whenever the **Value** property was changed. Because it is quite probable that it will be changed frequently throughout the execution of a program, it was necessary to implement a work-around.

The work-around consisted of calling the **Repaint** method rather than **Refresh**. The documentation for **Repaint** states that it will redraw the image without first erasing it. I tried it, and it worked—at least on one computer. Another machine that I tried the same code on caused the LED gauge to flicker away like mad. This rightly upset me. I didn't give up, however, and I soon discovered a work-around for my work-around. I did away with calling **Repaint** and decided to just call **Paint** directly. It worked, and continues to work, like a charm.

The second problem with calling **Refresh** every time a property is set is that it produces horribly inefficient code. Originally, the **Paint** method did absolutely everything necessary to draw the gauge: calculating the sizes of the LEDs, the space between them, and each placement for each LED. This was incredibly slow, mostly because determining the placement of each LED requires a multiplication and a division. The solution required to speed things up involved taking a good look at exactly what each property does. For example, if you change **Color**, there is no need to recalculate anything because all the sizes, spaces, and placements are unchanged from what they were before **Color** was changed. In the end, I decided to "break things up."

Paint now just draws the display—no more time-consuming calculations. These calculations still have to be done, however, so a separate routine—**Calculate**—was added for this purpose. It is called whenever the properties **Shape**, **Count**, or **Mirror** are changed. A side-effect quickly became evident; if the gauge is resized, the new size wouldn't be accounted for, and things would look strange. This is no good, of course, and some investigation into the inner workings of **TGraphicControl** had to be conducted to see if there was a method that could be overridden to respond to a size change. There wasn't, at least not directly.

There is a funny thing about **TGraphicControl** that needs to be mentioned. Even though components derived from it aren't real windows, the VCL emulates windows messages and sends them to instances of **TGraphicControl** (actually it sends them to all components descended from **TControl**). Mostly, these messages come from the parent of the component, which is usually a form. This is how **WM_MOUSEXXX** messages can be made available to a **TGraphicControl** component. In this sense, it may not be entirely accurate to call components that are directly descended of **TGraphicControl** noninteractive. However, they still can't receive input focus, so the name sticks. One such message that is emulated is **WM_WINDOWPOSCHANGED**, which can be intercepted with this declaration:

```
procedure WMWindowPosChanged(var Message:TWMWindowPosChanged);
  message WM_WINDOWPOSCHANGED;
```

This tells Delphi to call the **WMWindowPosChanged** procedure whenever a **WM_WINDOWPOSCHANGED** message is sent to the class via an eventual call to **Dispatch**, which is done internally in the VCL. The corresponding code for the preceding declaration looks like this:

```
procedure TLEDGauge.WMWindowPosChanged(var
  Message:TWMWindowPosChanged);
begin
  Calculate;
end;
```

Before this procedure gets called, however, the area corresponding to the new size is invalidated, meaning it is to be redrawn. At first, this might seem like a problem, because if the area is redrawn and *then* **Calculate** is called, you might think that the redraw would take place before **Calculate** had a chance to do its thing. Fortunately, this is not the case, because invalidating an area only *schedules* a redraw to occur; it doesn't actually do it at that very moment. The redraw will take place while the application that the component is in is processing messages—which can never be done while code is executing. Therefore, **Calculate** is called *before* the section of the form is repainted, giving the necessary values a chance to be set.

Breaking Up is Good to Do

I said it before, and I'll say it again: I dislike inefficiency in a program and producing efficient code in Delphi is an uphill battle because of its flexibility. So every enhancement that you make to your own code counts big time. This dislike prompted me to "break up" the **Calculate** routine even more. To be exact, I removed the code that calculated the **StopCount** value and placed it into its own routine, **CalculateStopCount**. The purpose of **StopCount** first needs some explanation.

StopCount indicates which LED corresponds with the current setting of the **Value** property. For example, if **Count** (the number of LEDs) was set to 10, **Maximum** was set to 100, and **Value** was set to 80, **StopCount** would be 8, meaning LEDs from 1 to 8 would be light. **StopCount** itself is calculated with a simple multiplication and division:

```
procedure TLEDGauge.CalculateStopCount;
begin
  StopCount:=MulDiv(FValue,FCount,FMaximum);
end;
```

Going back to the inefficiency problem, if **CalculateStopCount** is called only where it is needed, whenever **Count**, **Maximum**, or **Value** are set, some overhead is eliminated. The same has been done for the calculations involving the start positions of the yellow and red LEDs when **Style** is set to **stStereo**:

```
procedure TLEDGauge.CalculateStereoPositions;
begin
  YellowCount:=MulDiv(FCount,FYellowPercent,100);
  RedCount:=MulDiv(FCount,FRedPercent,100);
end;
```

YellowCount is the first LED that is yellow; whereas **RedCount** is the first LED that is red. These values are determined respectively by the **FYellowPercent** and **FRedPercent** variables, mirror images of the **YellowPercent** and **RedPercent** properties, which get scaled down to a number between zero and **FCount**, the mirror image of the **Count** property. **CalculateStereoPosition** is called when the **Count**, **YellowPercent**, or **RedPercent** properties change.

The most inefficient process, originally in **Paint**, but moved to **Calculate**, was determining the X and Y positions of the LEDs, because each LED required a multiplication and a division. Once removed from **Paint**, however, the positions had to be saved somehow. It would be quite wrong to use an instance to **TList**, a generic list class, to do this because it's inefficient in its own right and mostly overkill. It would have been possible to dynamically allocate some memory exactly to the size required, as determined by the **Count** property, to store the positions in, but I opted for the straightforward, and somewhat wasteful, approach of simply declaring two standard arrays to hold the positions:

```
LEDXPos:array[1..MaxLEDs] of Word;
LEDYPos:array[1..MaxLEDs] of Word;
```

Actually, this is doubly wasteful because only one of the arrays will actually contain different values; the other will contain values that are all the same. For the purpose of clarity, however, it seemed to be a reasonable trade-off. For a project, I invite you to de-bloat this aspect of **TLEDGauge**.

Other Properties

In addition to the properties specific to **TLEDGauge**, there are also some others that have been inherited from **TGraphicControl** (see Table 5.2).

Table 5.2 Inherited Properties

Property	Description
Cursor	Determines the appearance of the cursor while it is placed over **TLEDGauge.**
Height	The height of the component in pixels.
Hint	Text for a hint as to the purpose of the component in an application. Often you will see such a hint in the status bar of a program, usually located at the bottom of the window.
Left	Placement of the left edge of the component, in pixels, on the form.

Property	Description
Name	The name of the component. Defaults to **LEDGaugeX**, where *X* is a number decided by Delphi. For your own programs, it is desirable to rename this default name to something more descriptive.
Tag	This is unused by the component and can be any value that the programmer desires.
Top	Placement of the top edge of the component, in pixels, on the form.
Width	The width of the component, in pixels.

The properties that you will end up setting the most, albeit indirectly, are **Left**, **Top**, **Width**, and **Height**, whenever you place and size the component.

Knowing where Your LEDs Are

As stated earlier, the **Calculate** method is ultimately responsible for determining the final positions of the LEDs. Because this where all the important stuff is, let's look at it under the microscope.

The very first thing that is done is the assignment of the local variables **XPos** and **YPos** to the value of zero. These variables hold the "working" position of the LED before it is permanently assigned to the **LEDXPos** and **LEDYPos** arrays. The reason that they have to be initialized right now is for the special case of when there is only one LED on the gauge. We'll discuss that in a moment.

The second thing that has to be determined is the gauge's orientation, which is one criteria on the list of features that **TLEDGauge** is to have. You will not, however, find a property for this. Here, I determined that the orientation is best decided by comparing the height of the component to its width. Obviously, if the component is wider than it is high, a vertical LED gauge would look pretty lousy. The same can be said for the horizontal LED gauge against a higher than wide component. With this knowledge, the orientation can be automated—tall and skinny LED gauges are vertical; whereas short and fat LED gauges are horizontal.

Depending on the orientation, one of two sections of code is executed—one for vertical gauges and the other for horizontal gauges. For now, we'll make the assumption that the gauge is vertical. This being the case, the following equation is used to calculate the height of the LED:

```
LEDHeight:=Height*2 div (3*FCount-1);
```

It is derived from the fact that the spacing between the LEDs is one-half of the LED's height. Solving for **Height** helps to illustrate this:

```
Height:=LEDHeight*FCount + LEDHeight * (FCount-1) div 2;
```

The first part, **LEDHeight*FCount**, returns the total height of all LEDs if they were stacked one on top of another without space between them. Because there is space between them—one half of the LED height—and there is a total of one less than the number of LEDs of these spaces, the second half of the equation must be used to obtain a true **Height** value. Thus, by solving for **LEDHeight**, we arrive at the original equation.

The width of the LED is much easier to determine. If the **FShape** variable is **shRound**, the height is the same as the width to give a reasonably round circle. I say reasonably because the aspect ratio of the screen has not been factored in; but for small circles like we have here, it really doesn't make much of a difference. If **FShape** is **shRectangular** or **shRoundedRect**, the LED width is the width of the component itself.

Next, the LEDs may have to be offset from the vertical edge to center them. This is determined as follows:

```
XPos:=(Width-LEDWidth) div 2;
```

This takes the width of the component and subtracts from it the width of the LED to determine the space not occupied by the LED. If we divide this by two, we will get a value that represents how much space is on either side of the LED if it is centered. It is then assigned to **XPos**.

With this preliminary initialization done and still assuming that the gauge is vertical, the actual positions can now be assigned. This involves setting up a loop that has one iteration for each LED. In the course of each iteration, the **YPos** variable is assigned a value. Before doing this, though, we first have to check to see if the count of LEDs is one. If it is, the normal flow of execution cannot continue because it entails dividing by the count of LEDs *minus one*, which would turn out to be zero in this case. Because division by zero is off-limits, we will rely on the fact that the very first thing done when entering **Calculate** was to initialize **YPos** to zero—the proper value for a one-LED gauge.

By the way, you're probably wondering why you'd want a one-LED gauge. One excellent use is as an on/off indicator. Assign the **Maximum** property to one, and a **Value** of zero will turn off the LED; a **Value** of one will turn it on.

If the gauge has more than one LED, the position calculation can proceed normally:

```
YPos:=Height-MulDiv(i-1,Height-LEDHeight,FCount-1)
```

Here, the vertical position is being scaled from one less than its index value, **i**, to a value between zero and **Height-LEDHeight**. One less than the index value is used to produce a scaled value of zero for the first LED to get the proper position. The maximum scaled value is **Height-LEDHeight** because that is the start position for the final LED, even though the LED will actually be drawn beyond this position. Finally, the result of the **MulDiv** has to be subtracted from **Height** because the pixel positions at the bottom of the component have a higher value than those at the top—that is, pixel zero is at the top of the component.

Calculating LED positions for a horizontal gauge is similar to the procedure just discussed, except that scaling occurs in the X direction instead of the Y direction. Another difference is that pixel zero is at the left-hand side of the component—where the first LED is—so it is not necessary to do the same sort of subtraction as in the preceding discussion.

Drawing the Gauge

Drawing the gauge occurs in the **Paint** method, which as you learned, is called when one of two things happens: Windows asks for it to be done by posting a message to the form that owns it, or a property value changes.

Regardless of the cause, once the **Paint** method is called, a **For** loop starts, with one iteration for each LED in the gauge. At the beginning of each iteration, some logic is used to determine if the LED is to be on or off. It should be on if the mode is **moBar** and its position is less than or the same as the **StopCount** variable. If, however, the mode is **moDot**, the LED should only come on if its position is equal to **StopCount**. If both cases are false, it is in the "off" state, and the brush color—the color for drawing the inside of the LEDs—is set to **FOffColor**. But, If either case is true, it is then determined whether the style is **stSolid** or **stStereo**. If it is **stSolid**, the brush color is set to **FColor**, the "on" color. If the style is **stStereo**, the color of the LED is resolved by comparing the loop index to the **YellowCount** and **RedCount** variables. If it is greater than or equal to **RedCount**, the LED is red. If it is less than **RedCount** but greater than or equal to **YellowCount**, the LED is yellow. If neither situation is true, the LED is green.

After the color has been decided, the LED must be drawn. The shape of the LED is determined by the **FShape** variable, and depending on its value, one of the **Canvas** member functions, **Ellipse**, **Rectangle**, or **RoundRect**, will be called. All the functions are called by passing a bounding rectangle as a parameter. For **RoundRect**, it is also necessary to pass the width and height of the ellipse that is used to round each corner. This value is simply determined by using one quarter of the width of the LED and one quarter of its height, respectively. The bounding rectangle that is passed to each function is calculated swiftly by using the **LEDXPos** and **LEDYPos** arrays. **LEDXPos** is the left edge of the rectangle; **LEDYPos** is its bottom; **LEDWidth** added to **LEDXPos** is the right edge; and **LEDHeight** subtracted from **LEDYPos** is the top edge.

Because **LEDXPos** and **LEDYPos** are arrays, they obviously need an index to get the proper position of the rectangle. If we did not want the option of mirroring the gauge, we could use the loop index directly. Because we do want this option, we must alter the index value if **FMirror** is set to **True**. This alteration is quite simple:

```
if FMirror then
  Index:=FCount-i+1
else
  Index:=i;
```

The variable, **i**, is the loop index, and if **FMirror** is **False**, is assigned directly to **Index**. If **FMirror** is **True**, **Index** is assigned a value that is the same as **i**, except starting from the other end of the gauge. For example, on a mirrored gauge with ten LEDs where **i** was 2, **Index** would be 9. If **i** was 4, **Index** would be 7, and so on. Needless to say, the preceding piece of code is executed prior to actually drawing the LED.

The Code

That wraps up the discussion of **TLEDGauge**. All that remains is to give you the code, **\DC\CHAP05\LEDGAUGE.PAS**:

Listing 5.1 LEDGauge.PAS

```
unit LEDGauge;

interface

uses
  SysUtils, WinTypes, WinProcs, Messages, Classes, Graphics, Controls,
  Forms, Dialogs;

const
  MaxLEDs=50;

type
  TStyle=(stSolid,stStereo);
  TMode=(moBar,moDot);
  TShape=(shRound,shRectangular,shRoundedRect);
  TCount=1..MaxLEDs;
  TPercent=0..100;

const
  StyleDefault=stSolid;
  ModeDefault=moBar;
  ShapeDefault=shRound;
```

```
CountDefault=10;
ColorDefault=clRed;
MirrorDefault=False;
OffColorDefault=clBlack;
MaximumDefault=100;
ValueDefault=MaximumDefault;
YellowPercentDefault=60;
RedPercentDefault=90;

type
  TLEDGauge = class(TGraphicControl)
  private
    LEDXPos:array[1..MaxLEDs] of Word;
    LEDYPos:array[1..MaxLEDs] of Word;
    LEDHeight:Word;
    LEDWidth:Word;
    StopCount:Word;
    YellowCount:Word;
    RedCount:Word;

    FStyle:TStyle;
    FMode:TMode;
    FShape:TShape;
    FCount:TCount;
    FColor:TColor;
    FMirror:Boolean;
    FOffColor:TColor;
    FMaximum:LongInt;
    FYellowPercent:TPercent;
    FRedPercent:TPercent;
    FValue:LongInt;
    procedure SetStyle(AStyle:TStyle);
    procedure SetMode(AMode:TMode);
    procedure SetShape(AShape:TShape);
    procedure SetCount(ACount:TCount);
    procedure SetColor(AColor:TColor);
```

```
        procedure SetMirror(AMirror:Boolean);
        procedure SetOffColor(AOffColor:TColor);
        procedure SetMaximum(AMaximum:LongInt);
        procedure SetYellowPercent(AYellowPercent:TPercent);
        procedure SetRedPercent(ARedPercent:TPercent);
        procedure SetValue(AValue:LongInt);
        procedure Calculate;
        procedure CalculateStereoPositions;
        procedure CalculateStopCount;
        procedure WMWindowPosChanged(var Message:TWMWindowPosChanged);
          message WM_WINDOWPOSCHANGED;
    protected
    public
        constructor Create(AOwner:TComponent);override;
        procedure Paint;override;

    published
        property Style:TStyle read FStyle write SetStyle default
    StyleDefault;
        property Mode:TMode read FMode write SetMode default ModeDefault;
        property Shape:TShape read FShape write SetShape default
    ShapeDefault;
        property Count:TCount read FCount write SetCount default
    CountDefault;
        property Color:TColor read FColor write SetColor;
        property Mirror:Boolean read FMirror write SetMirror default
    MirrorDefault;
        property OffColor:TColor read FOffColor write SetOffColor;
        property Maximum:LongInt read FMaximum write SetMaximum
          default MaximumDefault;
        property YellowPercent:TPercent read FYellowPercent write
    SetYellowPercent
          default YellowPercentDefault;
        property RedPercent:TPercent read FRedPercent write SetRedPercent
          default RedPercentDefault;
        property Value:LongInt read FValue write SetValue default
    MaximumDefault;
```

```
    end;

procedure Register;

implementation

procedure TLEDGauge.SetStyle(AStyle:TStyle);
begin
  FStyle:=AStyle;
  Paint;
end;

procedure TLEDGauge.SetMode(AMode:TMode);
begin
  FMode:=AMode;
  Paint;
end;

procedure TLEDGauge.SetShape(AShape:TShape);
begin
  FShape:=AShape;
  Calculate;
  Refresh;
end;

procedure TLEDGauge.SetCount(ACount:TCount);
begin
  FCount:=ACount;
  CalculateStopCount;
  CalculateStereoPositions;
  Calculate;
  Refresh;
end;

procedure TLEDGauge.SetColor(AColor:TColor);
begin
```

```
    FColor:=AColor;
    Paint;
end;


procedure TLEDGauge.SetMirror(AMirror:Boolean);
begin
    FMirror:=AMirror;
    Calculate;
    Paint;
end;


procedure TLEDGauge.SetOffColor(AOffColor:TColor);
begin
    FOffColor:=AOffColor;
    Paint;
end;


procedure TLEDGauge.SetMaximum(AMaximum:LongInt);
begin
    FMaximum:=AMaximum;
    CalculateStopCount;
    Paint;
end;


procedure TLEDGauge.SetYellowPercent(AYellowPercent:TPercent);
begin
    FYellowPercent:=AYellowPercent;
    CalculateStereoPositions;
    Paint;
end;


procedure TLEDGauge.SetRedPercent(ARedPercent:TPercent);
begin
    FRedPercent:=ARedPercent;
    CalculateStereoPositions;
    Paint;
```

```
end;

procedure TLEDGauge.SetValue(AValue:LongInt);
begin
  FValue:=AValue;
  CalculateStopCount;
  Paint;
end;

procedure TLEDGauge.WMWindowPosChanged(var
Message:TWMWindowPosChanged);
begin
  Calculate;
end;

constructor TLEDGauge.Create(AOwner:TComponent);
begin
  inherited Create(AOwner);
  FStyle:=StyleDefault;
  FMode:=ModeDefault;
  FShape:=ShapeDefault;
  FCount:=CountDefault;
  FColor:=ColorDefault;
  FOffColor:=OffColorDefault;
  FMaximum:=MaximumDefault;
  FYellowPercent:=YellowPercentDefault;
  FRedPercent:=RedPercentDefault;
  FValue:=ValueDefault;
  CalculateStereoPositions;
  CalculateStopCount;
end;

procedure TLEDGauge.Calculate;
var
  i:Word;
  XPos:Word;
```

```
    YPos:Word;
begin
  XPos:=0;
  YPos:=0;

  if Height>Width then
  begin
    LEDHeight:=Height*2 div (3*FCount-1);
    case FShape of
      shRound:LEDWidth:=LEDHeight;
      shRectangular,shRoundedRect:LEDWidth:=Width;
    end;
    XPos:=(Width-LEDWidth) div 2;
  end
  else
  begin
    LEDWidth:=Width*2 div (3*FCount-1);
    case FShape of
      shRound:LEDHeight:=LEDWidth;
      shRectangular,shRoundedRect:LEDHeight:=Height;
    end;
    YPos:=Height-(Height-LEDHeight) div 2
  end;

  for i:=1 to FCount do
  begin
    if FCount<>1 then
    begin
      if Height>Width then
        YPos:=Height-MulDiv(i-1,Height-LEDHeight,FCount-1)
      else
        XPos:=MulDiv(i-1,Width-LEDWidth,FCount-1);
    end;
    LEDXPos[i]:=XPos;
    LEDYPos[i]:=YPos;
  end;
```

```
end;

procedure TLEDGauge.CalculateStereoPositions;
begin
  YellowCount:=MulDiv(FCount,FYellowPercent,100);
  RedCount:=MulDiv(FCount,FRedPercent,100);
end;

procedure TLEDGauge.CalculateStopCount;
begin
  StopCount:=MulDiv(FValue,FCount,FMaximum);
end;

procedure TLEDGauge.Paint;
var
  i:Word;
  Index:Word;
begin
  for i:=1 to FCount do
  begin
    if (i<=StopCount) and (FMode=moBar) or
      (i=StopCount) and (FMode=moDot) then
    begin
      if FStyle=stStereo then
      begin
        if i>=RedCount then
          Canvas.Brush.Color:=clRed
        else if i>=YellowCount then
          Canvas.Brush.Color:=clYellow
        else
          Canvas.Brush.Color:=clLime;
      end
      else
        Canvas.Brush.Color:=FColor;
    end
    else
      Canvas.Brush.Color:=FOffColor;

    if FMirror then
```

```
        Index:=FCount-i+1
     else
        Index:=i;

     case FShape of
        shRound:Canvas.Ellipse(LEDXPos[Index],LEDYPos[Index],
          LEDXPos[Index]+LEDWidth,LEDYPos[Index]-LEDHeight);
        shRectangular:Canvas.Rectangle(LEDXPos[Index],LEDYPos[Index],
          LEDXPos[Index]+LEDWidth,LEDYPos[Index]-LEDHeight);
        shRoundedRect:Canvas.RoundRect(LEDXPos[Index],LEDYPos[Index],
          LEDXPos[Index]+LEDWidth,LEDYPos[Index]-LEDHeight,LEDWidth div
4,
          LEDHeight div 4);
     end;
   end;
end;

procedure Register;
begin
   RegisterComponents('Additional', [TLEDGauge]);
end;

end.
```

To complete the component, its bitmap, **\DC\CHAP05\LEDGAUGE .DCR**, is shown in Figure 5.1.

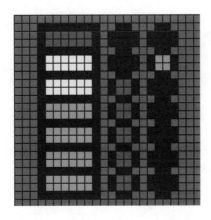

Figure 5.1 Palette bitmap for **TLEDGauge**.

The Demonstration Program

To demonstrate the features of **TLEDGauge**, I have written a small program consisting of two files **LGDEMO.DPR** and **LGMAIN.PAS**, which are shown here, but can also be found in the **\DC\CHAP05** directory:

Listing 5.2 LgDemo.DPR

```
program Lgdemo;

uses
  Forms,
  Lgmain in 'LGMAIN.PAS' {Form1};

{$R *.RES}

begin
  Application.CreateForm(TForm1, Form1);
  Application.Run;
end.
```

Lisitng 5.3 LGMain.PAS

```
unit LGMain;

interface

uses
  SysUtils, WinTypes, WinProcs, Messages, Classes, Graphics, Controls,
  Forms, Dialogs, LEDGauge, ExtCtrls, StdCtrls;

type
  TForm1 = class(TForm)
    LEDGauge1: TLEDGauge;
    LEDGauge2: TLEDGauge;
    Timer1: TTimer;
```

```
      Bevel1: TBevel;
      Bevel2: TBevel;
      LEDGauge4: TLEDGauge;
      Label1: TLabel;
      LEDGauge5: TLEDGauge;
      LEDGauge3: TLEDGauge;
      LEDGauge6: TLEDGauge;
      LEDGauge7: TLEDGauge;
      LEDGauge8: TLEDGauge;
      LEDGauge9: TLEDGauge;
      LEDGauge10: TLEDGauge;
      Bevel3: TBevel;
      LEDGauge11: TLEDGauge;
      Button1: TButton;
      procedure Timer1Timer(Sender: TObject);
      procedure Button1Click(Sender: TObject);
      procedure Button1Enter(Sender: TObject);
    private
      WarnCount:Word;
      CanFlash:Boolean;
      FlashCount:Word;
      Progress:Word;
    end;

var
  Form1: TForm1;

implementation

{$R *.DFM}

procedure TForm1.Timer1Timer(Sender: TObject);
var
  TempValue:Word;
begin
  LEDGauge1.Value:=Random(100);
```

```
LEDGauge2.Value:=LEDGauge1.Value;
LEDGauge5.Value:=Progress;
LEDGauge6.Value:=Progress;
LEDGauge7.Value:=Progress;
LEDGauge8.Value:=Progress;
LEDGauge9.Value:=Progress;
LEDGauge10.Value:=Progress;
LEDGauge11.Value:=Progress;
inc(Progress);
if Progress>100 then Progress:=0;

inc(WarnCount);
if WarnCount=10 then
begin
  TempValue:=LEDGauge3.Value;
  inc(TempValue);
  if TempValue=11 then TempValue:=1;
  CanFlash:=TempValue>6;
  LEDGauge3.Value:=TempValue;
  WarnCount:=0;
end;

if  CanFlash then
begin
  inc(FlashCount);
  if FlashCount=2 then
  begin
    if LEDGauge4.Value=0 then
      LEDGauge4.Value:=1
    else
      LEDGauge4.Value:=0;
    FlashCount:=0;
  end;
end;

end;
```

```
procedure TForm1.Button1Click(Sender: TObject);
begin
  Close;
end;

procedure TForm1.Button1Enter(Sender: TObject);
begin
  WarnCount:=0;
  CanFlash:=False;
  FlashCount:=0;
  Progress:=0;
end;

end.
```

CHAPTER • 6

CREATING AN INTERACTIVE COMPONENT

In the last chapter, we looked at how the **TGraphicControl** class can be used to create a non-interactive component. In this chapter, we will focus on the creation of an interactive component, an X-Y check box, that is to be derived from **TCustomControl.** As with every chapter, the goal here is to demonstrate the techniques used to create the example component:

- Working with fonts
- Processing mouse input
- Processing keyboard input

Component Specifications

I strive for nothing less than to give you commercial quality components that you can use in your own applications. This component is no exception; its specification boasts the following list of features:

- Descriptive text for both rows and columns
- Up to 20 rows and columns
- Three modes of operation: Normal, row-exclusive, and column-exclusive
- Automatic sizing

Drawing the Check Grid

Drawing the check grid component, **TCheckGrid,** occurs in two steps: determining where everything goes and actually painting it. Like the **TLEDGauge** component of the previous chapter, these two steps have been separated for efficiency.

Rectangles Abound!

TCheckGrid has three visible areas that it needs to maintain, as shown in Figure 6.1. Compare this to the image of an actual component shown in Figure 6.2. The column text area and the row text area are self-explanatory; they are used to display some descriptive text for each column and row of the grid area. The grid area is where the columns and rows are contained, with each intersection being a check or no check possibility. Because these areas are rectangles, three **TRect** records—**ColumnText Rect, RowTextRect**, and **CheckBoxRect**—are used to store their location and size relative to the confinements of the component. All the appropriate calculations used to determine their sizes are done in the **CalculateRects** method.

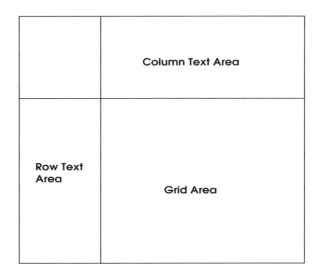

Figure 6.1 The three areas of **TCheckGrid**.

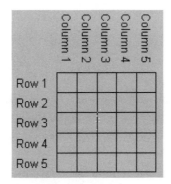

Figure 6.2 Appearance of **TCheckGrid**.

It is not possible to determine the bounds of any single rectangle without taking three factors into consideration:

- The size of the component
- The column and row text, as well as the font used for displaying it
- The bounds of the other rectangles

Component Size

The role of the component's size is obvious: If the width of the component is increased, the width of both the column text area and the grid area will increase. The same holds true if the width is decreased. Notice that no mention was made of the row text area's width changing. This is because it is dependent on the text it contains rather than the size of the component. If the height of the **TCheckGrid** is altered, a change occurs in the height of the row text area and the grid area, but not the column text area because its height is also a fixed value depending on the text inside it.

Formally stated, the bounds of the component rectangle form two bounds for each of the subrectangles. For the column text area, the top and right bounds of the component rectangle are used to define its top and right bounds. The right and bottom bounds of the component rectangle define the right and bottom bounds of the grid area rectangle. Finally, the left and bottom bounds define the left and bottom bounds of the row text area rectangle. This can be expressed with code like this:

```
ColumnTextRect.Top:=0;
ColumnTextRect.Right:=Width-1;
RowTextRect.Left:=0;
RowTextRect.Bottom:=Height-1;
CheckGridRect.Right:=Width-1;
CheckGridRect.Bottom:=Height-1;
```

Because coordinates within a component are relative to its upper-left corner, you will notice that a rectangle boundary that falls either on the top or left edge of the component has a value of zero. Boundaries on the right or bottom side are assigned values of **Width-1** and **Height-1**. It is necessary to subtract one to form the **Width** and **Height** properties because the drawing origin is zero and not one. If you are uneasy with this concept, consider a very small rectangle only two pixels wide. If the left edge of the rectangle is at zero, the right edge could not possibly be at two because that would make it three pixels wide—pixel number zero, pixel number one, and pixel number two.

Text Size

You no doubt noticed that I just let a clue slip as to how the height of the column text area and the width of the row text area are determined: by their text. So, if we take the longest text item from the column text area, its height can be deduced. The same goes for the row text area's width. Right? Wrong. In Windows, text is not limited to just monospaced letters, numbers, and smiley faces like it is in DOS. Text has a "flavor" to it called a *font*. Windows' fonts can be any shape or size and can have various attributes such as bold, italic, underline, and so on. In addition, they are not restricted to being monospaced; they can be proportionally spaced depending on the character. In other words, an "I" does not take up as much space as an "M."

Because you clearly cannot count characters to determine the length of a piece of text on the screen, another way must be used. Luckily, the VCL saves the day because one of the **TCanvas** methods, **TextWidth**, does exactly what we want. I didn't mention it yet, but the text in the column text area is at a 90-degree angle, because there wouldn't be room for it if it was horizontal like the row text. A puzzling question may now be forming on your lips: If the text is rotated, what will **TextWidth** return—its height or its width? It would be nice if it returned its width for the purpose of determining the bounding rectangle of text that is at an angle that is not a multiple of 90, but it doesn't. **TextWidth** returns the same number regardless of the angle of the text.

Now that we know how to get the height and width that the text will occupy on the screen, we have to set up two loops: one for the column text, contained in the **FColumnText** array, and one for row text, contained in the **FRowText** array, with an iteration for each string as determined by the **FColumns** and **FRows** variables:

```
RowWidthMax:=0;
for i:=1 to FRows do
begin
  WidthSize:=Canvas.TextWidth(FRowText[i]);
  if WidthSize>RowWidthMax then RowWidthMax:=WidthSize;
```

```
end;
RowTextRect.Right:=RowWidthMax+10;

ColumnWidthMax:=0;
for i:=1 to FColumns do
begin
  HeightSize:=Canvas.TextWidth(FColumnText[i]);
  if HeightSize>ColumnHeightMax then ColumnHeightMax:=HeightSize;
end;
ColumnTextRect.Bottom:=ColumnHeightMax+10;
```

When this code has been executed, both the bottom bound of the column text area and the right bound of the row text area will be defined. Notice that the constant value of **10** has been added to each. This is so that the text won't appear "scrunched up" against the check grid area.

If you were to run the preceding code, a problem would become apparent. The **TextWidth** function returns the width of a string as it would appear on the screen with the appropriate font assigned. However, we have not taken into account that a font, other than the default one, will be used. Therefore, before executing any of the preceding code, it is necessary to first make the following call:

```
Canvas.Font:=Font;
```

This makes the **Font** property of **Canvas** have the same attributes as the **Font** member of **TCheckGrid**. If you peruse the source code, you will not find a declaration for **Font** because it is an inherited member from **TCustomControl**.

The preceding assignment might confuse you. How can you simply assign one property to another? Isn't that what the **Assign** method is for, copying attributes from one class instance to another? You might think that a maneuver such as this would create a memory leak because everything associated with **Canvas.Font** before the assignment would still remain in memory. And you would be correct—except in this particular case. Notice that the **Font** part of **Canvas.Font** is not a true class instance, it is a property that pretends to be a class instance. Do you see where I'm going with this? We've done it enough times by now for you to know that you can assign a value to a property and have it call a procedure in lieu of a simple assignment. If that procedure calls **Assign**, it completes the illusion just described. This magic is not restricted to just **TFont** classes; it works with most properties that are classes, such as **TPen**, and **TBrush**. I have to admit that this "feature" frightens me somewhat. It is all too easy to forget yourself and do the same thing to a non-property class instance, creating a buggy program in the process:

```
var
   A:TSomeClass;
   B:TSomeClass;

begin
   A:=TSomeClass.Create;
   B:=TSomeClass.Create;
   B:=A;
end.
```

After the **B:=A** assignment is made, the original instance of class **B** is lost forever, as is the memory associated with it.

Other Rectangle Sizes

It is impossible to define the bounds of one rectangle without first taking the bounds of the others into consideration. Of course, to get the bounds of those other rectangles, you need information about the first one. This may sound like a catch-22 situation, but it is not. The secret is that the rectangles do not have to be fully defined before they can be used to define other rectangles. For example, the left edge of the column text area and the left edge of the grid area are at the same position as the right edge of the row text area. We know that the right edge of the row text area depends on the text that it contains, so once we figure that out, we have solved one coordinate of each rectangle. This also applies for the top edge of both the row text area and the grid area because they are at the same position as the bottom edge of the column text area, which can be determined from its text.

Determining Column and Row Positions

Determining the placement of the columns and rows within the check grid area is similar to how the positions of the LEDs were determined in the last chapter. The width of the grid area is divided into an equal number of sections, as dictated by **FColumns**. Each of these sections represents a single column and through the use of a loop, its position is stored in the **ColumnPos** array:

```
for i:=1 to FColumns+1 do
  ColumnPos[i]:=MulDiv(CheckGridRect.Right-CheckGridRect.Left,
    i-1,FColumns)+CheckGridRect.Left;
```

Those of you with eagle eyes will notice that the loop does not count from the first to the last column, but rather from the first to the last column *plus one*. The explanation for this is that two consecutive **ColumnPos** values define the bounds of the column. For example, **ColumnPos[1]** is the start of the first column, and **ColumnPos[2]** is the start of the second column; but it is also the end of the first column. By counting one more than the number of columns, we ensure that the bounds of the final column are defined. This technique works equally well for determining the position of the rows:

```
for i:=1 to FRows+1 do
  RowPos[i]:=MulDiv(CheckGridRect.Bottom-CheckGridRect.Top,i-1,
    FRows)+CheckGridRect.Top;
```

Check, Please

After the positions for the columns and rows have been determined, the size of a single cell can be calculated by simply subtracting the position of a column or row from the position of the next column or row. Because column one and row one are always defined, the process looks like this:

```
ColumnWidth:=ColumnPos[2]-ColumnPos[1];
RowWidth:=RowPos[2]-RowPos[1];
```

Using this relationship, two values can be calculated:

```
CheckXOffset:=(ColumnPos[2]-ColumnPos[1]) div 4;
CheckYOffset:=(RowPos[2]-RowPos[1]) div 4;
```

CheckXOffset is a value that indicates how far away from the left and right edges of the column the check will be. It is calculated by taking one quarter of the cell width. That means that the check mark (which is really an "X") occupies one half of the cell because one quarter of the cell is blank on the check's left, and one quarter of the cell is blank on the check's right. The same is done for the **CheckYOffset** variable.

The **CheckThickness** variable is used to provide a thickness for the pen that the check will be with:

```
CheckThickness:=(CheckXOffset+CheckYOffset) div 4;
```

It is evaluated to be one half of the average of **CheckXOffset** and **CheckYOffset**. The one half part was determined experimentally and is used because it produces a good-looking check mark.

Text Placement

The placement for the column and row text is also determined in the **CalculateRects** routine. For aesthetic results, the text should be right justified along the check grid area, as well as centered within either the column or row to which it belongs. The right justification calculation takes place whenever the text is drawn in the **Paint** method, so I'll put off describing it until we reach that point. The centering of the text, however, is fair game for our investigation.

It's quite simple to center something in something else, provided you know the size of each item. In Pascal, the general equation goes like this:

```
Offset = (BigObjectSize-SmallObjectSize) div 2;
```

The subtraction returns the area not occupied by the small object. If this area is divided by two, the result will be how much of that empty space can fit on one side of the small object with the same amount of empty space on the other side. Applying this to text involves plugging values into the equation:

```
ColumnTextOffset = (CellWidth - FontHeight) div 2;
```

We know that the cell width can be calculated by subtracting **ColumnPos[1]** from **ColumnPos[2]**:

```
ColumnTextOffset = ((ColumnPos[2]-ColumnPos[1]) - FontHeight) div 2;
```

The inner parentheses are only for clarity; operator precedence ensures that the expression would be evaluated properly without them. The font height can be obtained by calling the **Height** property of the **Font** property of **TCheckGrid**:

```
ColumnTextOffset = ((ColumnPos[2]-ColumnPos[1]) - Font.Height) div 2;
```

The equation looks correct, but if you try to use it, you will be startled by the result, which will be anything but centered. The snafu that crept in has to do with the **Height** property of the **TFont** class. You see, despite its name, it doesn't really return the height of the font! Instead, it returns the *negative* height of the font. This is nonintuitive to say the least! This is a leftover from the days of pre-Delphi when programmers had to use the Windows API directly. The API functions **CreateFont** and **CreateFontIndirect** needed the height parameter to be negative to indicate that the character height was being specified instead of the cell height. Delphi just adopted this tradition. If the programmers would have just changed a few lines, this mess could have been avoided.

Now that we know what the problem is, the solution is pretty obvious: change the sign of **Height**, or simply do an addition instead of a subtraction:

```
ColumnTextOffset = (ColumnPos[2]-ColumnPos[1] + Font.Height) div 2;
```

This is how the expression appears in the final code. Notice that the inner parentheses have been removed. The centering of row text is identical:

```
RowTextOffset:=(RowPos[2]-RowPos[1]+Font.Height) div 2;
```

Draw, Pardner

After the placement calculations have been completed, the component is ready to be painted, via the **Paint** method. Painting occurs whenever

Windows requests it, when the component is first displayed, or when one of the following properties change: **ColumnText**, **RowText**, **Columns**, **Rows**, **Font**, **Color**, or **BackgroundColor**. Changing the **Color** or **BackgroundColor** properties causes the component to paint over itself; it is not first erased as occurs when any of the other properties change.

The actual process of painting **TCheckGrid** takes place in five steps:

1. Setting **TCanvas** properties
2. Drawing the border of the check grid area
3. Drawing the column text
4. Drawing the row text
5. Drawing the check marks

Setting **TCanvas** Properties

It is extremely important to set all of **TCanvas**'s properties prior to doing any drawing because if it isn't done, things will end up looking peculiar. The explanation for this is that a check mark can be drawn *outside* the **Paint** method. Specifically, this occurs whenever the user clicks on a cell or presses the space bar when the cell is highlighted. **TCanvas** doesn't care where in the code the check mark is drawn, but it will remember the properties that were used to draw it, such as its thickness and color. Therefore, it is necessary to initialize certain properties:

```
Canvas.Font:=Font;
Canvas.Pen.Color:=Color;
Canvas.Pen.Width:=1;
Canvas.Brush.Color:=FBackgroundColor;
Canvas.Brush.Style:=bsSolid;
```

Drawing the Check Grid Border

Refer back to Figure 6.2. You will notice that there is a border around the check grid area of the component. This gives it a more professional appearance than if it had just been left open in a tic-tac-toe fashion. In the act of doing so, it also fills in the background of the grid area to the color specified by the **FBackgroundColor** variable. The code for accomplishing this is straightforward:

```
Canvas.Rectangle(CheckGridRect.Left,CheckGridRect.Top,
  CheckGridRect.Right,CheckGridRect.Bottom);
```

Drawing the Columns

Drawing the column text proved to be somewhat tricky because it is to be rotated clockwise by 90 degrees. Windows supports doing this, but the VCL's **TFont** does not. Without going into the details, let me state that it would have been so easy for Borland to do—less than ten lines of code. I contacted someone at Borland about this, and the explanation was that "[Delphi] was done at white heat, and so sometimes we don't include all the possible details." Not being one to cry over underdeveloped development environments, I set about the task myself.

My first attempt looked something like this:

```
procedure RotateFont(Angle:Integer);
var
   LogFont:TLogFont;
   NewLogFont:TLogFont;
   NewFont:HFont;
   OldFont:HFont;
begin
   GetObject(Font.Handle,SizeOf(TLogFont),@LogFont);
   NewLogFont:=LogFont;
   NewLogFont.lfEscapement:=Angle;
   NewFont:=CreateFontIndirect(NewFont);
   OldFont:=SelectObject(Canvas.Font.Handle,NewFont);
   DeleteObject(OldFont);
   Canvas.Font.Handle:=NewFont;
end;
```

Essentially, what I was trying to do was make a copy of the attributes of the **Canvas**'s current font, modify the **lfEscapement** field, which is used to set the angle of rotation, create a new font based on the modified attributes, and finally replace the **Canvas.Font** handle with the new one. Didn't work; wacky things kept happening. I'm ashamed to admit it, but I fell victim to the very pitfall I warned you about earlier in this chapter. I told you that you can do something like:

```
Canvas.Font:=Font;
```

and it will work because **Canvas.Font** is a property not a true instance, and a procedure is called to copy properties over. It was my intention for

```
Canvas.Font.Handle:=NewFont;
```

to do a simple assignment. It does, but it calls a procedure that selects the font into the device context (which I already did), and it also kills the current font (again, which I already did). You can probably see why this caused me grief. However, out of that grief came a better understanding of Delphi, which I can pass along to you. Here is the final code for rotating fonts:

```
procedure TCheckGrid.RotateFont(Angle:Integer);
var
  LogFont:TLogFont;
begin
  GetObject(Canvas.Font.Handle,SizeOf(TLogFont),@LogFont);
  LogFont.lfEscapement:=Angle;
  Canvas.Font.Handle:=CreateFontIndirect(LogFont);
end;
```

Notice that it is basically the same as what I was trying to accomplish before, but without **SelectObject** and **DeleteObject**. Creating the font and assigning it to **Canvas.Font.Handle** is all that is necessary.

Whenever the **RotateFont** procedure is called, it is passed a parameter specifying in *tenths* of a degree the angle to rotate the font associated with **Canvas**—i.e., **Canvas.Font**—counter-clockwise. Because it is our desire to rotate the column text by 90 degrees *clockwise*, the parameter is passed as -900.

With the font's angle set, it is time to output the text to the form. Doing so simply involves iterating through a loop once for each column:

```
for i:=1 to FColumns do
begin
  Canvas.TextOut(ColumnPos[i+1]-ColumnTextOffset,
    ColumnTextRect.Bottom-ColumnTextHeight[i]-10,
    FColumnText[i]);
  Canvas.MoveTo(ColumnPos[i],CheckGridRect.Top);
  Canvas.LineTo(ColumnPos[i],CheckGridRect.Bottom);
end;
```

The first parameter of **TextOut** indicates the position of the left edge of the text, which should be centered over the column. This value can be obtained by taking the start position of the column, which is stored in the **ColumnPos** array, and subtracting the **ColumnTextOffset** value from it.

The next parameter is where the top edge of the text is positioned. Because we want the text right justified, we have to take the text's width into consideration. Remember, the text is rotated, so the width value is really how tall its bounding rectangle is, which is why the pre-calculated **ColumnTextHeight** array is used.. By subtracting the width (height) from **ColumnTextRect.Bottom**, we get a value that is close to being correct. To finalize it, we have to subtract ten from it because we don't want the text to be squished up against the check grid area.

In the preceding code, there is also a call to **MoveTo** and **LineTo**. They result in the drawing of the separating lines between columns.

Drawing the Rows

Drawing the rows portions of the component is very similar to what happens when drawing the column portions. The only difference is that the text is not rotated.

```
for i:=1 to FRows do
begin
  Canvas.TextOut(RowTextRect.Right-RowTextWidth[i]-10,RowPos[i]+
    RowTextOffset,FRowText[i]);
  Canvas.MoveTo(CheckGridRect.Left,RowPos[i]);
  Canvas.LineTo(CheckGridRect.Right,RowPos[i]);
end;
```

Drawing the Check Marks

To draw the check marks, the current pen thickness is first set to **CheckThickness**, to ensure that they will appear properly. Next, two loops are employed. The first loop simply counts up to the number of columns that the grid has. The second loop is nested in the first, and counts the number of rows. When executed, they provide the column and row coordinates necessary for drawing every cell:

```
for i:=1 to FColumns do
begin
  for j:=1 to FRows do
    DrawCell(i,j);
end;
```

As you can see from the preceding code, the procedure **DrawCell** is called for every cell, and it does the actual drawing. The reason that it is a separate procedure is to avoid duplicating code because cells also have to be drawn and erased as a result of user interaction. Needless to say, it wouldn't be desirable to call **Paint** every time the user clicks on a cell to place a check mark.

DrawCell first has to decide whether the check is visible by referring to the **FChecked** array:

```
if FChecked[Column,Row] then
  Canvas.Pen.Color:=FColor
else
  Canvas.Pen.Color:=FBackgroundColor;
```

If **FChecked** for the cell is **True**, the pen color is set to **FColor**, a mirror of the **Color** property that identifies the color of the check box. If, however, **FChecked** is **False**, the color is set to the background color, resulting in an invisible check mark being drawn.

To draw the "X," the diagonal corners of the check box, minus the values of **CheckXOffset** and **CheckYOffset**, are connected with lines:

```
Canvas.MoveTo(ColumnPos[Column]+CheckXOffset,RowPos[Row]+CheckYOffset)
;
```

```
Canvas.LineTo(ColumnPos[Column+1]-CheckXOffset,
   RowPos[Row+1]-CheckYOffset);
Canvas.MoveTo(ColumnPos[Column+1]-
   CheckXOffset,RowPos[Row]+CheckYOffset);
Canvas.LineTo(ColumnPos[Column]+CheckXOffset,
   RowPos[Row+1]-CheckYOffset);
```

Drawing the "X" isn't the only thing that occurs in **DrawCell**. Whenever a Windows control has the focus, it is normally indicated by drawing a dotted rectangle, or a *focus rectangle*, in it or around it. This is important. If your interactive components don't do this, you might as well rename them all to **TCrap** because that is the kind of application that will result.

For **TCheckGrid**, the focus rectangle is drawn inside the cell that has the current focus. A cell can get the focus in one of two ways: the user can click on it or use the Tab key to move from another component to ours. Once the focus has been achieved, the arrow keys can be used to move the focus rectangle from cell to cell. Knowing what cell to put the focus in requires the use of two variables, **CurrentColumn** and **CurrentRow**. We'll talk about how they are assigned their values when we discuss mouse and keyboard input later in the chapter.

Regardless of how focus is obtained, Windows sends a **WM_SETFOCUS** message to the component to notify it. When this happens, the **HasFocus** variable is assigned a value of **True**:

```
procedure TCheckGrid.WMSetFocus(var Message: TWMSetFocus);
var
   FocusRect:TRect;
begin
   HasFocus:=True;
   DrawCell(CurrentColumn,CurrentRow);
   inherited;
end;
```

Notice that **DrawCell** is also called whenever the component gains the focus. This is done so that the focus rectangle can be drawn. One point should be mentioned concerning the **Inherited** statement on the last line of the preceding code sample. Normally, when you use **Inherited**, you have to specify what method you are inheriting the functionality of. For example:

```
inherited Create(AOwner);
```

For the line I just pointer out, however, **Inherited** stands alone. This may puzzle you because it is not clear just what is being inherited. A logical guess would be that the **WMSetFocus** method of **TCheckGrid**'s parent, **TCustomControl** was being called. This is logical, but impossible. **TCustomControl** does declare or inherit the **WMSetFocus** method. A new question arises: If **WMSetFocus** does not come from an ancestor of **TCustomControl**, how can **Inherit** be used at all? Looking at the declaration for this method might shed some light:

```
procedure WMSetFocus(var Message: TWMSetFocus); message WM_SETFOCUS;
```

It is declared as **Message**, meaning it intercepts messages created by calling **Dispatch**. This being the case, calling **Inherited** without specifying the parent results in the message being redispatched to the immediate ancestor, **TCustomControl**. Because **TCustomControl** nor any of its ancestors intercept the **WM_SETFOCUS** message, the default handler for it is called. This is why you must always call **Inherited** when intercepting a Windows message. If you don't, Windows just may bite you. Actually, it's a bit severe to say that you have to call **Inherited** for all messages; if you're a seasoned API veteran, you're probably aware that many messages don't require default handling because they don't do anything beyond providing your program with information. If you haven't waged the "Windows War" at this level, you're best off calling **Inherited** regardless of whether it is required, just to be safe.

When **TCheckGrid** loses focus because the user tabbed away from it or clicked on another component, Windows sends a **WM_KILLFOCUS** message. This is intercepted with the **WMKillFocus** method:

```
procedure TCheckGrid.WMKillFocus(var Message: TWMKillFocus);
begin
```

```
  HasFocus := False;
  DrawCell(CurrentColumn,CurrentRow);
  inherited;
end;
```

It's almost identical to **WMSetFocus** except that it sets the **HasFocus** flag to **False** rather than **True**.

We now know whether we have the focus, and we can apply it to displaying our focus rectangle in **DrawCell**:

```
if (Column=CurrentColumn) and (Row=CurrentRow) then
begin
  FocusRect.Left:=ColumnPos[CurrentColumn]+2;
  FocusRect.Top:=RowPos[CurrentRow]+2;
  FocusRect.Right:=ColumnPos[CurrentColumn+1]-1;
  FocusRect.Bottom:=RowPos[CurrentRow+1]-1;
  Canvas.Brush.Color:=FBackgroundColor;
  Canvas.FrameRect(FocusRect);

  if HasFocus then
    Canvas.DrawFocusRect(FocusRect);
end;
```

First, it is verified that the **Column** and **Row** parameters match the **CurrentColumn** and **CurrentRow** variables, indicating that the focus, be it visible or not, belongs to the cell at the coordinates dictated by **Column** and **Row**. If they don't match, there isn't much point executing the code contained in the **If** statement. If they do match, then we're in business.

The bounds of the focus rectangle have to be determined. This is done easily by using the bounds of the cell and "deflating" it a little, and storing the results in **FocusRect**. Before you get cranky at me for not calling **Canvas.InflateRect** to do this more efficiently, take a closer look at the code. You will see that the **Left** and **Top** edges are increased by two, but the **Right** and **Bottom** edges are decreased by only *one*. The reason? When **DrawFocusRect** is called—when any Windows rectangle drawing function is called—-it doesn't actually draw the **Right** and **Bottom** edges where you'd expect. It draws them one pixel shy.

Once the bounds have been determined, a rectangle the same color as the **FBackgroundColor** is drawn exactly in the location where the focus rectangle will end up. This is done for two purposes. First, even though we know that this cell technically has the focus, in reality the component may not, or it may be in the process of losing it, when **WMKillFocus** is called, for example. Whatever the cause, drawing this "invisible" rectangle will get rid of an existing focus rectangle.

The second reason for drawing the rectangle has to do with some peculiar goings-on concerning the call to **DrawFocusRect**. Things are not what they seem when you use this function. What it is supposed to do is draw a dotted rectangle pixel by pixel by using two colors and **XORing** them together. The first color comes from the pixel that will be overwritten as a result of drawing the rectangle. The second color is user definable and in the days of pre-Delphi was set using the Windows API **SetBkColor** function. **TCanvas** does not have any equivalent of **SetBkColor** because it was observed by some Borland employee that things could be made simpler if it was combined with the **Brush** property of **TCanvas**. That is, whenever you change the brush color, **SetBkColor** is called with the same color value. True, it is somewhat simpler, but it is not without its flaws, some of them serious.

For example, **SetBkColor** has a purpose that is quite different from the purpose of a Windows brush. A *brush* is normally used to paint the interior of solid objects such as rectangles and ellipses; but it also has the occasional bizarre use, like in the case of **FrameRect**, where it is used to draw a border. Also, a brush need not be a solid color; it can posses a *style* that allows the interior of objects to be filled with various types of hatching such as horizontal, vertical, diagonal, and so on. Of course, the brush still specifies the color of the hatching. But what about the voids in the hatching; what color will they be? Depending on the current mode, set with **SetBkMode**, the voids can either be **TRANSPARENT**, letting the original background through, or they can be **OPAQUE**, a solid fill of color. This is where **SetBkColor** enters the picture; its job is to set the void color. Because the VCL calls **SetBkColor** with the same color as the brush, any hatching you do with an **OPAQUE** background will appear to be a solid block with no hatching whatsoever, which is not a good thing.

For the time being this is something that we have to live with, but knowing that it is a problem makes it less threatening. In the hatching scenario just described, the solution involves making a few API calls:

```
Canvas.Brush.Color:=clRed;
Canvas.Brush.Style:=bsDiagCross;
SetBkMode(Canvas.Handle,OPAQUE);
SetBkColor(Canvas.Handle,clBlue);
Rectangle(Canvas.Handle,10,10,50,50);
```

This code results in a solid blue rectangle with red cross hatching.

Going back to the problem at hand, drawing the focus rectangle, **SetBkColor** must be called for it to be displayed correctly. Now, we know that setting the brush does this, but it doesn't do it right away. It waits for something that requires a brush to be drawn—like the invisible rectangle we just drew. In the process of drawing it, **SetBkColor** was called with the correct value for drawing the focus rectangle. At this point, calling **FocusRect** will produce the desired result.

Notice, however, that the focus rectangle is only drawn if the **HasFocus** variable is set to **True**. If this wasn't done, the component would be confusing to the user because it would always indicate a state of focus.

Responding to Mouse Events

The most important capability of **TCheckGrid** is that it can be manipulated by the user. Although there are some die-hard keyboard fans out there, most people prefer using a mouse when it comes to interacting with controls. This tendency is so strong that there are actually controls on the market that simply don't work with the keyboard, and as such, *require* a mouse. This is not to say that they couldn't be made to work with the keyboard, just that the programmer was too lazy to be bothered with it. We won't go to that extreme, nor is it recommended for any of your own projects; but suffice it to say, it would be a far more serious mistake not to support mouse input. Not wanting to commit this heinous crime, we will now investigate how to use the mouse for our own component.

TCheckGrid inherits several methods from **TControl**, such as **Click**, **DblClick**, **MouseDown**, **MouseMove**, and **MouseUp** that can be overridden for the purpose of capturing a mouse event. For our purpose, there are two possible candidates, **Click** and **MouseDown**. **Click**, although it sounds promising, is somewhat of a let-down because it does not live up to its name, which implies that it is called when the mouse button is clicked. In fact, the opposite happens; it is called when the mouse button is released. Good for some things perhaps, but it's not quite what we have in mind. By default we are therefore left with intercepting the **MouseDown** method. Actually, that is not a 100% true statement because it is also possible to take the brute force approach and intercept the **WM_LBUTTONDOWN** message directly. However, I don't recommend this when the cleaner alternative of overriding a preexisting method, such as **MouseDown**, is available.

The declaration to override **MouseDown** should be placed in the **Protected** section of the class declaration so that any future descendants have a crack at intercepting the method as well. Here is its format:

```
procedure MouseDown(Button:TMouseButton;Shift:TShiftState;
 X,Y:Integer);override;
```

The parameter **Button** is used to identify which mouse button is currently depressed. It does this through the use of the enumerated type **TMouse Button**:

```
TMouseButton = (mbRight, mbLeft, mbMiddle);
```

If, for example, **Button** held the value **mbLeft**, it would indicate that the left mouse button was currently down. The **Shift** parameter, of type **TShiftState,** is a little different:

```
TShiftState = set of (ssShift, ssAlt, ssCtrl, ssRight, ssLeft,
 ssMiddle, ssDouble);
```

Unlike **TMouseButton**, **TShiftState** is a set, meaning that **Shift** can contain any of the above "**ss**" flags in it. These flags are used to get extra information about the nature of the call to **MouseDown**. For instance, if the user clicked on a component with the right mouse button while holding down the **Alt** key, both **ssRight** and **ssAlt** would be present in **Shift**. Detecting this particular sequence in code is easy:

```
if (ssRight in Shift) and (ssAlt in Shift) then MessageBeep(0);
```

Alternatively, this could be rewritten using the **Button** parameter to detect if the right button was down:

```
if (Button=mbRight) and (ssAlt in Shift) then MessageBeep(0);
```

The two final parameters of **MouseDown** are **X** and **Y**. They provide information about where in the form the user clicked, and like the coordinate system used for **TCanvas**, the upper-left corner of the form corresponds to 0,0.

To make sense of how all these parameters interact, I have written a small program, **CKDEMO.DPR**, that simply displays the values of the **Button**, **Shift**, **X**, and **Y** parameters whenever you click on an unoccupied location on the form. The program works by responding to **TForm's** **OnClick** event, which is called whenever the **Click** method is using the same parameters.

```
program CKdemo;

uses
  Forms,
  CKmain in 'CKMAIN.PAS' {Form1};

{$R *.RES}

begin
  Application.CreateForm(TForm1, Form1);
  Application.Run;
```

```
end.

unit CKmain;

interface

uses
  SysUtils, WinTypes, WinProcs, Messages, Classes, Graphics, Controls,
  Forms, Dialogs, StdCtrls, ExtCtrls;

type
  TForm1 = class(TForm)
    Label1: TLabel;
    Label2: TLabel;
    Label3: TLabel;
    Label4: TLabel;
    Label5: TLabel;
    Label6: TLabel;
    Label7: TLabel;
    Label8: TLabel;
    Button1: TButton;
    Bevel1: TBevel;
    procedure Button1Click(Sender: TObject);
    procedure FormMouseDown(Sender: TObject; Button: TMouseButton;
      Shift: TShiftState; X, Y: Integer);
  end;

var
  Form1: TForm1;

implementation

{$R *.DFM}

procedure TForm1.Button1Click(Sender: TObject);
begin
```

```
      Close;
end;


procedure TForm1.FormMouseDown(Sender: TObject; Button: TMouseButton;
   Shift: TShiftState; X, Y: Integer);
var
   ShiftString:String;
begin
   case Button of
      mbRight:Label5.Caption:='mbRight';
      mbLeft:Label5.Caption:='mbLeft';
      mbMiddle:Label5.Caption:='mbMiddle';
   end;
   ShiftString:='';
   if ssShift in Shift then ShiftString:=ShiftString+'ssShift, ';
   if ssAlt in Shift then ShiftString:=ShiftString+'ssAlt, ';
   if ssCtrl in Shift then ShiftString:=ShiftString+'ssCtrl, ';
   if ssRight in Shift then ShiftString:=ShiftString+'ssRight, ';
   if ssLeft in Shift then ShiftString:=ShiftString+'ssLeft, ';
   if ssMiddle in Shift then ShiftString:=ShiftString+'ssMiddle, ';
   if ssDouble in Shift then ShiftString:=ShiftString+'ssDouble, ';
   if Length(ShiftString)<>0 then dec(ShiftString[0],2);
   Label6.Caption:=ShiftString;
   Label7.Caption:=IntToStr(X);
   Label8.Caption:=IntToStr(Y);
end;


end.
```

Now that you have workings of **MouseDown** freshly implanted in your brain, let's see how this all applies to **TCheckGrid**.

Whenever **MouseDown** is called, it is done so without regard to which button has actually been clicked. It doesn't really matter to our component which button was clicked; just knowing that a button was clicked is enough information to check or uncheck a box. For this reason, the **Button** parameter is not used in any way, nor is the **Shift** parameter. The same cannot be said about the **X** and **Y** parameters because their usage is essential for determining just which cell was clicked on.

The process for deciding which cell was clicked on is actually fairly simple. We already know the bounds of each cell because they are the same ones we used to draw the check mark. This time, instead of drawing in each cell, we just check to see if the **X** and **Y** coordinates reside in a certain cell. One method of accomplishing this would be to individually check each cell to see if the cursor is located within it. However, the performance of this technique is somewhat wasteful of processor power because it checks each row and each column more than once. Consider Figure 6.3.

Columns

	1	2	3	4	5
1	1,1	2,1	3,1	4,1	5,1
2	1,2	2,2	3,2	4,2	5,2
Rows 3	1,3	2,3	3,3	4,3	5,3
4	1,4	2,4	3,4	4,4	5,4
5	1,5	2,5	3,5	4,5	5,5

Figure 6.3 A Mockup of **TCheckGrid**.

The diagram is a mock-up of the grid area of **TCheckGrid**. The process we just discussed might work by checking row one, columns one through five, row two, columns one through five, all the way through to row five. Of course, if the cursor was found to be in the cell being checked, further checks would not be necessary. Even with this optimization, the procedure is still wasteful because it checks the same column more than once. For example, if cell 4,1 was checked, and it was determined that the cursor was not in the column bounds of the cell, it is a sure bet that it also wouldn't be in any other cells that intersect column four, namely 4,2; 4,3; 4,4; or 4,5. This being the case, we can use it to our advantage, as shown in the following code:

```
procedure TCheckGrid.MouseDown(Button:TMouseButton;Shift:TShiftState;
  X,Y:Integer);
```

```
var
  i,j:Byte;
  FoundBox:Boolean;
begin
  FoundBox:=False;
  i:=0;
  repeat
    inc(i);
    if (X>=ColumnPos[i]) and (X<=ColumnPos[i+1]) then
    begin
      j:=0;
      repeat
       inc(j);
       if (Y>=RowPos[j]) and (Y<=RowPos[j+1]) then
       begin
         {We found the cell that the mouse clicked on}
         FoundBox:=True;
       end;
      until (j>FRows) or FoundBox;
    end;
  until (i>FColumns) or FoundBox;
  inherited MouseDown(Button,Shift,X,Y);
end;
```

The preceding code checks each column and each row only once and improves speed by about a factor of five. You may be wondering how I came up with this value. For the cell-by-cell method, four comparisons are needed for each bound of the cell. If we multiply this by the number of cells, 25, the total number of comparisons is 100. Compare this to the row-once column-once method that requires only two comparisons for each row and column. This gives us a total of ten comparisons needed to figure out which row the cursor is in, as well as only ten comparisons to figure out which column it is in, for a total of 20 comparisons. You don't have to be a math whiz to know that 100:20 is 5:1. To be fair, this value is the *maximum* performance gain. The actual gain depends on the exact cell that was clicked: The cell at column one, row one would be detected equally fast with either scheme; and the cell at column three, row three would show an improvement of only 13:3, which is still considerable.

If it was determined that a click occurred inside a cell, it is necessary to perform some actions to make that click take effect. For example, when the **Mode** property is set to **moNormal**, clicking a cell causes it to invert—if there is no check, one is added, but if the cell was already checked, it is removed. Here is the code for acting on a click:

```
if TabStop or HasFocus then
begin
  SetFocus;
  HasFocus:=False;
  DrawCell(CurrentColumn,CurrentRow);
  HasFocus:=True;
end;
CurrentColumn:=i;
CurrentRow:=j;
FChecked[i,j]:=not FChecked[i,j];
CheckCell(i,j);
if Assigned(FOnChange) then
  FOnChange(CurrentColumn,CurrentRow,FChecked[CurrentColumn,
    CurrentRow]);
FoundBox:=True;
```

The first part, comprising the **if** statement, has the simple job of hiding the focus from the current cell. This is done because it just wouldn't be right to have two cells "active. Notice that the stuff inside the **If** statement is only executed if either the component's **TabStop** property is **True** or the component has the focus, indicated by the **HasFocus** variable being **True**. This needs some explanation. **TabStop** is a property that most interactive components have. Its purpose is to tell Windows whether the control may gain the input focus by tabbing to it. At first, you may think that there is little point to even making this an option, and that all controls should have this capability by default. What about label controls (**TLabel**)? They are normally used to display information and can do very little else. If it was mandatory that it be on the list of controls that could be tabbed to, it would produce some confusion among users.

When **TabStop** is **True**, we know for a fact that **TCheckGrid** is capable of receiving the input focus. If, on the other hand, **TabStop** is **False**, it does not mean that interaction is not possible, it simply means that the component can never gain the focus permanently. Obviously, the only method of interaction while **TabStop** is **False** is with the mouse or some other pointing device, because the keyboard can only be used if the component can gain the focus.

If **HasFocus** is **True**, we also know for a fact that **TCheckGrid** is capable of receiving the input focus. Why do we have to bother checking the state of **HasFocus**? How can it possibly be **True** without **TabStop** also being **True**? There is one and only one special case when this can happen: when there is only one component on the form. Regardless of the state of **TabStop**, a lone component on a form will *always* have the current focus. When this happens, it is unreliable to check the state of **TabStop** because it may be **False**, but the component may indeed have the focus.

You know the mechanics of why **TabStop** and **HasFocus** are used as conditions of the **If** statement, let's now see what happens within it. I already said that it is used to hide the current focus rectangle. For the benefit of when **TabStop** is **True** and **HasFocus** is **False**, the first operation is to call **SetFocus** to officially give the focus to the component while removing it from the component that had it previously. Next, **HasFocus** is set to **False**. This is needed to fool the call to **DrawCell** into thinking that there is no need to draw the focus rectangle, and as a result it will end up erasing it. Finally, **HasFocus** is set to **True** so that when it comes time to draw the new focus rectangle, it will be visible.

Past the **if** block is the code used to set the new current cell to its new state and draw it. Making the clicked on cell the current one requires setting **CurrentColumn** to the same value as the index "i" of the **For** loop used to determine the column that was clicked in. In an identical manner, the index "j" is used to set **CurrentRow** to its new value. Next, the check state of the cell has to be inverted. This operation simply requires noting the current state. To draw the cell, **CheckCell** is called.

CheckCell does a little bit more work than simply drawing the cell; after all, that is the purpose of **DrawCell**. It implements **Mode** property to provide the three available modes **moNormal**, **moRowExclusive**, and **moColumnExclusive**:

```
procedure TCheckGrid.CheckCell(Column:TColumns;Row:TRows);
var
```

```
    i:Byte;
begin
  Canvas.Pen.Width:=CheckThickness;
  case FMode of
    moNormal:
      DrawCell(Column,Row);
    moColumnExclusive:
    begin
      for i:=1 to FRows do
      begin
        FChecked[Column,i]:=i=Row;
        DrawCell(Column,i);
      end;
    end;
    moRowExclusive:
    begin
      for i:=1 to FColumns do
      begin
        FChecked[i,Row]:=i=Column;
        DrawCell(i,Row);
      end;
    end;
  end;
end;
```

As you can see, **CheckCell** requires the coordinates of the cell that was just checked or unchecked to be passed as the parameters **Column** and **Row**. Inside the procedure, the **Width** of the current pen is set. It is done here rather inside of **DrawCell** for performance reasons—remember **DrawCell** will be called many times in succession during the course of the **Paint** method. Next, using a **Case** statement combined with the **FMode** variable, an appropriate action is executed. If **FMode** is **moNormal**, **DrawCell** is called directly. If, however, **FMode** is either **moColumnExclusive** or **moRowExclusive** it is necessary to do some cleanup. In the case of **moColumnExclusive**, this cleanup involves unchecking every single cell in the column indicated by the **Column** parameter, except for the one also indicated by the **Row** parameter. **MoRowExclusive** is the opposite; every cell in the row indicated by the **Row** parameter is cleared, except for the one that intersects with the column indicated by the **Column** parameter.

Getting back to the main code, one of the events that **TCheckGrid** handles is **OnChange**, a mirror of the **FOnChange** variable. This event, if assigned, is called whenever a cell is clicked on. The test for determining whether it is assigned is done via the **Assigned** function, which returns true if **FOnChange** contains a valid address. If the address is valid, the **OnChange** event handler is called with parameters specifying which cell was clicked, and the state of the cell.

Responding to Keyboard Events

In the early days of personal computing, the types of input devices you could connect to your system was severely limited. This is not to say that such devices did not exist; the back section of every computer magazine always had (and still has) weird gadgets whose purpose was to get data from you. The real problem was twofold. First, the fact that every device was radically different from one another meant that there was no standard. Second, software manufacturers, realizing that a standard device did not exist, chose to take the easy route and support none of them. Then some magic happened: the Apple Macintosh was introduced. Emerging from its body, at the end of a long cord, was a certain something. Something old, yet unknown to many until that very moment. Something called a *mouse*.

The next thing that happened was mostly predictable; the IBM compatible software industry, fearing loss of sales to the ridiculously easy to use Macintosh, adopted the mouse as a major input device. Not everyone was sold, however. Early mice were awkwardly shaped and prone to getting their little mouse feet dirty from whatever happened to be on the table. Besides, everybody looked at you. So for awhile, nobody really cared that they could use a mouse on their computer. Then Windows 1.0 came about, an environment superbly suited for a mouse. Unfortunately, everybody just laughed at it. A couple of years later, Windows 2.0 and all of its various incarnations appeared; again, laughter abounded. Then something totally unexpected happened: A version of Windows was released that people didn't laugh at—

Windows 3.0. Although it made 386s run like Gameboys, for the first time in the history of the IBM PC, normal, non-technically inclined people felt at home on a computer. This was of course thanks to the innovative Program Manager, the capability of being able to layer windows on top of one-another, and many other oohs and ahhs that the Macintosh sported for years. People liked Windows 3.0 so much that they started to buy it (much to Microsoft's relief), and with it they bought a mouse. Now, two generations of Windows later, there on your desk is one of these beasts. Everybody has a mouse; you can't buy a computer without getting one. It's now almost as standard as the keyboard. *Almost* but not quite.

The keyboard is still the primary input device of choice since its invention, and it won't be going anywhere soon. Other schemes do exist, or are on the verge of existing. For example, it is possible to have an on-screen representation of a keyboard which when combined with a mouse would emulate normal keyboard input. However, except in rare cases, no one would choose to do this as an efficient means of entering manual input. Nor would they choose voice recognition. It may be great for microwaves and toasters, but can you imagine an office full of people talking to their computers? And besides, voice input is somewhat ambiguous. How often during a conversation with someone have you found it helpful, if not necessary, to draw a diagram of what you are trying to explain? So by default, we are left with the keyboard as the universal device for entering information.

In Windows, keyboard events are sent to the window to which they belong in the form of messages. Like mouse messages, the VCL captures the keyboard messages and allows them to be intercepted by overriding the appropriate methods. Three separate methods contained in **TWinControl** are used for this purpose: **KeyPress**, **KeyDown**, and **KeyUp**. **KeyPress** is the simplest of the three:

```
procedure KeyPress(var Key:Char);
```

This procedure is called whenever a Windows **WM_CHAR** message is sent to the form, which in turn occurs whenever a key is pressed that is capable of producing a single ASCII value. By this I mean that the key press could very well be represented by a single symbol contained in a text file. Some keys such as the arrow keys and function keys, do not produce a single ASCII value, and instead produce what is known as an *extended key code*. In DOS, an extended key code is represented by an ASCII 0 followed by a value representative of the key that was pressed. At the application level, Windows does not support extended key codes in this manner, so a **WM_CHAR** message will not be generated in response to such a key, and therefore **KeyPress** will not be called either. This does not render **KeyPress** useless, however; it does an exemplary job at what it is designed for: capturing ASCII key presses. A good example of where this would come in handy is with an editor component, which would expect the text to be entered in ASCII form.

For processing keys that produce extended key codes, the more general-purpose **KeyDown** method is available:

```
procedure TWinControl.KeyDown(var Key: Word; Shift: TShiftState);
```

This method is called whenever the **WM_KEYDOWN** Windows message is sent to the form. Instead of ASCII codes, it passes *virtual key codes* to the **Key** parameter. A virtual key code is identified by a **VK_XXX** constant, where *XXX* is dependent on the keystroke being identified. For instance, the Page Down key has a virtual key code of **VK_NEXT**, and the F7 key has a code of **VK_F7**. Of course, these codes are not limited only to extended keys; codes such as **VK_P** and **VK_3** exist for "normal" keystrokes. One thing is worth mentioning here: there is no difference between uppercase and lowercase letters. That is, a **VK_P** will be generated for both a capital P and a small P. This is not to say that the two cannot be differentiated; this is what the **Shift** parameter is for:

```
TShiftState = set of (ssShift, ssAlt, ssCtrl, ssRight, ssLeft, ssMiddle,
  ssDouble);
```

You probably remember this declaration from our discussion on mouse methods and events. For consistency, keyboard methods and events use the same type, with the same rules. For example, determining whether a P is capitalized only requires checking to see if **ssShift** exists in **Shift**:

```
if Key=VK_P then
begin
```

```
  if ssShift in Shift then
    {Capital P}
  else
    {Small P};
end;
```

One concern that you may have is the role that the **Caps Lock** key plays in all this. That is, if **Caps Lock** is on, is **ssShift** included in the **Shift** set? The answer is no, which may be good or bad depending on what you are trying to accomplish. However, this does not mean that you cannot determine if the **Caps Lock** key has been pressed; a **KeyDown** event is generated for it, just like every other key, and can be detected by comparing the **Key** parameter to the constant, **VK_CAPITAL**.

The final method, **KeyUp**, is called exactly when you think it would be: when a key is released. Here is its declaration:

```
procedure TWinControl.KeyUp(var Key: Word; Shift: TShiftState);
```

As you can see, the declaration is identical to that of **KeyDown**, as is its operation. The primary reason for wanting to detect a key release has to do with the way the PC keyboard operates. By its very nature, it can send only one command at a time, such as a "KeyPress". For example, if you press the A key, the keyboard sends a command over its cable to the computer that essentially says "Hey, the 'A' key has been pressed." After that, everything is silent. The problem that quickly arises from this limitation is that there is no way to detect simultaneous keypresses. So how do the **Shift**, **Alt**, and **Ctrl** keys work? First, you must understand that they are not treated any differently from any other key. For instance, when you press the **Alt** key, it sends a command over your keyboard's cable that tells the computer "Hey, the **Alt** key has been pressed," followed by silence. It retains this silence until another key has been pressed, or the **Alt** key (or any other key for that matter) is released. If the silence is broken due to a keypress, an "A" for example, but the **Alt** key release command has not been sent, what in effect has been received is an **Alt-A** key combination.

Because the **Shift**, **Alt**, and **Ctrl** keys operate identically to all the other keys, it stands to reason that any key could be used to indicate a state. When I say state, I mean the **Shift** in **Shift-P** or the **Ctrl** in **Ctrl-X**.

So, for example, you could have the key combination **S-1** that worked by first waiting for the **KeyDown** method to be called with **VK_S**, and then waiting for it to be called again with **VK_1**, only if **KeyUp** was not called with **VK_S** between the two calls to **KeyDown**.

You're probably at a loss to think of a use for what I just told you, but believe it or not, there is an excellent one. Games! Haven't you ever marveled at how responsive PC games appear while using the keyboard? In a fast-paced action game, you are almost certain to press more than one key at the same time, and yet it seems to make little difference to the computer or game play. Another use would be to put an "Easter egg" into your program that requires an odd combination of keypresses before displaying its message. Sadly, Windows itself limits the number of **KeyUp/KeyDown** messages that may be nested, except for special cases such as the **Alt, Ctrl,** and **Shift** keys.

TCheckGrid overrides the **KeyDown** method to handle user entry:

```
procedure TCheckGrid.KeyDown(var Key: Word; Shift: TShiftState);
begin
  inherited KeyDown(Key,Shift);
  case Key of
    VK_LEFT:
    begin
      HasFocus:=False;
      DrawCell(CurrentColumn,CurrentRow);
      dec(CurrentColumn);
      if CurrentColumn=0 then CurrentColumn:=FColumns;
      HasFocus:=True;
      DrawCell(CurrentColumn,CurrentRow);
    end;
    VK_RIGHT:
    begin
      HasFocus:=False;
      DrawCell(CurrentColumn,CurrentRow);
      inc(CurrentColumn);
      if CurrentColumn>FColumns then CurrentColumn:=1;
      HasFocus:=True;
```

```
      DrawCell(CurrentColumn,CurrentRow);
    end;
  VK_DOWN:
  begin
    HasFocus:=False;
    DrawCell(CurrentColumn,CurrentRow);
    inc(CurrentRow);
    if CurrentRow>FRows then CurrentRow:=1;
    HasFocus:=True;
    DrawCell(CurrentColumn,CurrentRow);
  end;
  VK_UP:
  begin
    HasFocus:=False;
    DrawCell(CurrentColumn,CurrentRow);
    dec(CurrentRow);
    if CurrentRow=0 then CurrentRow:=FRows;
    HasFocus:=True;
    DrawCell(CurrentColumn,CurrentRow);
  end;
  VK_SPACE:
  begin
    FChecked[CurrentColumn,CurrentRow]:=
      not FChecked[CurrentColumn,CurrentRow];
    CheckCell(CurrentColumn,CurrentRow);
    if Assigned(FOnChange) then
    FOnChange(CurrentColumn,CurrentRow,FChecked[CurrentColumn,
  CurrentRow]);
    end;
  end;
end;
```

The key presses in question that it handles are the arrow keys for navigating among the various cells, and the space key for checking or unchecking the cell that has the focus. Let's spend a moment investigating how the left arrow key works. Because the other arrow keys are similar, I'll leave them for you to look at yourself.

Unfortunately, the VCL throws a small hurdle our way concerning the use of the arrow keys. Normally they are used to navigate among components on the form such as buttons, check boxes, radio buttons, and so forth. As such, arrow key notifications are not directly passed to components, and it becomes necessary to override this default behavior. Happily, it is easy to do, if you know the trick. The VCL emulates a standard Windows message, **WM_GETDLGCODE**, that when overridden, allows arrow key notifications to be received:

```
procedure TCheckGrid.WMGetDlgCode(var Message: TWMGetDlgCode);
begin
  Message.Result := DLGC_WANTARROWS;
end;
```

The **DLGC_WANTARROWS** constant that is used tells the form that when the **TCheckGrid** component has the focus, it wants to handle the arrow key messages directly. **WM_GETDLGCODE** also supports two other constants:

Constant	Description
DLGC_WANTTAB	Allows a Tab keypress to be detected inside of a component
DLGC_WANTALLKEYS	Allows all keys to be detected inside of a component

When any key is pressed, the preceding **KeyDown** method is called. The first task performed is the calling of the ancestor **KeyDown** function to ensure that keyboard action normally handled by Windows takes place. Next, a **case** statement is used to determine if the key that was pressed is one of the keys that we are interested in. In the case of the left arrow key, the **Key** parameter is compared to **VK_LEFT**. If the two match, the following section of code is executed:

```
HasFocus:=False;
DrawCell(CurrentColumn,CurrentRow);
```

```
dec(CurrentColumn);
if CurrentColumn=0 then CurrentColumn:=FColumns;
HasFocus:=True;
DrawCell(CurrentColumn,CurrentRow);
```

The first thing that has to be done is to "fool" the component into think-ing that it does not have the input focus by setting **HasFocus** to **False**. This is necessary because it is our intention to transfer the focus to a dif-ferent cell, meaning that we first have to "unfocus" the current cell. The actual "unfocusing" occurs in the next line when **DrawCell** is called with the current column and row coordinates. Remember, in addition to draw-ing the check mark, **DrawCell** is also responsible for drawing the focus rectangle, provided, of course, that the component has the input focus. Because we are in the process of fooling it, the focus will not be visible after the cell has been redrawn.

The next action to be performed has to do with the movement of the current cell. Because we are pressing the left arrow key, we expect the focus to move to the left, which is exactly what is accomplished by execut-ing **dec(CurrentColumn)**. It is important to be careful here, however. If **CurrentColumn** held a value of one, decrementing it would produce the invalid column coordinate of zero. To save us from this embarrassment, the line that follows it checks to see if such a condition has occurred, and if so, sets **CurrentColumn** to the value of the **FColumns** member. This effectively causes the focus to wrap around to the rightmost column, which is a typical action for such situations.

Now that the **CurrentColumn** variable has been updated to its new value, the focus rectangle can be made visible. This requires setting **HasFocus** to **True** and calling **DrawCell** with the new coordinates.

As mentioned, **KeyDown** also checks to see if the space bar has been pressed. This occurs in the same **case** statement just discussed by compar-ing the **Key** parameter to **VK_SPACE**. If a successful match has been detected, the following code is executed:

```
FChecked[CurrentColumn,CurrentRow]:=
  not FChecked[CurrentColumn,CurrentRow];
CheckCell(CurrentColumn,CurrentRow);
```

```
if Assigned(FOnChange) then
  FOnChange(CurrentColumn,CurrentRow,FChecked[CurrentColumn,
    CurrentRow]);
```

The first line inverts the state of the cell. That is, if it is currently checked, the check is removed; or if there is no check mark, one is added. The second line makes a call to **CheckCell** to make the inverting operation take effect; at least this is the case when **Mode** property is set to **moNormal**. If **Mode** is either **moRowExclusive** or **moColumnExclusive**, the call to **CheckCell** alters this standard operation. For more information concerning exactly what happens in **CheckCell**, refer to the earlier section titled "Responding to Mouse Events."

Finally, the **FOnChange** variable, which corresponds to the **OnChange** event property is checked to see if it is a valid address by calling **Assigned** function. If the function returns **True**, the address is valid, and the event handler is called, passing the **CurrentRow** and **CurrentColumn** values, as well as the check/uncheck state of the current cell.

Column and Row Text

The column and row text of **TCheckGrid** can be set two different ways. The first way is to assign the **ColumnText** and **RowText** properties at run time to the desired strings:

```
ColumnText[1]:='Eggs';
ColumnText[2]:='Bacon';
ColumnText[3]:='Pancakes';
ColumnText[4]:='Sausages';
ColumnText[5]:='Hashbrowns';
ColumnText[6]:='Toast';
ColumnText[7]:='Orange Juice';
ColumnText[8]:='Milk';
RowText[1]:='Monday';
RowText[2]:='Tuesday';
```

```
RowText[3]:='Wednesday';
RowText[4]:='Thursday';
RowText[5]:='Friday';
```

The main drawback to assigning the text at run time is that it makes it difficult to position and size the component at design time. The reason that these strings cannot be assigned at design time has to do with what properties Delphi permits to be published—arrays are off limits. This does not mean that it can't be done, however. In Chapter 9, we will discuss how to create *property editors* that allow for such otherwise impossible feats. When we get there, we'll return to **TCheckGrid** and enhance it so that the column and row text can be set directly. For the time being, we will employ a little trickery to accomplish the same thing, although in a limited fashion.

TCheckGrid has two additional properties, **ColumnString** and **RowString** that accept the individual column and row items separated by commas:

```
ColumnString:='Eggs,Bacon,Pancakes,Sausages,Hashbrowns,Toast,
    Orange Juice,Milk';
RowString:='Monday,Tuesday,Wednesday,Thursday,Friday';
```

Because these properties are not arrays, they can be published and are therefore accessible at design time. The limitation that I mentioned is that both **ColumnString** and **RowString** can be no longer than 255 characters.

Whenever **ColumnString** and **RowString** are read, the members **FColumnString** and **FRowString** are accessed directly. When they are written to, the **SetColumnString** and **SetRowString** procedures are called to parse the strings into their individual column and row items:

```
procedure TCheckGrid.SetColumnString(ColumnString:String);
var
  i:Byte;
  Column:Byte;
  Text:String;
begin
  FColumnString:=ColumnString;
```

```
    Text:='';
    Column:=1;
    For i:=1 to Length(ColumnString) do
    begin
      if ColumnString[i]<>',' then
        Text:=Text+ColumnString[i]
      else
      begin
        ColumnText[Column]:=Text;
        Text:='';
        inc(Column);
      end;
    end;
    ColumnText[Column]:=Text;
end;


procedure TCheckGrid.SetRowString(RowString:String);
var
  i:Byte;
  Row:Byte;
  Text:String;
begin
  FRowString:=RowString;
  Text:='';
  Row:=1;
  For i:=1 to Length(RowString) do
  begin
    if RowString[i]<>',' then
    Text:=Text+RowString[i]
    else
    begin
      RowText[Row]:=Text;
      Text:='';
      inc(Row);
    end;
  end;
  RowText[Row]:=Text;
end;
```

One thing to be aware of is that if you assign text to the **ColumnText** and **RowText** arrays manually, **ColumnString** and **RowString** will *not* be updated accordingly. Consider the following line of code:

```
ColumnString:='Eggs,Bacon,Pancakes,Sausages,Hashbrowns,Toast,
  Orange Juice,Milk';
```

Now, suppose that for some reason, you decided to make a change to one of the **ColumnText** items:

```
ColumnText[3]:='Ham';
```

Once this line was executed, a visual change would occur immediately. However, if you were to inspect what was contained in **FColumnString**, you would find that it would be unchanged from its original assignment. This is because no provision has been made to reconstruct the **FColumnString** and **FRowString** strings whenever **ColumnText** or **RowText** is changed. In light of the future property editor enhancement we will be making, this problem is really quite trivial.

Other Properties

To prevent programmers from growling at you, it is always a good idea to publish any properties inherited from the ancestors of your component class. **TCheckGrid** publishes the following inherited properties: **DragCursor, DragMode, Enabled, ParentFont, ParentShowHint, ShowHint, TabOrder, TabStop, Visible, OnClick, OnDragDrop, OnDragOver, OnEndDrag, OnEnter, OnExit, OnKeyDown, OnKeyPress, OnKeyUp, OnMouseDown, OnMouseMove,** and **OnMouseUp.**

Finally...

Here we are, at the end of another chapter. To wrap things up, I will now provide you with the complete source code for **TCheckGrid**, which can also be found as **\DC\CHAP06\CHKGRID.PAS**. In the same directory, you will also find **CGDEMO.DPR**, a small demonstration program, and the bitmap for **TCheckGrid**, **CHKGRID.DCR**, as shown in Figure 6.4.

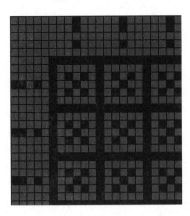

Figure 6.4 Component Palette bitmap for **TCheckGrid**.

Listing 6.1 Chkgrid.PAS

```
unit Chkgrid;

interface

uses
  SysUtils, WinTypes, WinProcs, Messages, Classes, Graphics,
  Controls, Forms, Dialogs, StdCtrls;

const
  RowsMax=20;
  ColumnsMax=20;

type
  TColumns=1..ColumnsMax;
  TRows=1..RowsMax;
  TMode=(moNormal,moColumnExclusive,moRowExclusive);

const
  RowsDefault=5;
  ColumnsDefault=5;
  ModeDefault=moNormal;
```

```
  ColorDefault=clBtnText;
  BackgroundColorDefault=clBtnFace;
  FontNameDefault='Arial';
  FontSizeDefault=10;

type
  TChangeEvent=procedure(Column:TColumns;Row:TRows;
    State:Boolean) of Object;

  TCheckGrid = class(TCustomControl)
  private
    ColumnTextRect:TRect;
    RowTextRect:TRect;
    CheckGridRect:TRect;

    ColumnPos:array[1..ColumnsMax+1] of Integer;
    RowPos:array[1..RowsMax+1] of Integer;

    CheckXOffset:Word;
    CheckYOffset:Word;

    ColumnTextHeight:array[1..ColumnsMax] of Word;
    RowTextWidth:array[1..RowsMax] of Word;

    ColumnTextOffset:Word;
    RowTextOffset:Word;

    CurrentColumn:Byte;
    CurrentRow:Byte;

    HasFocus:Boolean;
    CheckThickness:Word;
    HasBeenCalculated:Boolean;


    FChecked:array[1..ColumnsMax,1..RowsMax] of Boolean;
    FColumns:TColumns;
```

```
FRows:TRows;
FMode:TMode;
FColor:TColor;
FBackgroundColor:TColor;
FRowText:array[1..RowsMax] of String;
FColumnText:array[1..ColumnsMax] of String;
FOnChange:TChangeEvent;
FColumnString:String;
FRowString:String;


procedure RotateFont(Angle:Integer);
procedure CalculateRects;
procedure DrawCell(Column:TColumns;Row:TRows);
procedure CheckCell(Column:TColumns;Row:TRows);


procedure SetColumns(AColumns:TColumns);
procedure SetRows(ARows:TRows);
procedure SetMode(AMode:TMode);
procedure SetColor(AColor:TColor);
procedure SetBackgroundColor(ABackgroundColor:TColor);
procedure SetColumnText(Index:TColumns;AColumnText:String);
function GetColumnText(Index:TColumns):String;
procedure SetRowText(Index:TRows;ARowText:String);
function GetRowText(Index:TRows):String;
procedure SetChecked(Column:TColumns;Row:TRows;
  AChecked:Boolean);
function GetChecked(Column:TColumns;Row:TRows):Boolean;
procedure SetColumnString(ColumnString:String);
procedure SetRowString(RowString:String);
procedure WMSize(var Message:TWMSIZE); message WM_SIZE;
procedure WMSetFocus(var Message: TWMSetFocus);
  message WM_SETFOCUS;
procedure WMKillFocus(var Message: TWMKillFocus);
  message WM_KILLFOCUS;
procedure WMGetDlgCode(var Message: TWMGetDlgCode);
  message WM_GETDLGCODE;
```

```
    procedure ChangeFont(Sender:TObject);
protected
    procedure MouseDown(Button:TMouseButton;Shift:TShiftState;
      X,Y:Integer);override;
    procedure Paint;override;
    procedure KeyDown(var Key: Word; Shift: TShiftState);override;
public
    constructor Create(AOwner:TComponent);override;
    property ColumnText[Index:TColumns]:String read GetColumnText
      write SetColumnText;
    property RowText[Index:TRows]:String read GetRowText
      write SetRowText;
    property Checked[Column:TColumns;Row:TRows]:Boolean
      read GetChecked write SetChecked;
published
    property Columns:TColumns read FColumns write SetColumns
      default ColumnsDefault;
    property Rows:TRows read FRows write SetRows
      default RowsDefault;
    property Mode:TMode read FMode write SetMode
      default ModeDefault;
    property Color:TColor read FColor write SetColor
      default ColorDefault;
    property BackgroundColor:TColor read FBackgroundColor
      write SetBackgroundColor default BackgroundColorDefault;
    property OnChange: TChangeEvent read FOnChange
      write FOnChange;
    property ColumnString:String read FColumnString
      write SetColumnString;
    property RowString:String read FRowString write SetRowString;

    property DragCursor;
    property DragMode;
    property Enabled;
    property Font;
    property ParentFont;
```

```
      property ParentShowHint;
      property ShowHint;
      property TabOrder;
      property TabStop;
      property Visible;
      property OnClick;
      property OnDragDrop;
      property OnDragOver;
      property OnEndDrag;
      property OnEnter;
      property OnExit;
      property OnKeyDown;
      property OnKeyPress;
      property OnKeyUp;
      property OnMouseDown;
      property OnMouseMove;
      property OnMouseUp;
    end;

procedure Register;

implementation

procedure TCheckGrid.RotateFont(Angle:Integer);
var
   LogFont:TLogFont;
begin
   GetObject(Canvas.Font.Handle,SizeOf(TLogFont),@LogFont);
   LogFont.lfEscapement:=Angle;
   Canvas.Font.Handle:=CreateFontIndirect(LogFont);
end;

procedure TCheckGrid.CalculateRects;
var
   i:Byte;
   ColumnHeightMax:Word;
```

```
  RowWidthMax:Word;
  WidthSize,HeightSize:Word;
begin
  if csLoading in ComponentState then exit;
  HasBeenCalculated:=True;
  Canvas.Font:=Font;
  RowTextRect.Left:=0;
  RowTextRect.Bottom:=Height-1;
  ColumnTextRect.Top:=0;
  ColumnTextRect.Right:=Width-1;

  RowWidthMax:=0;
  for i:=1 to FRows do
  begin
    WidthSize:=Canvas.TextWidth(FRowText[i]);
    RowTextWidth[i]:=WidthSize;
    if WidthSize>RowWidthMax then RowWidthMax:=WidthSize;
  end;
  RowTextRect.Right:=RowWidthMax+10;
  ColumnTextRect.Left:=RowWidthMax;

  ColumnHeightMax:=0;
  for i:=1 to FColumns do
  begin
    HeightSize:=Canvas.TextWidth(FColumnText[i]);
    ColumnTextHeight[i]:=HeightSize;
    if HeightSize>ColumnHeightMax then
      ColumnHeightMax:=HeightSize;
  end;

  RowTextRect.Top:=ColumnHeightMax;
  ColumnTextRect.Bottom:=ColumnHeightMax+10;

  CheckGridRect.Left:=RowTextRect.Right;
  CheckGridRect.Top:=ColumnTextRect.Bottom;
  CheckGridRect.Right:=Width-1;
```

```
  CheckGridRect.Bottom:=Height-1;

  for i:=1 to FColumns+1 do
    ColumnPos[i]:=MulDiv(CheckGridRect.Right-CheckGridRect.Left,
      i-1,FColumns)+CheckGridRect.Left;

  for i:=1 to FRows+1 do
    RowPos[i]:=MulDiv(CheckGridRect.Bottom-CheckGridRect.Top,i-1,
      FRows)+CheckGridRect.Top;

  CheckXOffset:=(ColumnPos[2]-ColumnPos[1]) div 4;
  CheckYOffset:=(RowPos[2]-RowPos[1]) div 4;
  CheckThickness:=(CheckXOffset+CheckYOffset) div 4;

  ColumnTextOffset:=(ColumnPos[2]-ColumnPos[1]+Font.Height) div 2;
  RowTextOffset:=(RowPos[2]-RowPos[1]+Font.Height) div 2;
end;

procedure TCheckGrid.DrawCell(Column:TColumns;Row:TRows);
var
  i:Byte;
  FocusRect:TRect;
begin
  if FChecked[Column,Row] then
    Canvas.Pen.Color:=FColor
  else
    Canvas.Pen.Color:=FBackgroundColor;

  Canvas.MoveTo(ColumnPos[Column]+CheckXOffset,RowPos[Row]+
    CheckYOffset);
  Canvas.LineTo(ColumnPos[Column+1]-CheckXOffset,RowPos[Row+1]-
    CheckYOffset);

  Canvas.MoveTo(ColumnPos[Column+1]-CheckXOffset,RowPos[Row]+
    CheckYOffset);
  Canvas.LineTo(ColumnPos[Column]+CheckXOffset,RowPos[Row+1]-
```

```
    CheckYOffset);

  if (Column=CurrentColumn) and (Row=CurrentRow) then
  begin
    FocusRect.Left:=ColumnPos[CurrentColumn]+2;
    FocusRect.Top:=RowPos[CurrentRow]+2;
    FocusRect.Right:=ColumnPos[CurrentColumn+1]-1;
    FocusRect.Bottom:=RowPos[CurrentRow+1]-1;
    Canvas.Brush.Color:=FBackgroundColor;
    Canvas.FrameRect(FocusRect);

    if HasFocus then
      Canvas.DrawFocusRect(FocusRect);
  end;
end;


procedure TCheckGrid.CheckCell(Column:TColumns;Row:TRows);
var
  i:Byte;
begin
  Canvas.Pen.Width:=CheckThickness;
  case FMode of
    moNormal:
      DrawCell(Column,Row);
    moColumnExclusive:
    begin
      for i:=1 to FRows do
      begin
        FChecked[Column,i]:=i=Row;
        DrawCell(Column,i);
      end;
    end;
    moRowExclusive:
    begin
      for i:=1 to FColumns do
      begin
```

```
        FChecked[i,Row]:=i=Column;
        DrawCell(i,Row);
      end;
    end;
  end;
end;

procedure TCheckGrid.SetColumns(AColumns:TColumns);
begin
  FColumns:=AColumns;
  CalculateRects;
  Invalidate;
end;

procedure TCheckGrid.SetRows(ARows:TRows);
begin
  FRows:=ARows;
  CalculateRects;
  Invalidate;
end;

procedure TCheckGrid.SetMode(AMode:TMode);
begin
  FMode:=AMode;
end;

procedure TCheckGrid.SetColor(AColor:TColor);
begin
  FColor:=AColor;
  Paint;
end;

procedure TCheckGrid.SetBackgroundColor(ABackgroundColor:TColor);
begin
  FBackgroundColor:=ABackgroundColor;
  Paint;
end;
```

```
procedure TCheckGrid.ChangeFont(Sender:TObject);
begin
  CalculateRects;
  Invalidate;
end;

procedure TCheckGrid.SetColumnText(Index:TColumns;
  AColumnText:String);
begin
  FColumnText[Index]:=AColumnText;
  CalculateRects;
  Invalidate;
end;

function TCheckGrid.GetColumnText(Index:TColumns):String;
begin
  GetColumnText:=FColumnText[Index];
end;

procedure TCheckGrid.SetRowText(Index:TRows;ARowText:String);
begin
  FRowText[Index]:=ARowText;
  CalculateRects;
  Invalidate;
end;

function TCheckGrid.GetRowText(Index:TRows):String;
begin
  GetRowText:=FRowText[Index];
end;

procedure TCheckGrid.SetChecked(Column:TColumns;Row:TRows;
  AChecked:Boolean);
begin
  FChecked[Column,Row]:=AChecked;
  CheckCell(Column,Row);
```

```
end;

function TCheckGrid.GetChecked(Column:TColumns;Row:TRows):Boolean;
begin
  GetChecked:=FChecked[Column,Row];
end;

procedure TCheckGrid.SetColumnString(ColumnString:String);
var
  i:Byte;
  Column:Byte;
  Text:String;
begin
  FColumnString:=ColumnString;
  Text:='';
  Column:=1;
  For i:=1 to Length(ColumnString) do
  begin
    if ColumnString[i]<>',' then
      Text:=Text+ColumnString[i]
    else
    begin
      ColumnText[Column]:=Text;
      Text:='';
      inc(Column);
    end;
  end;
  ColumnText[Column]:=Text;
end;

procedure TCheckGrid.SetRowString(RowString:String);
var
  i:Byte;
  Row:Byte;
  Text:String;
begin
```

```
    FRowString:=RowString;
    Text:='';
    Row:=1;
    For i:=1 to Length(RowString) do
    begin
      if RowString[i]<>',' then
        Text:=Text+RowString[i]
      else
      begin
        RowText[Row]:=Text;
        Text:='';
        inc(Row);
      end;
    end;
    RowText[Row]:=Text;
end;


constructor TCheckGrid.Create(AOwner:TComponent);
var
  i,j:Byte;
begin
  inherited Create(AOwner);
  FRows:=RowsDefault;
  FColumns:=ColumnsDefault;
  FMode:=ModeDefault;
  FColor:=ColorDefault;
  FBackgroundColor:=BackgroundColorDefault;
  Font.Name:=FontNameDefault;
  Font.Size:=FontSizeDefault;
  Font.OnChange:=ChangeFont;
  FOnChange:=nil;

  CurrentColumn:=1;
  CurrentRow:=1;
  HasFocus:=False;
  HasBeenCalculated:=False;
```

```
  for i:=1 to ColumnsMax do
  begin
    for j:=1 to RowsMax do
    begin
      FChecked[i,j]:=False;
    end;
  end;

  for i:=1 to RowsMax do
    FRowText[i]:='Row '+IntToStr(i);

  for i:=1 to ColumnsMax do
    FColumnText[i]:='Column '+IntToStr(i);
end;

procedure TCheckGrid.Paint;
var
  i,j:Byte;
begin
  if not HasBeenCalculated then CalculateRects;
  Canvas.Font:=Font;
  Canvas.Pen.Color:=Color;
  Canvas.Pen.Width:=1;
  Canvas.Brush.Color:=FBackgroundColor;
  Canvas.Brush.Style:=bsSolid;

  Canvas.Rectangle(CheckGridRect.Left,CheckGridRect.Top,
    CheckGridRect.Right,CheckGridRect.Bottom);

  Canvas.Brush.Style:=bsClear;

  RotateFont(-900);
  for i:=1 to FColumns do
  begin
    Canvas.TextOut(ColumnPos[i+1]-ColumnTextOffset,
      ColumnTextRect.Bottom-ColumnTextHeight[i]-10,
```

```
      FColumnText[i]);
    Canvas.MoveTo(ColumnPos[i],CheckGridRect.Top);
    Canvas.LineTo(ColumnPos[i],CheckGridRect.Bottom);
  end;

  RotateFont(0);
  for i:=1 to FRows do
  begin
    Canvas.TextOut(RowTextRect.Right-RowTextWidth[i]-10,RowPos[i]+
      RowTextOffset,FRowText[i]);
    Canvas.MoveTo(CheckGridRect.Left,RowPos[i]);
    Canvas.LineTo(CheckGridRect.Right,RowPos[i]);
  end;

  Canvas.Pen.Width:=CheckThickness;
  for i:=1 to FColumns do
  begin
    for j:=1 to FRows do
      DrawCell(i,j);
  end;
end;

procedure TCheckGrid.MouseDown(Button:TMouseButton;
  Shift:TShiftState;X,Y:Integer);
var
  i,j:Byte;
  FoundBox:Boolean;
begin
  FoundBox:=False;
  i:=0;
  repeat
    inc(i);
    if (X>=ColumnPos[i]) and (X<=ColumnPos[i+1]) then
    begin
      j:=0;
      repeat
        inc(j);
```

```
              if (Y>=RowPos[j]) and (Y<=RowPos[j+1]) then
              begin
                if TabStop or HasFocus then
                begin
                  SetFocus;
                  HasFocus:=False;
                  DrawCell(CurrentColumn,CurrentRow);
                  HasFocus:=True;
                end;
                CurrentColumn:=i;
                CurrentRow:=j;
                FChecked[i,j]:=not FChecked[i,j];
                CheckCell(i,j);
                if Assigned(FOnChange) then
                  FOnChange(CurrentColumn,CurrentRow,
                    FChecked[CurrentColumn,CurrentRow]);
                FoundBox:=True;
              end;
            until (j>FRows) or FoundBox;
        end;
    until (i>FColumns) or FoundBox;
    inherited MouseDown(Button,Shift,X,Y);
  end;

  procedure TCheckGrid.WMSize(var Message:TWMSIZE);
  begin
    CalculateRects;
    Invalidate;
  end;

  procedure TCheckGrid.WMSetFocus(var Message: TWMSetFocus);
  var
    FocusRect:TRect;
  begin
    HasFocus:=True;
    DrawCell(CurrentColumn,CurrentRow);
    inherited;
```

```
end;

procedure TCheckGrid.WMKillFocus(var Message: TWMKillFocus);
begin
  HasFocus := False;
  DrawCell(CurrentColumn,CurrentRow);
  inherited;
end;

procedure TCheckGrid.KeyDown(var Key: Word; Shift: TShiftState);
begin
  inherited KeyDown(Key,Shift);
  case Key of
    VK_LEFT:
    begin
      HasFocus:=False;
      DrawCell(CurrentColumn,CurrentRow);
      dec(CurrentColumn);
      if CurrentColumn=0 then CurrentColumn:=FColumns;
      HasFocus:=True;
      DrawCell(CurrentColumn,CurrentRow);
    end;
    VK_RIGHT:
    begin
      HasFocus:=False;
      DrawCell(CurrentColumn,CurrentRow);
      inc(CurrentColumn);
      if CurrentColumn>FColumns then CurrentColumn:=1;
      HasFocus:=True;
      DrawCell(CurrentColumn,CurrentRow);
    end;
    VK_DOWN:
    begin
      HasFocus:=False;
      DrawCell(CurrentColumn,CurrentRow);
      inc(CurrentRow);
      if CurrentRow>FRows then CurrentRow:=1;
```

```
      HasFocus:=True;
      DrawCell(CurrentColumn,CurrentRow);
    end;
  VK_UP:
  begin
    HasFocus:=False;
    DrawCell(CurrentColumn,CurrentRow);
    dec(CurrentRow);
    if CurrentRow=0 then CurrentRow:=FRows;
    HasFocus:=True;
    DrawCell(CurrentColumn,CurrentRow);
  end;
  VK_SPACE:
  begin
    FChecked[CurrentColumn,CurrentRow]:=
      not FChecked[CurrentColumn,CurrentRow];
    CheckCell(CurrentColumn,CurrentRow);
    if Assigned(FOnChange) then
      FOnChange(CurrentColumn,CurrentRow,FChecked[CurrentColumn,
      CurrentRow]);
  end;
  end;
end;


procedure TCheckGrid.WMGetDlgCode(var Message: TWMGetDlgCode);
begin
  Message.Result := DLGC_WANTARROWS;
end;



procedure Register;
begin
  RegisterComponents('Additional', [TCheckGrid]);
end;


end.
```

CHAPTER • 7

INHERITING EXISTING FUNCTIONALITY

All the components that we have created so far have the common link that they needed to provide total functionality for every minute detail. While this is sometimes necessary, often the features and capabilities of another component can be "stolen" and put to work for you. This is not a difficult proposition either; the procedure for doing so is identical to inheriting any component class and expanding on it. In this chapter, we will explore this notion, and in the process, you will become acquainted with the following:

- Inheriting from a working component
- Using combo boxes
- Owner drawing
- Initializing after properties have been loaded

To demonstrate these points, I have chosen an example component that is often needed for day-to-day programming, but is sadly missing from Delphi. It is a variation of the standard combo box, but instead of displaying text, it allows the user to select a specific color from a list in a manner similar to that seen in Word for Windows and, for that matter, most other Microsoft programs.

TColorDrop

Shown in Figure 7.1 is the aptly named **TColorDrop** component. From an operational standpoint, it is a rather simple component. The user merely clicks on the drop-down box and selects the color that he or she desires. From a programming standpoint, it is also a simple component, a perfect starting place for our discussion on inheriting functionality.

7.1 TColorDrop in action.

Choosing the Ancestor

TColorDrop obtains its combo box functionality from its ancestor, **TCustomComboBox**, and provides the relatively trivial color enhancements itself. Like all components descended from another one, total functionality is transferred, not just bits and pieces. This explains why **TCustomComboBox** was chosen over **TComboBox**. Had it been the other way around, the color drop component would indeed function— **TCustomComboBox** and **TComboBox** are identical—but it would also contain needless properties specifically suited for **TComboBox**, such as **Text**, **Items**, and **ItemHeight**.

Sometimes, you will want to create a descendant from a component that does not have a "pre" class like **TCustomComboBox**. In this situation, you may think this means that you are stuck with having needless published properties. Happily, there is some magic you can perform to effectively *unpublish* a property. All you have to do is redefine the property in your descendant and make it read-only. Remember, read-only properties do not show up in the Object Inspector because they can't be set. Consider the **Tag** property in the following bit of code:

```
TNewComponent=class(TComponent)
private
  FTag:LongInt;
property
  Tag:LongInt read FTag;
end;
```

Here, we see that **Tag** is redefined. It is therefore this **Tag** and not the one inherited from **TComponent** that gets the opportunity to be published. Because **Tag** is read-only—because of how the property is declared with only the **read** keyword—it will not appear in the Object Inspector at design-time. In the preceding code, I decided to make **Tag** a **LongInt**, just like in the original declaration, but it could have been any type at all because it is a dummy variable.

We can go one step farther in unpublishing a property. If we change the access variable to a function, we can declare that function as **abstract**, preventing accidental access to the property:

```
type
  TUnpublish=Byte;

  TNewComponent=class(TComponent)
  private
    function Unpublish:TUnpublish;virtual;abstract;
  property
    Tag:TUnpublish read Unpublish;
  end;
```

Now, whenever **Tag** is accessed, an exception will be raised because the **read** function is abstract. Notice that the type **TUnpublish** is of type **byte**. Again, this decision is entirely arbitrary.

The two techniques for unpublishing a property that we just looked at raise an important question: What happens to the original **Tag** property? Nothing. It is still there, but it's a little harder to access. From inside the component's code, all that is needed is the **inherited** keyword:inherited Tag:=12;

From outside the component's code, in the owner's form, for example, its instance must be typecast to the ancestor's type:

```
NewComponent:=TNewComponent.Create;
TComponent(NewComponent).Tag:=12;
```

For **TColorDrop**, we don't need to unpublish anything because **TCustomComboBox** publishes only one property, **TabStop**, which we will need anyhow. There is, however, a small handful of properties that we will want to publish ourselves to make **TColorDrop** more Delphi-like. These are listed in Table 7.1.

Table 7.1 TColorDrop's Published Properties

Property	Description
Ctl3D	Determines whether the component has a 3-D look.
Cursor	Used to specify the cursor shape.
DragCursor	Used to specify the cursor shape during a drag operation.
DragMode	Specifies the drag mode, automatic or manual.
DropDownCount	Indicates how many items will be dropped when **TColorDrop** opens.
Enabled	Specifies whether **TColorDrop** is enabled.
HelpContext	Specifies what help screen should be displayed when the user needs help with **TColorDrop**.

Property	Description
Hint	Contains the text string that is displayed whenever the user moves the cursor over the **TColorDrop**.
ParentColor	If this property is **True**, **TColorDrop** uses its parent's **Color** property instead of its own.
ParentCtl3D	If this property is **True**, **TColorDrop** uses its parent's **Ctl3D** property instead of its own.
ParentFont	If **True**, the parent's **Font** property is used instead of **TColorDrop**'s.
ParentShowHint	If this property is **True**, the parent's **ShowHint** property is used instead of the **TColorDrop**'s.
PopupMenu	When the user right-clicks on **TColorDrop**, the menu coressponding to the **TPopupMenu** class pointed to by this property will be displayed.
ShowHint	If this property is **True**, the text contained in the **Hint** property will be displayed when the mouse cursor is placed over the **TColorDrop** component for a moment.
TabOrder	Every time the Tab key is pressed in a form, the focus goes from one component to another in a predetermined order. This property is used to specify where in that order a **TColorDrop** component will be.
Visible	Determines if **TColorDrop** is visible.
Font	Font of the text used in **TColorDrop**.
Color	Color of the current selection in the edit portion of **TColorDrop**.
OnChange	Event that is called when the color selection changes.

(Continued)

Property	Description
OnClick	Called when **TColorDrop** is clicked on.
OnDblClick	Called when **TColorDrop** is double-clicked on.
OnDragDrop	Called when an object is dropped onto **TColorDrop**.
OnDragOver	Called when an object is dragged over **TColorDrop**.
OnEndDrag	Called when **TColorDrop** has been dropped on an object
OnEnter	Called when the focus shifts to **TColorDrop**.
OnExit	Called when the focus shifts away from **TColorDrop**.

Understanding Owner Drawing

The capability of **TColorDrop** to display colored squares is achieved by giving up the automatic text-only scheme that Windows provides and by adopting a technique known as *owner drawing*. In the context of Delphi, this term is riddled with mind-numbing confusion. To see why I say this, consider this example: Drop a **TComboBox** on a form and select the **Events** tab in the Object Inspector. You will see all the properties associated with it, including one called **OnDrawItem**. This event is called when any custom drawing needs to be done by **TComboBox**, which occurs whenever the **Style** property is set to **csOwnerDrawFixed** or **csOwnerDrawVariable**. Notice that the **OnDrawItem** event is contained entirely within the component, and has nothing to do with the owner—be it a form or a container component such as **TPanel**—whatsoever. This is where the confusion takes root.

The reason the term *owner drawing* exists at all has to do with how Windows works internally. If a *control* (built-in Windows version of a component) needs custom drawing to be done, it sends a **WM_DRAWITEM** message to the window that houses it or its *owner*. Remember, this is low-level Windows; it has to happen this way or not at all regardless of the development environment being used. But as we just saw, in Delphi, it is the component that responds to the request to do custom drawing, not the form that owns it. How can this be? This is where things start to get clever. Realizing that it is more desirable to custom draw within the component code, Borland introduced a mechanism where all Delphi windowed components derived from **TWinControl**—including forms—intercept the **WM_DRAWITEM** message. When this happens, a custom message, **CN_DRAWITEM** is sent to the proper component. The custom message is necessary because if **WM_DRAWITEM** was to be sent instead, the component would think that one of the components it owned, if any, needed to be custom drawn, which would obviously not be the desired result.

With the explanation I just gave in mind, I should note that I feel it was careless of Delphi's developers to use the **csOwnerDrawFixed** and **csOwnerDrawVariable** identifiers. They describe the inner workings, and the whole point of Delphi is that the inner workings are hidden. It would have been much more appropriate to call them **csCustomDrawFixed** and **csCustomDrawVariable**, or something similar.

It's a Colorful World

The colors listed in **TColorDrop** have been purposely limited to those that Windows keeps on hand for its own purposes. Although it certainly would have been possible to have an impressive palette of 256 colors drop down, I for one would not be willing to give each of them a name! Even if I were willing, there is a more profound reason for sticking to Windows stock colors: they are always available. Well, almost. If you are working in monochrome, a laptop computer for example, you are out of luck. Other than this situation, however, the colors used are always reserved by Windows and never go anywhere. The same cannot be said for any other color. If you have ever played with 256 color wallpaper, you know what I'm talking about. Sure, the wallpaper is pretty and everything, but as soon as you open up an application that redefines any of the colors used in it, the image transforms into a psychedelic alteration of its former glory. For some programs, such as painting programs, I'm willing to accept it. But the majority of programs do not benefit one iota from using hordes of colors. Generally, the handful of stock colors is good enough to suit anybody's needs.

Initializing TColorDrop

Like the majority of all components, **TColorDrop** has to override the **Create** constructor so it may perform some preliminary custom initialization before fully creating the component. One such initialization that must take place is setting the **Style** property to **csDropDown** to ensure that the component supports owner drawing. For an owner-drawn component, it is also important to set the **OnDrawItem** event handler to point to the procedure that is to be called whenever the component needs to be drawn. For **TColorDrop**, the procedure that does the drawing is **DrawItemProc**. The final step in completing the initialization sequence is to set the published properties to their default values. Note, that this does not apply to published properties that were inherited from **TCustomComboBox** because they are set to the proper values when the ancestor's **Create** constructor is called. In this component, there is only one unique published property, **FSelectedColor**, and it is set to its default value of **SelectedColorDefault**. Here, expressed in code, is what I just explained:

```
constructor TColorDrop.Create(AOwner:TComponent);
begin
  inherited Create(AOwner);
  Style:=csOwnerDrawFixed;
  OnDrawItem:=DrawItemProc;
  FSelectedColor:=SelectedColorDefault;
end;
```

Further Initialization

One of the problems that you are sure to run into when programming visual components is trying to decide where to perform initialization after the component's published properties have been loaded. Remember, published properties are loaded after **Create** has been called, so it is impossible to do such initialization there. As we have seen before, the **Loaded** method is called after the published properties have been loaded, so it can be used, but it has two major drawbacks. First of all, if you create a component on-the-fly at run time, **Loaded** is not automatically called and will have to be called manually. For example:

```
MyComponent:=TMyComponent.Create(Self);
MyComponent.Parent:=Self;
MyComponent.Loaded;
```

As you can probably guess, it is *very* easy to forget to make the call to **Loaded**. With nonvisual components, we are stuck with this because there isn't any method that can be hooked into to provide initialization for both components loaded from a stream and components created at run time. Visual components are, however, a completely different story. In the preceding section of code, notice that after the component has been created, the **Parent** property must be assigned to **Self**. When this action is performed, the actual window that houses the component is created. If we can hook into a method that is called as a result of this, the necessary initialization can be performed there. But where to place the hook? There are two likely candidates, but as it turns out, there is really only one reliable method that can be overridden to do what we want. Before we get to it, however, let's look at why the alternative does not work.

The first candidate is **CreateWnd**. Like its name implies, this is where the "big bang" of window creation occurs. Logic would dictate that initialization for published properties could be done here. And it can, if certain conditions are met.

There are two possible scenarios for doing initialization in **CreateWnd**: the initialization is done before the call to the inherited method, or it is done after the call. Each choice has its own drawbacks. In the first case, initialization may be performed, but it may not involve anything to do with the window being created. No drawing, no getting the client size, nothing. The reason couldn't be simpler—the window hasn't been created yet because the original **CreateWnd** has not been called!

The second case, initializing after the inherited call, can indeed use the window, but this is often too late to do anything useful. During the inherited call, not only is the window created, but it is sized and painted as well. It doesn't do much good to calculate a value crucial to how a window is painted if the window has already been painted. True, **Refresh** or **Repaint** could be called at this point, but that would be just plain stupid. Especially in light of the alternative that's available.

From the two possibilities just discussed, it is evident that the ideal time to perform initialization would be at the point just after the window has been created, but before it has been sized and painted. Although there isn't any method that can be hooked into directly to accomplish this, it is nevertheless achievable through the interception of the **WM_CREATE** message, which is no more difficult than intercepting any other message:

```
type
  TMyComponent=class(TCustomControl)
    procedure WMCreate(var Message:TWMCreate);message WM_Create;
  end;


procedure TMyComponent.WMCreate(var Message:TWMCreate);
begin
  inherited;
  {Do initialization here}
end;
```

This is as close to a catch-all that Delphi provides.

Although either the **CreateWnd** method override or the **WMCreate** message interception technique would work for **TColorDrop**, I decided to stick with **WMCreate** because it provides a solution that works 100 percent of the time regardless of the particulars of the component.

TColorDrop uses the owner draw style **csOwnerDrawFixed**, indicating that the size height of the custom drawing is always the same size regardless of the index of the item selected.

Managing the Color List

Information is added, modified, and deleted from all **TComboBox** components through the use of the **Items** property, which is of type **TStrings**. **TStrings** itself originates from the type **TList**, but has been specifically designed to manage a list of strings rather than objects. At first glance, this might seem like it is going to be a problem for us because, although we do need strings to display the name of the color, we also need to know what color is associated with what string so that we can draw a small colored box beside the name. The top-of-the-head solution for this problem is quite simple.

As the combo box fills up with items, they are added in the order that they are received, unless the **Sorted** property is **True**. Therefore, the first item added has an index of zero; the second has an index of one; and so on. The owner draw function knows what item to draw because it is passed a parameter called **Index**, the index of the item. The intended purpose of **Index** is to point at the appropriate item in the **Items** property and use the resultant value as the data for the owner drawing. For **TColorDrop**, the relationship between the index and the data is shown in Table 7.2.

Table 7.2 The Item Index and Corresponding Color

Index	Color Name
0	Black
1	Maroon
2	Green
3	Olive
4	Navy
5	Purple
6	Teal
7	Gray
8	Silver
9	Red
10	Lime
11	Yellow
12	Blue
13	Fuchsia
14	Aqua
15	Light Gray
16	Dark Gray
17	White

In real life, the index for the color name is one more than shown here because the array that it is declared in, **ColorStrings**, starts at one rather than zero; but it is a simple matter to make the necessary adjustment by adding or subtracting one when needed. What you should notice is that even though the owner draw procedure's **Index** parameter is normally used to retrieve the name of the color from the **Items** property, the same index—plus one—also corresponds to the **ColorStrings** array. This means that the string information could just as easily be obtained from the **ColorStrings** array. If this holds true, it's a sure bet that the color for drawing the little box can be obtained using the same index—plus one, but this time pointing to the **Colors** array instead.

The method just described will work fine, provided that you never want to use the **Sorted** property with a value other than **False**. If **Sorted** was **True**, the color names would be added to the **Items** list, but instead of appearing in the order that they were added, they would be dynamically sorted. No longer will "black" be the first color in the list, because "aqua" will take its place. The thing about aqua being first is that it is at index zero—the same index zero where the **clBlack** constant is going to be. Obviously, aqua is not black, and something more clever needs to be done if things are to work properly for a sorted list.

Foreseeing this sort of problem, Borland added a back door to the **Items** property that allows it to not only have a string associated with an individual item, but an object as well. This is accomplished by calling **AddObject** in place of **Add**:

```
function AddObject(const S:string;AObject:TObject):Integer;
```

The parameter **S** is the string that you want to be associated with the item, and the **AObject** parameter specifies the class that is to be associated. The return value of the function is how many items were in the list, before **AddObject** was called. For a nonsorted list, this also corresponds to the index of the item just added.

The capability to associate an object with an item opens up a whole realm of possibilities that can be accomplished with owner drawn combo boxes. For our purpose, however, using a class to encapsulate a single value would be overkill to say the least; so instead, a simple typecast is done to make each item of the **Colors** array "fit":

```
for i:=1 to NumColors do
  Items.AddObject(ColorStrings[i],TObject(Colors[i]));
```

It should be pointed out that the only reason this typecasting trick works at all is because the bit length of each **Colors** member is compatible with the bit length of a class instance—both are 32 bits. If you ever need to store more information than will fit into 32 bits, there are a couple of options. First, you could pass a pointer to a record instead of a simple type. Second, you could opt to store your information in a class and pass an instance of it for each item you want to store. Both methods have their advantages. Passing a record uses less memory than a class, but a class allows you to embed routines that manipulate the data.

Regardless of the method you choose, there is one important point to remember: You are responsible for allocating and deallocating the memory for each individual item. For a record, this involves calling **New** and **Dispose**; and for a class, you must call the **Create** constructor and **Free** destructor. Should you fail to release memory, it will not be done automatically for you when the **TComboBox** component frees the strings associated with **Items**.

Drawing the Cell

When it comes time to draw any portion of **TColorDrop**, the procedure **DrawItemProc** is called once for each cell:

```
procedure DrawItemProc(Control:TWinControl;Index:Integer;Rect:TRect;
  State:TOwnerDrawState);
```

The **Control** parameter tells the procedure which component is responsible for calling it. When the **OnDrawItem** event is assigned to a procedure within the component from which it originates, as it is with ours, this parameter has little meaning and can be safely ignored. As an aside, I should note that it's a completely different story if the **OnDrawItem** event is assigned to a procedure that is external to the component itself, an owning form, for example. Should this be the situation, the event handler can be reused multiple times. For instance, suppose that you had a form that had several owner drawn combo boxes and you wanted each to display the exact same thing—various line thicknesses. It would certainly be possible to write a separate **OnDrawItem** handler for each combo box, but this would be a waste of valuable resources. It is much more logical to write a single event handler and then point each **OnDrawItem** property to it.

The second parameter of the preceding declaration is **Index**. The value that it provides is an index to the **Items** property, which can be used to extract the previously stored color name and color value. The third parameter, **Rect**, defines the bounds of the rectangle that you are allowed to draw in. Note that the upper left corner of this rectangle is never 0,0, so it is very important to use the **Rect.Left** and **Rect.Top** values as the origin instead.

The final parameter is **State**, of type **TOwnerDrawState**:

```
TOwnerDrawState=set of (odSelected,odGrayed,odDisabled,
  odChecked, odFocused);
```

This provides extra information to the programmer that allows the correct state of the cell to be drawn. It would be entirely inappropriate to ignore this parameter and draw all the cells the same regardless of the state they are in because it would confuse the user greatly and render the component practically useless. A minimal implementation has been done for **TColorDrop**, just enough to show the user which cell is currently selected:

```
if odSelected in State then
  Canvas.Brush.Color:=clHighLight
else
  Canvas.Brush.Color:=Color;
Canvas.FillRect(Rect);
```

What happens here is that if the current cell is selected, its background is drawn with the **clHighlight** color; otherwise, the default color assigned to the component is used.

As mentioned previously, each cell consists of some text that names the color and a square that is filled with the color itself. The code needed for doing this simple procedure goes like this:

```
Canvas.Pen.Color:=Font.Color;
Canvas.TextOut(Rect.Bottom-Rect.Top+4,Rect.Top,Items[Index]);
```

```
Canvas.Brush.Color:=TColor(Items.Objects[Index]);
Canvas.Rectangle(4,Rect.Top+2,Rect.Bottom-Rect.Top,Rect.Bottom-2);
SetBkColor(Canvas.Handle,Color);
```

The first two lines are responsible for drawing the text—the first line sets the color, and the second line draws it. The next two lines draw the colored box. The final line sets the background color to the value of the **Color** property. This ensures that when the focus rectangle is drawn, it is the proper color.

Finishing Touches

That just about wraps up the discussion of **TColorDrop**. The palette bitmap is shown in Figure 7.2.

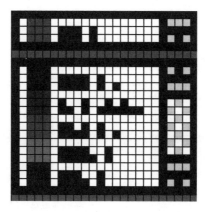

Figure 7.2 Palette bitmap for **TColorDrop**.

As always, here is the complete code for the component, which you can also find in the **\DC\CHAP07** directory:

Listing 7.1 ColorDrop.PAS

```
unit ColorDrop;

interface

uses
```

```
SysUtils, Windows, Messages, Classes, Graphics, Controls, Forms,
Dialogs, StdCtrls;

const
  NumColors=18;
  ColorStrings:array[1..NumColors] of AnsiString=('Black',
     'Maroon','Green','Olive','Navy','Purple','Teal','Gray',
     'Silver','Red','Lime','Yellow','Blue','Fuchsia','Aqua',
     'Light Gray','Dark Gray','White');
  Colors:array[1..NumColors] of TColor=(clBlack,clMaroon,clGreen,
     clOlive,clNavy,clPurple,clTeal,clGray,clSilver,clRed,clLime,
     clYellow,clBlue,clFuchsia,clAqua,clLtGray,clDkGray,clWhite);

const
  SelectedColorDefault=clBlack;

type
  TColorDrop = class(TCustomComboBox)
  private
    FSelectedColor:TColor;
    procedure SetFont(AFont:TFont);
    procedure SetSelectedColor(ASelectedColor:TColor);
  protected
    procedure SetColors;
    procedure SetHeights;
    procedure DrawItemProc(Control:TWinControl;Index:Integer;
      Rect:TRect;State:TOwnerDrawState);
    procedure Change;override;
    procedure WMCreate(var Message:TWMCreate);message WM_Create;
    procedure DoFontChange(Sender:TObject);
  public
    constructor Create(AOwner:TComponent);override;
  published
    property SelectedColor:TColor read FSelectedColor
      write SetSelectedColor;
    property Ctl3D;
    property Color;
```

```
    property Cursor;
    property DragCursor;
    property DragMode;
    property DropDownCount;
    property Enabled;
    property HelpCcntext;
    property Hint;
    property ParentColor;
    property ParentCtl3D;
    property ParentFont;
    property ParentShowHint;
    property PopupMenu;
    property ShowHint;
    property TabOrder;
    property Visible;
    property Font;
    property OnChange;
    property OnClick;
    property OnDblClick;
    property OnDragDrop;
    property OnDragOver;
    property OnEndDrag;
    property OnEnter;
    property OnExit;
  end;

procedure Register;

implementation

procedure TColorDrop.DoFontChange(Sender:TObject);
begin
  SetHeights;
end;

procedure TColorDrop.SetFont(AFont:TFont);
begin
```

```
    inherited Font:=AFont;
end;


procedure TColorDrop.SetSelectedColor(ASelectedColor:TColor);
var
  i:Byte;
begin
  for i:=1 to NumColors do
  begin
    if ASelectedColor=Colors[i] then
    begin
      ItemIndex:=i-1;
      FSelectedColor:=Colors[i];
      break;
    end;
  end;
end;


procedure TColorDrop.Change;
begin
  FSelectedColor:=Colors[ItemIndex+1];
  inherited Change;
end;


procedure TColorDrop.SetColors;
var
  i:Byte;
begin
  for i:=1 to NumColors do
    Items.AddObject(ColorStrings[i],TObject(Colors[i]));
end;


procedure TColorDrop.SetHeights;
begin
  SendMessage(Handle,CB_SETITEMHEIGHT,0,-Font.Height+4);
  SendMessage(Handle,CB_SETITEMHEIGHT,Word(-1),-Font.Height+4);
end;
```

```
procedure TColorDrop.DrawItemProc(Control:TWinControl;
  Index:Integer;Rect:TRect;State:TOwnerDrawState);
var
  ColorRect:TRect;
  Offset:Byte;
begin
  if odSelected in State then
    Canvas.Brush.Color:=clHighLight
  else
    Canvas.Brush.Color:=Color;
  Canvas.FillRect(Rect);

  Canvas.Pen.Color:=Font.Color;
  Canvas.TextOut(Rect.Bottom-Rect.Top+4,Rect.Top,Items[Index]);
  Canvas.Brush.Color:=TColor(Items.Objects[Index]);
  Canvas.Rectangle(4,Rect.Top+2,Rect.Bottom-Rect.Top,
    Rect.Bottom-2);
  SetBkColor(Canvas.Handle,Color);
end;

constructor TColorDrop.Create(AOwner:TComponent);
begin
  inherited Create(AOwner);
  Style:=csOwnerDrawFixed;
  OnDrawItem:=DrawItemProc;
  FSelectedColor:=SelectedColorDefault;
  Font.OnChange:=DoFontChange;
end;

procedure TColorDrop.WMCreate(var Message:TWMCreate);
begin
  inherited;
  SetColors;
  SetHeights;
  SetSelectedColor(FSelectedColor);
end;
```

```
procedure Register;
begin
  RegisterComponents('Additional', [TColorDrop]);
end;

end.
```

Finally, I have created a small demo program, shown in Figure 7.3, so that you may test drive the component. Here is the code for the program, which is also in the **\DC\CHAP07** directory:

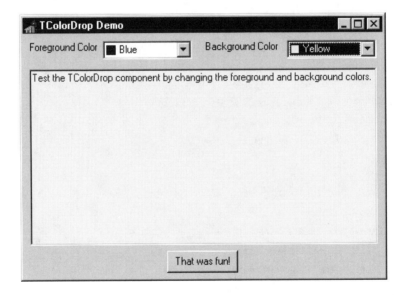

Figure 7.3 TColorDrop in action.

Listing 7.2 ColorDropDemo.DPR

```
program ColorDropDemo;

uses
  Forms,
  ColorDropDemoForm in 'ColorDropDemoForm.pas' {Form1};

{$R *.RES}
```

```
begin
  Application.Initialize;
  Application.CreateForm(TForm1, Form1);
  Application.CreateForm(TForm1, Form1);
  Application.Run;
end.
```

Listing 7.3 ColorDropDemoForm.PAS

```
unit ColorDropDemoForm;

interface

uses
  Windows, Messages, SysUtils, Classes, Graphics, Controls, Forms,
Dialogs,
  ExtCtrls, StdCtrls, ColorDrop;

type
  TForm1 = class(TForm)
    ColorDrop1: TColorDrop;
    Memo1: TMemo;
    Label1: TLabel;
    Label2: TLabel;
    ColorDrop2: TColorDrop;
    Button1: TButton;
    procedure ColorDrop1Change(Sender: TObject);
    procedure ColorDrop2Change(Sender: TObject);
    procedure Button1Click(Sender: TObject);
  private
    { Private declarations }
  public
    { Public declarations }
  end;

var
  Form1: TForm1;
```

```
implementation

{$R *.DFM}

procedure TForm1.ColorDrop1Change(Sender: TObject);
begin
  Memo1.Font.Color:=ColorDrop1.SelectedColor;
end;

procedure TForm1.ColorDrop2Change(Sender: TObject);
begin
  Memo1.Color:=ColorDrop2.SelectedColor;
end;

procedure TForm1.Button1Click(Sender: TObject);
begin
  Close;
end;

end.
```

CHAPTER • 8

COMPONENTS THAT PRINT

When the personal computer was first introduced, its proponents were quick to point out that one of its greatest features would be the so-called paperless office. More than a decade later, we know that this is not the case, and indeed, the consumption of paper has been increasing rather than decreasing despite new heightened environmental awareness. Ironically, the primary reason for the increase is the computer itself—printing a document is as easy as selecting "print" from a menu.

Because printing is obviously still important in our world, it is only fitting to look at how a component can be made to print its contents. The example that I have chosen to demonstrate how this can be accomplished is an enhanced **TStringGrid** component that supports not only the printing, but also print preview. During the course of this chapter, you will become acquainted with the following topics:

- How to use the **TPrinter** class
- Adding forms to a component
- Supporting more than one unit in a component
- Publishing a class

The **TPrinter** Class

Tucked away in the **Printers** unit is the **TPrinter** class. It is the job of this class to wrap around the conventional Windows API calls needed for printing and provide a shiny Delphi-compatible interface. Its implementation has been so well done that you should rarely need to make any API level calls yourself.

Instead creating an instance of **TPrinter** yourself, you should use the built-in instance called **Printer**. To access this variable, it is only necessary to include **Printers** in your uses statement.

The most prominent feature of **TPrinter** is that, just like a form, it too has a **Canvas** property. This means that all the drawing commands you have already learned from your previous experiences with **Canvas** can be applied here.

In addition to **Canvas**, several other properties—and for that matter, methods—are unique to **TPrinter** that you will need to become familiar with before you take on the task of programming. For this reason, we'll now examine them in detail.

Properties

Aborted

```
property Aborted:Boolean;
```

The **Aborted** property is read-only. If set to true, it indicates that the print job has been aborted by the user. It is useful to frequently check this property during a lengthy drawing operation to provide a snappy response to the user.

Canvas

```
property Canvas:TCanvas;
```

The **Canvas** property, of type **TCanvas**, is read-only and is identical to the **Canvas** property supported by on-screen objects such as forms. One potential problem to be on the lookout for is that not all printers support graphics and therefore cannot properly process nontextual commands.

Capabilities

```
property Capabilities:TPrinterCapabilities;
```

The **Capabilities** property is read-only and provides the programmer with information on what features the current printer is able to support. It does this by returning a value of type **TPrinterCapabilities**, which is a set of type **TPrinterCapability**:

```
TPrinterCapability=(pcCopies,pcOrientation,pcCollation);
```

Currently, the values **pcCopies**, **pcOrientation**, and **pcCollation** are supported. If the **pcCopies** member is included in **Capabilities**, the printer is capable of printing out multiple copies of the entire document. If the **pcOrientation** member is present, the printer supports landscape (sideways) printing. Finally, if the **pcCollation** property is present, the printer is capable of reprinting an entire page without the need to send all the information to it.

Copies

```
property Copies:Integer;
```

The **Copies** property is read/write, and the value it contains specifies the number of copies of the current print job that are to be made.

Fonts

```
property Fonts:TStrings;
```

The read-only **Fonts** property is of type **TStrings** and contains a list of all the fonts on computer that the printer is capable of supporting. The number of fonts may be determined from the **Fonts.Count** member, and each individual name can be retrieved by accessing the **Fonts.Strings** array.

Handle

```
property Handle:HDC;
```

This read-only property returns a handle to the currently selected printer. During printing, this value is the same as the **Canvas.Handle** property. Its primary reason for existing is to support information functions at the API level such as **GetDeviceCaps** that need a valid device handle.

Orientation

```
property Orientation:TPrinterOrientation;
```

The read/write **Orientation** property is of type **TPrinterOrientation**:

```
TPrinterOrientation = (poPortrait, poLandscape);
```

When the **Orientation** property is set to **poPortrait**, pages will be printed normally—that is, the width is smaller that the height. If, however, **poLandscape** is selected, the pages will be printed sideways, with the width of the page being greater than its height.

PageHeight

```
property PageHeight:Integer;
```

The read-only property, **PageHeight**, returns the height of the page in pixels. Note that the value returned by this property depends on the orientation of the page. For example, if the **Orientation** property is set to **poLandscape**, **PageHeight** returns the *width* of the paper (its shortest dimension) rather than its height.

PageWidth

```
property PageWidth: Integer read GetPageWidth;
```

The read-only property, **PageWidth**, returns the width of the page in pixels. Like **PageHeight**, the value returned by this property depends on the orientation of the page. For example, if the **Orientation** property is set to **poLandscape**, **PageWidth** returns the *height* of the paper (its longest dimension) rather than its width.

PageNumber

```
property PageNumber:Integer;
```

This read-only property returns the current page number.

PrinterIndex

```
property PrinterIndex:Integer;
```

This read/write property specifies which printer, from the list of printers contained in the **Printers** property is currently selected. If this value is -1, the default printer will be used.

Printing

```
property Printing: Boolean;
```

This read-only property returns true if the printer is currently printing.

Printers

```
property Printers:TStrings;
```

This read-only property is of type **TStrings** and contains a list of the available printers. To select which printer is to be used for printing, pass the index of the printer you want to the **PrinterIndex** property.

Title

```
property Title:string;
```

This read/write property is used to specify the title of the document. It has a maximum length of 32 characters.

Methods

Abort

```
procedure Abort;
```

Calling the **Abort** method terminates the current print job.

BeginDoc

```
procedure BeginDoc;
```

BeginDoc is called to start the printing process and activate **Printer.Canvas**.

EndDoc

```
procedure EndDoc;
```

EndDoc is called to finish the printing process.

NewPage

```
procedure NewPage;
```

When all the necessary information has been written to the current page and it is time to proceed to the next one, call **NewPage**. This also has the effect of advancing the **PageNumber** property.

Using TPrinter

The steps involved in successfully using the **TPrinter** class are straightforward:

1. Set the **Title** property. This is not mandatory, but it gives your project a much more professional appearance.

2. Call **BeginDoc**.

3. Using the **Canvas** property, call the functions necessary to draw your page.

4. If you have more than one page to print, call **NewPage** and repeat step 3.

5. When all the pages have been drawn, call **EndDoc**.

As an example of the preceding steps, here is a short code sequence that will print 100 randomly placed circles on the first page and 100 randomly placed squares on the second page:

```
Printer.Title:='Shapes';

Printer.BeginDoc;

for i:=1 to 100 do
begin
  Radius:=Random(50)+20;
  X:=Random(Printer.PageWidth-2*Radius)+Radius;
  Y:=Random(Printer.PageHeight-2*Radius)+Radius;
  Printer.Canvas.Ellipse(X-Radius,Y-Radius,X+Radius,Y+Radius);
end;

Printer.NewPage;

for i:=1 to 100 do
begin
  Radius:=Random(50)+20;
  X:=Random(Printer.PageWidth-2*Radius)+Radius;
  Y:=Random(Printer.PageHeight-2*Radius+Radius);
  Printer.Canvas.Rectangle(X-Radius,Y-Radius,X+Radius,Y+Radius);
end;

Printer.EndDoc;
```

The above snippet specifies the position and size of the objects in pixels. Although this may be nice for a program that slaps some randomly placed shapes on a page, in real life, this is too limited because the size of a pixel on one printer can be vastly different from one on another. Therefore, you will often find yourself wanting to draw on the page in real-world units such as inches, thousandths of an inch or millimeters. Unless you're a seasoned API programmer, you probably won't have the foggiest notion of how to go about this because Delphi doesn't directly include support for this sort of thing.

The first thing that needs to be done is to determine the number of pixels per the unit of your choice by calling the **GetDeviceCaps** function:

```
function GetDeviceCaps(DC:HDC;Index:Integer):Integer;
```

This function accepts a handle to the device context, which for **TPrinter** is the **Handle** or **Canvas.Handle** property, and a constant value specifying what aspect of the device you want information on. In our case, the constants that we will need to use are **LOGPIXELSX** and **LOGPIXELSY**, which return values in pixels per *logical inch*. In case you're thrown off guard by the term *logical inch*, you should know that one logical inch is somewhat bigger than a real inch. The reason for this is that it was determined that small font sizes, about eight point or so, are practically illegible, especially with older video cards that have low resolution. Because many people wanted to use, and indeed see, such fonts on the screen, the logical inch was invented, which has the overall effect of making the text bigger. On a printer, little would be accomplished by having a logical inch differently sized from a regular inch, so the two values are the same.

Notice that there is one constant for each dimension, **LOGPIXELSX** for the horizontal, and **LOGPIXELSY** for the vertical. When used for a screen device, each constant returns a different value. For example, calling **GetDeviceCaps** with **LOGPIXELSX** returns a value different from what is returned when calling the function with **LOGPIXELSY**. This is because the number of pixels per unit in the vertical is different from the number of pixels in the horizontal. With a printer, this is generally not the case because a single pixel is usually a perfectly round dot, and passing **HORZSIZE** or **VERTSIZE** to **GetDeviceCaps** will return the same value. Even though you can usually rely on this relationship, I urge you not to do so. As mentioned earlier, the **TPrinter.Canvas** property is no different from any other **Canvas** property. This makes it ridiculously easy to implement a print preview and just use the different **LOGPIXELSX** and **LOGPIX-ELSY** values to achieve the *wysiwyg* (what you see is what you get) effect.

So how do you use **GetDeviceCaps**? First, you must call the function for each dimension:

```
XPixelsPerInch:=GetDeviceCaps(Printer.Handle,LOGPIXELSX);
YPixelsPerInch:=GetDeviceCaps(Printer.Handle,LOGPIXELSY);
```

With my printer, I get 360 for both values. Assigning the results to variables is much more efficient than calling the functions each time you need them. This allows you to draw objects of exact size and placement: a one-inch circle three inches to the right and one inch down, for example:

```
Printer.BeginDoc;

Printer.Canvas.MoveTo(0,0);
Printer.Canvas.LineTo(XPixelsPerInch*4-1,0);

Printer.Canvas.MoveTo(0,0);
Printer.Canvas.LineTo(0,YPixelsPerInch*4-1);

XRadius:=XPixelsPerInch div 2;
YRadius:=YPixelsPerInch div 2;

XCenter:=XPixelsPerInch*3-1;
YCenter:=YPixelsPerInch-1;

Printer.Canvas.Ellipse(XCenter-XRadius,YCenter-YRadius,
    XCenter+XRadius,YCenter+YRadius);

Printer.EndDoc;
```

Most printers cannot print on the edges of the paper, so the origin (0,0) is typically down and to the right a bit. In the preceding code, I indicate where this is by the intersection of two four-inch lines. It is from these lines that you may confirm that the circle is indented three inches and one inch down. Also notice that because the origin starts at 0,0 and not 1,1, all positions such as **XCenter** and **YCenter** have one taken away from them.

Working in inches is fine, but sometimes you will find yourself wanting to work in other units, millimeters, perhaps. To do this, you need to scale your millimeter dimensions to logical inch dimensions. As you undoubtedly know, one inch contains 25.4 millimeters, so one millimeter equates to 1/25.4th of the **XPixelsPerInch** and **YPixelsPerInch** values. It would be unwise to do this calculation immediately upon obtaining the **LOGPIXELSX** and **LOGPIXELSY** values:

```
XMillimetersPerInch:=MulDiv(GetDeviceCaps(Printer.Handle,LOGPIXELSX),
   10,254);
YMillimetersPerInch:=MulDiv(GetDeviceCaps(Printer.Handle,LOGPIXELSY),
   10,254);
```

Here I have used the **MulDiv** function to do the division by 25.4 because it avoids using floating point numbers, which it is always a good idea. With my computer, I get 14 for both values, meaning that there are about fourteen pixels per millimeter. In reality, there is a tad more that. Recall that my printer has a whopping 360 pixels per inch; dividing this by 25.4 yields a value of 14.17. This means that if I use the value 14 to do my drawing, I lose a pixel every six millimeters. Although it not seem worthy of a panic attack, it can produce really horrid results in the long run—lines may not meet up correctly, text may slightly touch other text, and so on.

A much better solution is to keep the **XPixelsPerInch** and **YPixelsPerInch** values and scale on-the-fly each time you need a new dimension. For example, suppose that you want to draw a 10 millimeter circle 94 millimeters to the right and 150 millimeters down. This could be done like so:

```
Printer.BeginDoc;

Printer.Canvas.MoveTo(0,0);
Printer.Canvas.LineTo(XPixelsPerInch*4-1,0);

Printer.Canvas.MoveTo(0,0);
Printer.Canvas.LineTo(0,YPixelsPerInch*4-1);
```

```
XRadius:=MulDiv(XPixelsPerInch,50,254);
YRadius:=MulDiv(YPixelsPerInch,50,254);

XCenter:=MulDiv(XPixelsPerInch,940,254)-1;
YCenter:= MulDiv(YPixelsPerInch,1500,254)-1;

Printer.Canvas.Ellipse(XCenter-XRadius,YCenter-YRadius,
  XCenter+XRadius,YCenter+YRadius);

Printer.EndDoc;
```

For reference purposes, I included the four-inch lines that intersect at the origin.

Programming **TPrintGrid**

The **TPrintGrid** component is fairly complex. In addition to merely printing the contents of its parent class, **TStringGrid**, it supports such niceties as different fonts for on-screen and printed text, print preview, and the capability to cancel the print job. It also provides a separate published class that allows the printer specific parameters to be set without having to wade through all the other properties in the Object Inspector.

Publishing the **TPrintSettings** Class

Normally, a component's published properties are simple types, sets, or records. Often, however, the need for something more elegant becomes apparent when the number of properties begins to grow too large to navigate efficiently, especially if the properties are intimately related. In an early incarnation, it was obvious to me that **TPrintGrid** was falling victim to this, and as a result, I opted to create **TPrintSettings**, a separate class to encapsulate the printer-specific properties and publish this single property in **TPrintGrid**.

Creating a published class is not terribly difficult. All you need to do is declare a class of type **TPersistent**. The fact that it is **TPersistent** is quite important—should the class be declared simply as **TObject**, none of the published properties will be saved with the form that is ultimately responsible for the class. As code, this looks like this:

```
type
  TMyPropertyClass=class(TPersistent)
  end;
```

Of course, a bare class such as this one doesn't do too much for us. To make it sing, it needs at least one property:

```
const
  MyIntegerDefault=17;

type
  TMyPropertyClass=class(TPersistant)
    FMyInteger:Integer;
  public
    constructor Create(AOwner:TComponent);
  published
    MyInteger:Integer read FMyInteger write FMyInteger
      default MyIntegerDefault;
  end;

constructor TMyProperty.Create(AOwner:TComponent);
begin
  inherited Create(AOwner);
  FMyInteger:=MyIntegerDefault;
end;
```

Here, we see that the property **MyInteger**, has been introduced, along with its underlying member **FMyInteger**. Also included is the **Create** constructor, which is needed to set the default value of **MyInteger**. You have no doubt noticed that adding properties to this class is no different from adding them to a component class. Because you already are armed with this knowledge from previous chapters, I'll leave it up to you to experiment with adding additional properties.

Creating the class to be published is just half of the work that needs to be done to properly integrate it into a component. Consider the following declaration:

```
type
  TMyComponent=class(TComponent)
  end;
```

This is just your run-of-the-mill do-nothing component. To add the TMyProperty class to it as a property, some modifications are needed:

```
type
  TMyComponent=class(TComponent)
    FMyProperty:TMyProperty;
  private
    procedure SetMyProperty(AMyProperty:TMyProperty);
  public
    constructor Create(AOwner:TComponent);
    destructor Destroy;
  published
    property MyProperty:TMyProperty read FMyProperty
      write SetMyProperty;
  end;

procedure TMyComponent.SetMyProperty(AMyProperty:TMyProperty);
begin
  FMyProperty.Assign(AMyProperty);
end;

constructor TMyComponent.Create(AOwner:TComponent);
begin
  inherited Create(AOwner);
  FMyProperty:=TMyProperty.Create(Self);
end;

destructor TMyComponent.Destroy;
begin
```

```
  FMyProperty.Destroy;
  inherited Destroy;
end;
```

What we see in the preceding code is that **FMyProperty**, the instance of **TMyProperty**, must first be created in the **Create** constructor. If this is not done, any accesses to **FMyProperty** will fail because it won't be initialized. We also see that the procedure **SetMyProperty** is called when the property is set. During the call, the **Assign** method of **FMyProperty** is called with the **AMyProperty** parameter as its parameter. It is important that this is done instead of a simple assignment; otherwise, **FMyProperty** will be pointing to the **AMyProperty** class instead of receiving a copy of it. This would quickly spell trouble. **FMyProperty** is freed when the component closes down by calling its **Destroy** destructor in **TMyComponent's Destroy** method. Technically, this is unnecessary because Delphi performs such cleanup automatically; but I prefer to clean up whatever mess I make myself rather than be left wondering whether it has truly been done for me.

The groundwork just laid down for you is key into understanding how **TPrinterSettings** works. There is a total of eleven published properties:

Table 8.1 TPainterSettings' Published Properties

Property	Description
TitleFont	The font used by the main title shown on page one
HeaderFont	The font used to print the title and page number on pages after the first one
TitleText	The text that is to be displayed as the title and page header of the printout
TextFont	The font used to print the contents of each cell
TextBackColor	The background color of each cell
FixedForeColor	The text color of fixed cells
FixedBackColor	The background color of the fixed cells
MarginTop	The top margin, in thousandths of an inch

Property	Description
MarginBottom	The bottom margin, in thousandths of an inch
MarginLeft	The left margin, in thousandths of an inch
MarginRight	The right margin, in thousandths of an inch

Other than these properties, there is nothing else particularly spectacular about the **TPrinterSettings** class that needs to be discussed in detail.

Printing the Grid

For all intents and purposes, **TPrintGrid** behaves exactly like the standard **TStringGrid** component. Our component, however, has a **Print** method. When this method is called, the first thing done is to determine whether there is anything to print, and if there is, initialize some variables. This is done by calling the method **PreparePrint**.

When PreparePrint begins to execute, it calls the method **GetGridExtents**:

```
function TPrintGrid.GetGridExtents(var PrintRect:TRect):Boolean;
```

This function figures out the first—the upper leftmost—cell that is not blank, and the last—the lower rightmost—cell that is not blank. It returns these values via the **var** declared **PrintRect** parameter. If all the cells are blank, meaning that there is nothing to print, **GetGridExtents** returns **False**. **PreparePrint** uses this information to pop up a dialog box stating the lack of data and then exits, returning **False** itself.

Should **GetGridExtents**, however, return **True**, the **ScreenPixelsPerInch** and **PrinterPixelsPerInch** variables, of type **TPoint** are filled. The information they contain is retrieved from the **GetScreenPixelsPerInch** and the **GetPrinterPixelsPerInch** functions, respectively, both of which call **GetDeviceCaps** much like we saw in the "Using **TPrinter**" section. For the curious, a handle to the screen is obtained by calling **GetDC** and passing it a value of 0, indicating the desktop. After the call to **GetDeviceCaps**, the handle is freed by calling **ReleaseDC**.

Next, the **TPrinterSettings** values **MarginTop**, **MarginBottom**, **MarginLeft**, and **MarginRight** are scaled to printer pixels and assigned to the **MarginRect** structure of type **TRect**. Also, the thickness to print grid lines is calculated by converting the number of screen pixels in the line's width to printer pixels. This sort of operation might seem tricky at first thought, but it's really quite simple. If we divide the line's screen width by the number of pixels per logical inch, **ScreenPixelsPerInch.X**, we are rewarded with the line's width in inches. To convert inches to printer pixels, we simply multiply the result by **PrinterPixelsPerInch.X**. This sequence is easily accomplished with the **MulDiv** function:

```
LineThickness.X:=MulDiv(GridLineWidth,PrinterPixelsPerInch.X,
  ScreenPixelsPerInch.X);
```

Finally, to wrap up the call to **PreparePrint**, some housekeeping is done by initializing variables. The class-wide variable **CurrentCol** is assigned the value of **PrintRect.Left**, which as you may recall, contains the first leftmost column that is not empty. Similarly, **CurrentRow** is assigned the value of **PrintRect.Top**, the topmost row that is not empty. The last variable to be set is **CurrentPage**, which is given a value of zero. If you're on the ball, you may have a question mark floating above your head as you attempt to puzzle out why a **CurrentPage** variable is needed because **TPrinter** already has a **PageNumber** property. The reason is that our goal is not only to support printing, but print preview as well. During a print preview, **TPrinter** is useless to us because it is limited to printing on paper, and not the screen.

When **PreparePrint** returns to the **Print** method, steps are taken to display a "printing" dialog box. The dialog box, a class derived from **TForm** called **TPrintingDialog**, as shown in Figure 8.1, resides in a unit separate from the main one in which the **TPrintGrid** class is declared in.

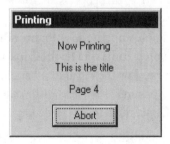

Figure 8.1 The **TPrintingDialog** dialog box.

The sequence used for displaying the dialog box goes like this:

```
Application.CreateForm(TPrintingDialog,PrintingDialog);
PrintingDialog.TitleLabel.Caption:=FPrintSettings.FTitleText;
WindowList:=DisableTaskWindows(PrintingDialog.Handle);
PrintingDialog.Show;
```

The first line actually creates the dialog box. The second line sets the text of the label **TitleLabel** to be the same as the title chosen for the document, **FPrintSettings.FTitleText**. The third line is probably unlike anything you have seen so far. The **DisableTaskWindows** function has the effect of disabling every window in the current application *except* for the one whose handle is passed to it. This creates what as known as a *modal* window. This step is included to prevent the user from manipulating the data currently being printed. This is needed because if the user were to change the data, it would be quite likely that the printout would reflect some of this change, resulting in a meaningless output. For extremely large print jobs, this may become annoying because the user is unable to do anything with the application. The solution that would fix this problem would be to quickly make a copy of the data somewhere in memory and use it to do the printing. I will leave this task to you for those days when you are feeling particularly energetic.

You may be wondering why the **ShowModal** method can't be used instead of going through the seemingly elaborate process of calling **DisableTaskWindows**. If we were to call **ShowModal** instead, we would find that the flow of execution of **PreparePrint** would grind to a halt while waiting for the user to close the dialog box. Obviously, this doesn't do us any good because while we are waiting for the dialog box to close, we can't be doing anything else. **DisableTaskWindows** rescues us by allowing the window to be modal without hindering the flow of execution.

The return value of **DisableTaskWindows** is assigned to a variable, **WindowList**, which is of type **Pointer**. This value will be needed later to reenable all the disabled windows by calling **EnableTaskWindows**. At this point, the dialog box is fully created, but it is somewhat useless because it is invisible. The final line of the preceding code cures this problem by calling the method **ShowWindow**.

After the **TPrintingDialog** dialog box has been displayed, it is time to start thinking about getting down to the job of doing some printing.

Before we can fully jump in, a bit of preliminary work is needed. First, the print job's title is set by assigning the document's title to the **Printer.Title** property. Next, the familiar **Printer.BeginDoc** method is called to get the ball in motion. Finally, the class wide variable **PrintCanvas** is assigned the value of **Printer.Canvas**. **PrintCanvas** provides the means to make print preview possible. By not hard coding **Printer.Canvas** everywhere, the canvas used during printing becomes generic—either a screen canvas or a printer canvas will work happily.

At this point, the **Print** method enters a loop, which has one iteration for each page. Inside the loop, the **PrintingDialog.PageLabel** property is set to indicate the page number. This keeps the user informed by displaying what page is currently being printed. Now we come to the heart of **TPrintGrid**. For each page, the **PrintPage** method is called. It is this method that draws each and every page. A detailed description of how this code works, is way beyond the scope of this chapter; however, I'll give you a run-down on the essentials so that you can get the gist of what is happening.

Depending on whether the current page is the first one, either a title or a header will be printed. Regardless of which, the **FPrintSettings.FTitleText** member is used as the text. For a title, the **FPrintSettings.FTitleFont** is used, and the text is centered at the top of the page. For a header, the **FPrintSettings.FHeaderFont** member dictates which font to use. Unlike the title, the header text is left-justified, and the page number is printed using the same font, but this time the text is right-justified.

After the title or header has been printed, **PrintPage** uses the values **CurrentCol** and **CurrentRow** as an index for the cell that is to be printed first on the page. For example, if **CurrentCol** is 17 and **CurrentRow** is 32, the starting cell on the page will be 17,32. Each cell is printed from left to right, top to bottom until either there is no more data to print, the user aborts the print job, or a cell has been reached that cannot be fully printed on the current page. For the first case, **PrintPage** exits normally with the **CurrentRow** value set to one more than the maximum printable row, which signals **Print** that there is nothing more to print. The second case, when the user aborts the job by pressing **TPrintingDialog**'s "abort" button, is detected by periodically calling **TPrinterDialog**'s **HasBeenAborted** method. If it returns **True**, the **PrintPage** function is immediately aborted, and control returns to **Print**, which also checks the state of **HasBeenAborted** and deals with it accordingly.

The final situation, where the current cell can't be printed on the page without overlap, comes in two varieties. The first, and the simplest, occurs when the cell can't be printed because it is at the bottom of the page. In this case, **PrintPage** exits with **CurrentRow** set to the row index of the cell that can't be printed. The other possible overlap happens when the current cell extends too far to the right. Should this take place, **PrintPage** exits with **CurrentCol** equal to column index of the cell that was unable to print. The next time **PrintPage** is called, the column that failed will be the first to be printed.

Previewing the Grid

One of the most requested features of any program that prints is a print preview function. This allows the user to see *exactly* how the printed page will appear without investing ink and paper. This is considerably more convenient than going through the print-edit-print cycle, which tends to eat up a surprisingly large amount of paper.

The foundation for making **TPrintGrid** preview compatible was laid down by not restricting the canvas used for drawing to **TPrinter.Canvas**. This allows us to pop up a form, pass its handle to **PrintHandle**, and go about our business of previewing. **TPrintGrid** sports the method **Preview** that gets things underway. The big difference from the **Print** method and **Preview** is that while **Print** was responsible for printing each page, **Preview** creates a modal **TPreviewDialog** form (see Figure 8.2) that takes on this responsibility.

The greater portion of the **TPreviewDialog** form is occupied by **TImage** component called **Page**. When **TPreviewDialog**'s form first becomes visible, the **PreparePreview** method is called to size **Page** depending on the size of the form and the size of the printer's paper. The result is a perfectly scaled rendition of a sheet of paper that is to be previewed. After **PreparePreview** has finished, the **PreviewNext** method is called, which, after determining the page that is next—in this case, the next page is one—calls **ShowPage** to do the on-screen magic.

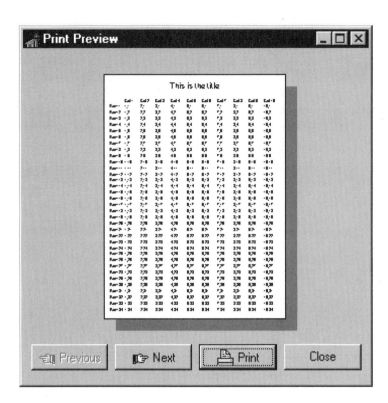

Figure 8.2 The **TPreviewDialog** dialog box.

The magic in question has to do with scaling the output of the **TPrintGrid.PrintPage** method. If left untouched, we would be greeted by a grossly oversized display that definitely would not fit in the **Page** component that we just scaled. Luckily, Windows itself provides the API functions that we need to accomplish this task. The first function that needs to be called is **SetMapMode**:

```
function SetMapMode(DC:HDC;fnMapMode:Integer):Integer;
```

This function accepts a handle to the device context of the window we are drawing on and one of the following constants

Table 8.2 SetMapMode Constants

Constant	Description
MM_ANISOTROPIC	This mode allows one logical unit (see below) to be mapped to any arbitrary unit.
MM_HIENGLISH	This mode equates one logical unit to one one-thousandth of an inch.
MM_HIMETRIC	This mode equates one logcial unit to one one-hundredth of a millimeter.
MM_ISOTROPIC	This mode equates one logical unit to any arbitrary unit, much like **MM_ANISOTROPIC** except the X and Y scales are the same. That is, one logical unit in the horizontal direction exactly equals one logical unit in the vertical direction.
MM_LOENGLISH	This mode equates one logical unit to one one-hundredth of an inch.
MM_LOMETRIC	This mode equates one logical unit to one one-tenth of a millimeter.
MM_TEXT	This mode maps one logical unit to one pixel. This is the default mode.
MM_TWIPS	This mode maps one logical inch to 1/1,440th of an inch, or one 20th of a font point size.

In the preceding descriptions, the term *logical unit* refers to the values passed to various graphical functions. For example, the **Rectangle** function accepts four values that determine the bounds of the drawn rectangle. These values are specified in logical units because depending on the mode chosen with

SetMapMode, the actual translation to pixels will vary. The wide variety of mapping modes makes it incredibly easy to do automatic scaling.

Of the preceding modes, we are primarily interested in **MM_ANISOTROPIC** because it allows us to do completely arbitrary scaling along both axes. To set the actual scale, two functions, **SetViewportExtEx** and **SetWindowExtEx** are used:

```
function SetViewportExtEx(DC:HDC;XExt,YExt:Integer;Size:PSize):BOOL;
function SetWindowExtEx(DC:HDC;XExt,YExt:Integer;Size:PSize):BOOL;
```

The relationship between these two functions is this:

```
P=(L*V)/W
```

Here, **P** is the number of pixels; **L** is the number of logical units; **V** is the value passed to **SetViewPortExtEx**; and **W** is the value passed to **SetWindowExtEx**. This relationship holds true regardless of which axis you are working with. For example, if **V** is set to 1 and **W** is set to 10, we will effectively get a 1:10 reduction of whatever we draw. To scale the output of the **TPrintGrid.PrintPage** method, these functions are use like this:

```
SetWindowExtEx(Page.Canvas.Handle,Printer.PageWidth,
   Printer.PageHeight,nil);
SetViewportExtEx(Page.Canvas.Handle,Page.Width,Page.Height,nil);
```

Page.Canvas.Handle identifies the device context of the window that we want to scale, which in this case belongs to our **Page** component. **SetWindowExtEx** is called with the size of the physical page because **TPrintGrid.PrintPage** outputs its graphical coordinates thinking that they are intended for a real page. But this is not the situation—our output is the **Page** component, so its size is passed to the **SetViewportExtEx** function. Now, almost everything that **TPrintGrid.PrintPage** outputs for the real page is properly scaled for the virtual page.

I said "almost" for a good reason. Sadly, the one item that is not scaled automatically is text that uses a device font. Interestingly, the default font that Delphi uses for everything, MS Sans Serif, is just such a font. To circumvent this little problem, the **SetFont** procedure, which is nested in **TPrintGrid.PrintPage**, searches to see if the same font exists in the scaled-down size that we need. If so, it is used. If not, the TrueType, and thus scalable, font Arial is chosen. Even though Arial may be completely different from the desired font, there is very little degradation in quality because of the small sizes that we are dealing with.

Another gottcha that needs to be taken care of has to do with the fact that when you are dealing with a screen canvas rather than a printer canvas, the **Size** property of the font is geared for the screen rather than the printer. As you can imagine, a 72-point font on the screen uses a lot less pixels than does its printer equivalent; so in the end, text just doesn't scale properly. To get around this, the **TFont's PixelsPerInch** property must be set to the number of pixels per inch on the printer, not the screen:

```
FontSize:=Canvas.Font.Size;
Canvas.Font.PixelsPerInch:=PrinterPixelsPerInch.Y;
Canvas.Font.Size:=FontSize;
```

The reason that the font's size must be saved and then restored is that changing the **PixelsPerInch** property only updates a variable within the **TFont** class and doesn't do anything meaningful to the **Height** property, which is used extensively in **TPrintGrid.PrintPage** for determining how tall, in pixels, text is. By first saving **Canvas.Font.Size** in the variable **FontSize** and then restoring it after **PixelsPerInch** is modified, a recalculation of **Height** is forced.

Presenting... The Code

With all the ugly details now taken care of, here is the code for the three units that comprise the **TPrintGrid** component, **PRINTGRID.PAS**, **PRINTINGDLG.PAS**, and **PREVDLG.PAS**. The source code for these units can be found in the **\DC\CHAP09** directory. The palette bitmap for the component, shown in Figure 8.3 can be found in the same directory and is called **PRINTGRID.DCR**.

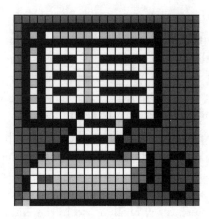

Figure 8.3 Palette bitmap for **TPrintGrid**.

Listing 8.1 PRINTGRID.PAS

```
unit printgrid;

interface

uses
  Windows, Messages, SysUtils, Classes, Graphics, Controls, Forms,
  Dialogs,Grids,Printers,ExtCtrls,Buttons,StdCtrls,PrevDlg,
  PrintingDlg;

type
  TMargin=0..3000;
  TPrintSettings=class(TPersistent)
    FTitleFont:TFont;
    FTitleText:String;
    FHeaderFont:TFont;
    FTextFont:TFont;
    FTextBackColor:TColor;
    FFixedForeColor:TColor;
    FFixedBackColor:TColor;
    FMarginTop:TMargin;
```

```
  FMarginBottom:TMargin;
  FMarginLeft:TMargin;
  FMarginRight:TMargin;
private
  procedure SetTitleFont(ATitleFont:TFont);
  procedure SetHeaderFont(AHeaderFont:TFont);
  procedure SetTextFont(ATextFont:TFont);
public
  constructor Create(AOwner:TComponent);
  destructor Destroy;override;
published
  property TitleFont:TFont read FTitleFont write SetTitleFont;
  property HeaderFont:TFont read FHeaderFont write SetHeaderFont;
  property TitleText:String read FTitleText write FTitleText;
  property TextFont:TFont read FTextFont write SetTextFont;
  property TextBackColor:TColor read FTextBackColor
    write FTextBackColor default clWhite;
  property FixedForeColor:TColor read FFixedForeColor
    write FFixedForeColor default clBlack;
  property FixedBackColor:TColor read FFixedBackColor
    write FFixedBackColor default clWhite;
  property MarginTop:TMargin read FMarginTop write FMarginTop
    default 250;
  property MarginBottom:TMargin read FMarginBottom
    write FMarginBottom default 250;
  property MarginLeft:TMargin read FMarginLeft
    write FMarginLeft default 250;
  property MarginRight:TMargin read FMarginRight
    write FMarginRight default 250;
end;

TPrintGrid = class(TStringGrid)
private
  LineThickness:TPoint;
  ScreenPage:TPoint;
  Margins:TRect;
```

```pascal
    FPrintSettings:TPrintSettings;
    PreviewDialog:TPreviewDialog;
    PrintingDialog:TPrintingDialog;
    function GetGridExtents(var PrintRect:TRect):Boolean;
    procedure SetPrintSettings(APrintSettings:TPrintSettings);
    function PreparePrint:Boolean;
  public
    CurrentCol,CurrentRow:LongInt;
    PrintRect:TRect;
    ScreenPixelsPerInch:TPoint;
    PrinterPixelsPerInch:TPoint;
    CurrentPage:Word;
    PrintCanvas:TCanvas;
    procedure PrintPage;
    procedure Print;
    procedure Preview;
    constructor Create(AOwner:TComponent);override;
    destructor Destroy;override;
  published
    property PrintSettings:TPrintSettings read FPrintSettings
      write SetPrintSettings;
  end;

procedure Register;

implementation

procedure Register;
begin
  RegisterComponents('Additional', [TPrintGrid]);
end;

procedure TPrintSettings.SetTitleFont(ATitleFont:TFont);
begin
  FTitleFont.Assign(ATitleFont);
end;
```

```
procedure TPrintSettings.SetHeaderFont(AHeaderFont:TFont);
begin
  FHeaderFont.Assign(AHeaderFont);
end;

procedure TPrintSettings.SetTextFont(ATextFont:TFont);
begin
  FTextFont.Assign(ATextFont);
end;

constructor TPrintSettings.Create(AOwner:TComponent);
begin
  inherited Create;

  FMarginLeft:=250;
  FMarginTop:=250;
  FMarginRight:=250;
  FMarginBottom:=250;

  FTitleText:='Title';

  FTitleFont:=TFont.Create;
  FTitleFont.Name:='Arial';
  FTitleFont.Size:=24;
  FTitleFont.Color:=clBlack;

  FHeaderFont:=TFont.Create;
  FHeaderFont.Name:='Arial';
  FHeaderFont.Size:=12;
  FHeaderFont.Color:=clBlack;

  FTextFont:=TFont.Create;
  FTextFont.Name:='Arial';
  FTextFont.Size:=8;
  FTextFont.Color:=clBlack;

  FTextBackColor:=clWhite;
```

```
    FFixedForeColor:=clBlack;
    FFixedBackColor:=clWhite;
end;

destructor TPrintSettings.Destroy;
begin
  FTitleFont.Free;
  FTextFont.Free;
  inherited Destroy;
end;

function TPrintGrid.GetGridExtents(var PrintRect:TRect):Boolean;
var
  ColIndex,RowIndex:Integer;
begin
  with PrintRect do
  begin
    Left:=ColCount;
    Top:=RowCount;
    Right:=0;
    Bottom:=0;
    for ColIndex:=FixedCols to ColCount-1 do
    begin
      for RowIndex:=FixedRows to RowCount-1 do
      begin
        if Trim(Cells[ColIndex,RowIndex])<>'' then
        begin
          if ColIndex<Left then Left:=ColIndex;
          if RowIndex<Top then Top:=RowIndex;
          Right:=ColIndex;
          Bottom:=RowIndex;
        end;
      end;
    end;
    GetGridExtents:=Left<>ColCount;
  end;
```

```
end;

procedure TPrintGrid.PrintPage;
var
  DoneFixedCols,DoneFixedRows:Boolean;
  ColIndex,RowIndex:LongInt;
  CellRect:TRect;
  XPos,YPos:Integer;
  TextRect:TRect;
  StartCol,StartRow:LongInt;

function EnumFontsProc(var LogFont:TLogFont;
  var TextMetric:TTextMetric; FontType:Integer;
  PrintGrid:TPrintGrid):Integer;stdcall;
var
  PointSize:TPoint;
begin
  if FontType and TRUETYPE_FONTTYPE<>0 then
    EnumFontsProc:=0
  else
  begin
    PointSize.Y:=MulDiv(LogFont.lfHeight,72,
      PrintGrid.ScreenPixelsPerInch.Y);
    PointSize.X:=MulDiv(PrintGrid.PrintCanvas.Font.Size,
      PrintGrid.ScreenPage.Y,Printer.PageHeight);
    if PointSize.Y=MulDiv(PrintGrid.PrintCanvas.Font.Size,
      PrintGrid.ScreenPage.Y,Printer.PageHeight) then
      EnumFontsProc:=0
    else
      EnumFontsProc:=1;
  end;
end;

procedure SetFont(Font:TFont);
var
  Match:Boolean;
```

```
    Name:String;
    DC:hDC;
    BadScale:Boolean;
    FontSize:Integer;
begin
  PrintCanvas.Font:=Font;
  FontSize:=PrintCanvas.Font.Size;
  PrintCanvas.Font.PixelsPerInch:=PrinterPixelsPerInch.Y;
  PrintCanvas.Font.Size:=FontSize;
  Name:=PrintCanvas.Font.Name;
  DC:=GetDC(0);
  if EnumFontFamilies(DC,PChar(Name),@EnumFontsProc,
    LongInt(Self)) then
      PrintCanvas.Font.Name:='Arial';
  ReleaseDC(0,DC);
end;

procedure PrintTitle;
var
  TitleRect:TRect;
begin
  SetFont(FPrintSettings.TitleFont);
  PrintCanvas.Brush.Color:=clWhite;
  TitleRect.Top:=YPos;
  TitleRect.Bottom:=YPos+PrintCanvas.TextHeight(
    FPrintSettings.TitleText);
  TitleRect.Left:=Margins.Left;
  TitleRect.Right:=Printer.PageWidth-Margins.Right;
  PrintCanvas.Font.Color:=FPrintSettings.TitleFont.Color;
  DrawText(PrintCanvas.Handle,PChar(FPrintSettings.TitleText),
    Length(FPrintSettings.TitleText),TitleRect,DT_CENTER);
  YPos:=TitleRect.Bottom;
end;

procedure PrintHeader;
var
```

```
    HeaderRect:TRect;
    PageString:String;
begin
    SetFont(FPrintSettings.HeaderFont);
    PrintCanvas.Brush.Color:=clWhite;
    HeaderRect.Top:=YPos;
    HeaderRect.Bottom:=YPos+PrintCanvas.TextHeight(
      FPrintSettings.TitleText);
    HeaderRect.Left:=Margins.Left;
    HeaderRect.Right:=Printer.PageWidth-Margins.Right;
    DrawText(PrintCanvas.Handle,PChar(FPrintSettings.TitleText),
      Length(FPrintSettings.TitleText),HeaderRect,DT_LEFT);
    PageString:='Page '+IntToStr(CurrentPage);
    DrawText(PrintCanvas.Handle,PChar(PageString),Length(PageString),
      HeaderRect,DT_RIGHT);
    YPos:=HeaderRect.Bottom;
end;

begin
    StartCol:=CurrentCol;
    StartRow:=CurrentRow;

    YPos:=Margins.Top;

    if CurrentPage=1 then
      PrintTitle
    else
      PrintHeader;

    inc(YPos,PrinterPixelsPerInch.Y div 4);

    CellRect.Top:=YPos;
    CellRect.Bottom:=YPos;
    SetFont(Font);

    DoneFixedRows:=False;
    RowIndex:=0;
```

```
repeat
  if not DoneFixedRows and (RowIndex+1>FixedRows) then
  begin
    RowIndex:=StartRow;
    DoneFixedRows:=True;
  end;

  inc(CellRect.Bottom,MulDiv(RowHeights[RowIndex],
    PrinterPixelsPerInch.Y,ScreenPixelsPerInch.Y));
  inc(CellRect.Bottom,LineThickness.Y*2);

  if CellRect.Bottom>Printer.PageHeight-Margins.Bottom then
  begin
    if CurrentCol=StartCol then
    begin
      CurrentRow:=RowIndex;
      CurrentCol:=PrintRect.Left;
    end;
    exit;
  end;

  DoneFixedCols:=False;
  CellRect.Left:=Margins.Left;
  CellRect.Right:=Margins.Left;
  ColIndex:=0;

  repeat
    if not DoneFixedCols and (ColIndex+1>FixedCols) then
    begin
      ColIndex:=StartCol;
      DoneFixedCols:=True;
    end;

    inc(CellRect.Right,MulDiv(ColWidths[ColIndex],
      PrinterPixelsPerInch.X,ScreenPixelsPerInch.X));

    inc(CellRect.Right,LineThickness.X*2);
```

```
if CellRect.Right>Printer.PageWidth-Margins.Right then
begin
  CurrentCol:=ColIndex;
  break;
end;

if (ColIndex=0) or (RowIndex=0) then
begin
  PrintCanvas.Brush.Color:=FPrintSettings.FixedBackColor;
  PrintCanvas.Font.Color:=FPrintSettings.FixedForeColor;
end
else
begin
  PrintCanvas.Brush.Color:=FPrintSettings.TextBackColor;
  PrintCanvas.Font.Color:=FPrintSettings.TextFont.Color;
end;
TextRect.Left:=CellRect.Left+LineThickness.X;
TextRect.Right:=CellRect.Right-LineThickness.X;
TextRect.Top:=CellRect.Top+LineThickness.Y;
TextRect.Bottom:=CellRect.Bottom-LineThickness.Y;
PrintCanvas.TextRect(TextRect,TextRect.Left,TextRect.Top+
  ((TextRect.Bottom-TextRect.Top)+
  PrintCanvas.Font.Height) div 2,Cells[ColIndex,RowIndex]);

PrintCanvas.Pen.Width:=0;
PrintCanvas.Pen.Style:=psClear;
PrintCanvas.Brush.Style:=bsSolid;
PrintCanvas.Brush.Color:=clBlack;

PrintCanvas.Rectangle(CellRect.Left,CellRect.Top,
  CellRect.Right,CellRect.Top+LineThickness.Y);
PrintCanvas.Rectangle(CellRect.Left,CellRect.Top,
  CellRect.Left+LineThickness.X,CellRect.Bottom);
PrintCanvas.Rectangle(CellRect.Right-LineThickness.X,
  CellRect.Top,CellRect.Right,CellRect.Bottom);
PrintCanvas.Rectangle(CellRect.Left,CellRect.Bottom-
```

```
            LineThickness.Y,CellRect.Right,CellRect.Bottom);

        dec(CellRect.Right,LineThickness.X);
        CellRect.Left:=CellRect.Right;

        inc(ColIndex);
      until ColIndex>PrintRect.Right;

      if Printer.Printing then
      begin
        Application.ProcessMessages;
        if PrintingDialog.HasBeenAborted then exit;
      end;

      dec(CellRect.Bottom,LineThickness.Y);
      CellRect.Top:=CellRect.Bottom;

      inc(RowIndex);
    until RowIndex>PrintRect.Bottom;
    if CurrentCol=StartCol then
    begin
      CurrentRow:=RowIndex;
      CurrentCol:=PrintRect.Left;
    end;
  end;

procedure TPrintGrid.Print;
var
  WindowList:Pointer;
begin
  if not PreparePrint then exit;
  Parent.Cursor:=crHourGlass;
  Application.CreateForm(TPrintingDialog,PrintingDialog);
  PrintingDialog.TitleLabel.Caption:=FPrintSettings.FTitleText;
  WindowList:=DisableTaskWindows(PrintingDialog.Handle);
  PrintingDialog.Show;
  Printer.Title:=FPrintSettings.FTitleText;
```

```
    Printer.BeginDoc;
    PrintCanvas:=Printer.Canvas;
    repeat
      CurrentPage:=Printer.PageNumber;
      PrintingDialog.PageLabel.Caption:='Page '+IntToStr(CurrentPage);
      PrintPage;
      if (CurrentRow<=PrintRect.Bottom) or
        (CurrentCol<>PrintRect.Left) then
        Printer.NewPage
      else
      begin
        Break;
      end;
    until PrintingDialog.HasBeenAborted;

    if PrintingDialog.HasBeenAborted then
      Printer.Abort
    else
      Printer.EndDoc;

    EnableTaskWindows(WindowList);
    PrintingDialog.Close;
    Parent.Cursor:=crDefault;
  end;

procedure TPrintGrid.Preview;
begin
  if not PreparePrint then exit;
  Application.CreateForm(TPreviewDialog, PreviewDialog);
  ScreenPage.X:=PreviewDialog.Page.Width;
  ScreenPage.Y:=PreviewDialog.Page.Height;
  PreviewDialog.PrintGrid:=Self;
  PreviewDialog.ShowModal;
end;

function TPrintGrid.PreparePrint:Boolean;
```

```
function GetScreenPixelsPerInch:TPoint;
var
  DC:hDC;
begin
  DC:=GetDC(0);
  GetScreenPixelsPerInch.X:=GetDeviceCaps(DC,LOGPIXELSX);
  GetScreenPixelsPerInch.Y:=GetDeviceCaps(DC,LOGPIXELSY);
  ReleaseDC(0,DC);
end;

function GetPrinterPixelsPerInch:TPoint;
begin
  GetPrinterPixelsPerInch.X:=GetDeviceCaps(Printer.Handle,
    LOGPIXELSX);
  GetPrinterPixelsPerInch.Y:=GetDeviceCaps(Printer.Handle,
    LOGPIXELSY);
end;

begin
  if not GetGridExtents(PrintRect) then
  begin
    MessageDlg('Nothing to print!',mtError,[mbOK],0);
    PreparePrint:=False;
    exit;
  end;
  ScreenPixelsPerInch:=GetScreenPixelsPerInch;
  PrinterPixelsPerInch:=GetPrinterPixelsPerInch;

  Margins.Top:=MulDiv(FPrintSettings.MarginTop,
    PrinterPixelsPerInch.Y,1000);
  Margins.Bottom:=MulDiv(FPrintSettings.MarginBottom,
    PrinterPixelsPerInch.Y,1000);
  Margins.Left:=MulDiv(FPrintSettings.MarginLeft,
    PrinterPixelsPerInch.X,1000);
  Margins.Right:=MulDiv(FPrintSettings.MarginRight,
    PrinterPixelsPerInch.X,1000);

  LineThickness.X:=MulDiv(GridLineWidth,PrinterPixelsPerInch.X,
    ScreenPixelsPerInch.X);
```

```
  LineThickness.Y:=MulDiv(GridLineWidth,PrinterPixelsPerInch.Y,
    ScreenPixelsPerInch.Y);

  CurrentCol:=PrintRect.Left;
  CurrentRow:=PrintRect.Top;
  CurrentPage:=0;
  PreparePrint:=True;
end;

procedure TPrintGrid.SetPrintSettings(
  APrintSettings:TPrintSettings);
begin
  FPrintSettings.Assign(APrintSettings);
end;

constructor TPrintGrid.Create(AOwner:TComponent);
begin
  inherited Create(AOwner);
  FPrintSettings:=TPrintSettings.Create(Self);
end;

destructor TPrintGrid.Destroy;
begin
  FPrintSettings.Destroy;
  inherited Destroy;
end;

end.
```

Listing 9.2 PRINTINGDLG.PAS

```
unit PrintingDlg;

interface

uses
  Windows, Messages, SysUtils, Classes, Graphics, Controls, Forms,
  Dialogs,StdCtrls,Printers;
```

```
type
  TPrintingDialog = class(TForm)
    Label1: TLabel;
    TitleLabel: TLabel;
    PageLabel: TLabel;
    Button1: TButton;
    procedure Button1Click(Sender: TObject);
    procedure FormCreate(Sender: TObject);
  private
    IsAborted:Boolean;
  public
    function HasBeenAborted:Boolean;
  end;

implementation

{$R *.DFM}

procedure TPrintingDialog.Button1Click(Sender: TObject);
begin
  IsAborted:=True;
end;

procedure TPrintingDialog.FormCreate(Sender: TObject);
begin
  IsAborted:=False;
end;

function TPrintingDialog.HasBeenAborted:Boolean;
begin
  HasBeenAborted:=IsAborted;
end;

end.
```

Listing 3 PREVDLG.PAS

```pascal
unit PrevDlg;

interface

uses
  Windows, Messages, SysUtils, Classes, Graphics, Controls, Forms,
  Dialogs,StdCtrls, Buttons, ExtCtrls,Printers;

type
  PPreviewNode=^TPreviewNode;
  TPreviewNode=record
    Next:PPreviewNode;
    Previous:PPreviewNode;
    Col:LongInt;
    Row:LongInt;
  end;

  TPreviewDialog = class(TForm)
    Page: TImage;
    NextButton: TBitBtn;
    PreviousButton: TBitBtn;
    PrintButton: TBitBtn;
    CloseButton: TButton;
    ShadowRight:TShape;
    ShadowBottom:TShape;
    procedure FormCreate(Sender: TObject);
    procedure FormShow(Sender: TObject);
    procedure FormSize(Sender: TObject);
    procedure PreviousButtonClick(Sender: TObject);
    procedure NextButtonClick(Sender: TObject);
    procedure PrintButtonClick(Sender: TObject);
    procedure FormClose(Sender: TObject; var Action: TCloseAction);
  private
```

```
      FirstPreviewNode:PPreviewNode;
      CurrentPreviewNode:PPreviewNode;
      OKToSizePage:Boolean;
      Sizing:Boolean;
      procedure PreparePreview;
      procedure ShowPage;
      procedure PreviewPrevious;
      procedure PreviewNext;
      procedure WMSysCommand(var Msg:TWMSysCommand);
        message WM_SYSCOMMAND;
      procedure WMEnterSizeMove(var Msg:TMsg);
        message WM_ENTERSIZEMOVE;
      procedure WMExitSizeMove(var Msg:TMsg);message WM_EXITSIZEMOVE;
      procedure WMGetMinMaxInfo(var Msg:TWMGetMinMaxInfo);
        message WM_GETMINMAXINFO;
    public
      PrintGrid:TObject;
    end;

implementation
uses PrintGrid;

{$R *.DFM}

procedure TPreviewDialog.FormCreate(Sender: TObject);
begin
  FirstPreviewNode:=nil;
  CurrentPreviewNode:=nil;
  OKToSizePage:=False;
  Sizing:=False;
  PrintGrid:=nil;
end;

procedure TPreviewDialog.FormShow(Sender: TObject);
begin
  PreparePreview;
```

```
    PreviewNext;
end;

procedure TPreviewDialog.FormSize(Sender: TObject);
begin
  if OKToSizePage then
  begin
    Page.Stretch:=True;
    PreparePreview;
    Sizing:=True;
  end;
end;

procedure TPreviewDialog.ShowPage;
var
  PG:TPrintGrid;
begin
  PG:=TPrintGrid(PrintGrid);
  Screen.Cursor:=crHourGlass;

  PG.CurrentCol:=CurrentPreviewNode^.Col;
  PG.CurrentRow:=CurrentPreviewNode^.Row;

  PG.PrintCanvas:=Page.Canvas;
  Page.Canvas.Brush.Color:=clWhite;
  Page.Canvas.Rectangle(0,0,Page.Width,Page.Height);
  SetMapMode(Page.Canvas.Handle,MM_ANISOTROPIC);
  SetWindowExtEx(Page.Canvas.Handle,Printer.PageWidth,
    Printer.PageHeight,nil);
  SetViewPortExtEx(Page.Canvas.Handle,Page.Width,Page.Height,nil);
  PG.PrintPage;
  PreviousButton.Enabled:=PG.CurrentPage>1;
  NextButton.Enabled:=(PG.CurrentRow<=PG.PrintRect.Bottom) or
    (PG.CurrentCol<>PG.PrintRect.Left);
  Screen.Cursor:=crDefault;
end;
```

```
procedure TPreviewDialog.PreviewPrevious;
var
  PG:TPrintGrid;
begin
  PG:=TPrintGrid(PrintGrid);
  CurrentPreviewNode:=CurrentPreviewNode^.Previous;
  PG.CurrentCol:=CurrentPreviewNode^.Col;
  PG.CurrentRow:=CurrentPreviewNode^.Row;
  dec(PG.CurrentPage);
  ShowPage;
end;


procedure TPreviewDialog.PreviewNext;
var
  PG:TPrintGrid;
begin
  PG:=TPrintGrid(PrintGrid);
  if FirstPreviewNode=nil then
  begin
    new(FirstPreviewNode);
    CurrentPreviewNode:=FirstPreviewNode;
    CurrentPreviewNode^.Next:=nil;
    CurrentPreviewNode^.Col:=PG.CurrentCol;
    CurrentPreviewNode^.Row:=PG.CurrentRow;
    CurrentPreviewNode^.Previous:=nil;
  end
  else
  begin
    if CurrentPreviewNode^.Next=nil then
    begin
      new(CurrentPreviewNode^.Next);
      CurrentPreviewNode^.Next^.Previous:=CurrentPreviewNode;
      CurrentPreviewNode:=CurrentPreviewNode^.Next;
      CurrentPreviewNode^.Next:=nil;
      CurrentPreviewNode^.Col:=PG.CurrentCol;
      CurrentPreviewNode^.Row:=PG.CurrentRow;
```

```
      end
    else
      CurrentPreviewNode:=CurrentPreviewNode^.Next;
  end;
  inc(PG.CurrentPage);
  ShowPage;
end;


procedure TPreviewDialog.WMSysCommand(var Msg:TWMSysCommand);
begin
  if (Msg.CmdType=SC_MAXIMIZE) or (Msg.CmdType=SC_RESTORE) then
  begin
    OkToSizePage:=True;
    FormSize(nil);
    PostMessage(Handle,WM_EXITSIZEMOVE,0,0);
  end;
  inherited;
end;


procedure TPreviewDialog.WMEnterSizeMove(var Msg:TMsg);
begin
  OkToSizePage:=True;
end;


procedure TPreviewDialog.WMExitSizeMove(var Msg:TMsg);
begin
  if Sizing then
  begin
    Page.Stretch:=False;
    Page.Picture.Assign(nil);
    ShowPage;
    Sizing:=False;
  end;
  OKToSizePage:=False;
  inherited;
end;
```

```
procedure TPreviewDialog.WMGetMinMaxInfo(var Msg:TWMGetMinMaxInfo);
begin
  if PrintGrid<>nil then
  begin
    Msg.MinMaxInfo^.ptMinTrackSize.x:=
      TPrintGrid(PrintGrid).ScreenPixelsPerInch.x*2;
    Msg.MinMaxInfo^.ptMinTrackSize.y:=
      TPrintGrid(PrintGrid).ScreenPixelsPerInch.y*3;
  end;
end;


procedure TPreviewDialog.PreviousButtonClick(Sender: TObject);
begin
  PreviewPrevious;
end;


procedure TPreviewDialog.NextButtonClick(Sender: TObject);
begin
  PreviewNext;
end;


procedure TPreviewDialog.PrintButtonClick(Sender: TObject);
var
  PG:TPrintGrid;
  SaveCurrentCol:LongInt;
  SaveCurrentRow:LongInt;
  SaveCurrentPage:Word;
begin
  PG:=TPrintGrid(PrintGrid);
  SaveCurrentCol:=PG.CurrentCol;
  SaveCurrentRow:=PG.CurrentRow;
  SaveCurrentPage:=PG.CurrentPage;
  PG.Print;
  PG.CurrentCol:=SaveCurrentCol;
  PG.CurrentRow:=SaveCurrentRow;
  PG.CurrentPage:=SaveCurrentPage;
```

```
end;

procedure TPreviewDialog.PreparePreview;
var
  TryHeight:Integer;
  PG:TPrintGrid;
begin
  PG:=TPrintGrid(PrintGrid);
  PreviousButton.Top:=ClientHeight-PreviousButton.Height-
    PG.ScreenPixelsPerInch.Y div 8;
  NextButton.Top:=PreviousButton.Top;
  PrintButton.Top:=PreviousButton.Top;
  CloseButton.Top:=PreviousButton.Top;

  Page.Top:=PG.ScreenPixelsPerInch.Y div 4;
  Page.Left:=PG.ScreenPixelsPerInch.X div 4;
  Page.Width:=ClientWidth-PG.ScreenPixelsPerInch.X div 2;
  Page.Height:=PreviousButton.Top-PG.ScreenPixelsPerInch.Y div 2;

  TryHeight:=MulDiv(MulDiv(MulDiv(Page.Width,1000,
    PG.ScreenPixelsPerInch.X),MulDiv(Printer.PageHeight,1000,
    PG.PrinterPixelsPerInch.Y),MulDiv(Printer.PageWidth,1000,
    PG.PrinterPixelsPerInch.X)),PG.ScreenPixelsPerInch.Y,1000);

  if TryHeight>Page.Height then
  begin
    Page.Width:=MulDiv(MulDiv(MulDiv(Page.Height,1000,
      PG.ScreenPixelsPerInch.Y),MulDiv(Printer.PageWidth,1000,
      PG.PrinterPixelsPerInch.X),MulDiv(Printer.PageHeight,1000,
      PG.PrinterPixelsPerInch.Y)),PG.ScreenPixelsPerInch.X,1000);
    Page.Left:=(ClientWidth-Page.Width) div 2;
  end
  else
  begin
    Page.Top:=Page.Top+(Page.Height-TryHeight) div 2;
    Page.Height:=TryHeight;
```

```
    end;

    ShadowRight.Brush.Color:=clDkGray;
    ShadowRight.Pen.Color:=clDkGray;
    ShadowRight.Left:=Page.Left+Page.Width;
    ShadowRight.Top:=Page.Top+PG.ScreenPixelsPerInch.Y div 8;
    ShadowRight.Width:=PG.ScreenPixelsPerInch.X div 8;
    ShadowRight.Height:=Page.Height;

    ShadowBottom.Brush.Color:=clDkGray;
    ShadowBottom.Pen.Color:=clDkGray;
    ShadowBottom.Left:=Page.Left+PG.ScreenPixelsPerInch.X div 8;
    ShadowBottom.Top:=Page.Top+Page.Height;
    ShadowBottom.Width:=Page.Width;
    ShadowBottom.Height:=PG.ScreenPixelsPerInch.Y div 8;
  end;

procedure TPreviewDialog.FormClose(Sender: TObject;
  var Action: TCloseAction);
begin
  while FirstPreviewNode<>nil do
  begin
    CurrentPreviewNode:=FirstPreviewNode^.Next;
    dispose(FirstPreviewNode);
    FirstPreviewNode:=CurrentPreviewNode;
  end;
end;

end.
```

CHAPTER • 9

PROPERTY AND COMPONENT EDITORS

The Object Inspector is a convenient tool for filling in property information. However, there are times when its simple interface may be too awkward, cumbersome, or completely unwilling to comply to your needs for some of the more exotic properties that you may want to create. Does this mean that all is lost? Certainly not! Enter a powerful duo called *property* and *component editors*.

A property editor comes in two flavors. The first is the text-based mechanism that you see in the right-hand pane of the Object Inspector. It is useful for entering string or numeric data, but not much else. The second is a custom dialog box that appears when you double-click on the edit portion of the property in the Object Inspector, or when you by single-click on the small button with the ellipsis that is also inside of the edit box. A good example of this is the **TFont** property editor that displays the standard Windows font dialog box, allowing the same data to be entered in a manner more intuitive than filling in the property's subproperties.

A component editor is used primarily for two reasons. The first is that you want to add menu items to the context menu that appears whenever you right-click on the component. The second reason is that you want to change the default action of double-clicking on one of the Object Inspector's property fields.

With these thoughts in mind, the goal of this chapter is to explore the various types of property and component editors that can be created with Delphi. As you read on, you will become acquainted with the following:

- Using predefined property editors
- How to create a custom property editor
- How to create component editors

Text-Based Property Editors

One thing that many Delphi programmers don't realize is that every cell in the right-hand pane of the Object Inspector has an associated property editor. Most often, the term *property editor* is thought of as a customization that Delphi permits, not an inherent part of the environment itself. The Object Inspector only understands strings and knows nothing about other types such as integers, sets, fonts, and so on. It is the property editor's job to act as a translator, changing the string entered into the property editor into the type that the component requires. The reverse is also true; when given a value of a certain type, the property editor must know how to change back into a string.

Delphi possesses many property editors that are built into the VCL, ready for immediate use in your components. As a component programmer, however, you really don't need to give very much thought to whether you will be using one—if one exists for the type of property you are editing, it will be used automatically.

Creating Your Own Text-Based Editor

The first thing you must do after deciding that a property editor is a must have is to decide exactly how you want it to display your property. For several components that I have programmed, I found it convenient to have the properties displayed in binary format instead of a decimal number. This is a very simple property editor with little code, and thus an excellent example.

I frequently use two types of binary property editors, as shown in Figure 9.1—one that edits 8-bit values and another that edits 16-bit values. Although the 16-bit version could easily accommodate the 8-bit values, the visual prompt of "0000000000000000" would potentially lead the programmer into thinking that a 16-bit value was required instead. Because the code for both property editors is practically identical, I decided to give them a common parent, **TBinaryProperty**.

Figure 9.1 The 8-bit and 16-bit binary property editors.

TBinaryProperty is not a predefined class of Delphi. Instead, it is one that we have to program ourselves. Before getting into that chore, however, a parent property editor must be decided upon. Delphi has many built-in property editors, but the only one that is really appropriate for our task is **TPropertyEditor**, the granddaddy of them all. Now that that decision has been made, a descendant can be declared:

```
type
  TBinaryProperty = Class(TPropertyEditor)
  end;
```

Not much to look at so far, but it's a start.

The actual mechanism for getting data into and out of the property editor is done through two methods, **GetValue** and **SetValue**, both of which must be overridden from **TPropertyEditor**:

```
type
  TBinaryProperty = Class(TPropertyEditor)
    function GetValue:String;override;
    procedure SetValue(const Value:String);override;
  end;
```

It is the job of **GetValue** to translate the value of the underlying property into a string to be displayed in the Object Inspector. Before doing the conversion, it is necessary to first retrieve the value. There are four methods used for this purpose—**GetFloatValue**, **GetMethodValue**, **GetOrdValue**, and **GetStrValue**—which return a floating point number, a pointer to a method, an ordinal value, and a string, respectively. Because it only takes an integer to hold our value, we'll be doing good by using **GetOrdValue**. This and the gory details of integer to binary string conversion are shown in the following block of code:

```
function TBinaryProperty.GetValue:String;
var
  i:Integer;
  OrdValue:Word;
begin
  OrdValue:=GetOrdValue;
  for i:=GetEditLimit-1 downto 0 do
  begin
    if OrdValue and (1 shl i) <> 0 then
      Result:=Result+'1'
    else
      Result:=Result+'0';
  end;
end;
```

If you read through the preceding segment of code, you may have noticed the identifier **GetEditLimit** thrown in. It is a function, originally declared as a member of **TPropertyEditor**, that returns a number specifying the maximum length that the string in the Object Inspector can be. The relationship between number of binary digits and string length is one-to-one. That is, to represent an 8-bit binary value, an 8-character string is needed. By overriding **GetEditLimit**, we gain a fairly sneaky way of allowing descendants of **TBinaryProperty** to provide information on the number of bits that they are meant to manipulate, and of course, prevent the user from entering more information than is necessary. To make it blatantly obvious that **GetEditLimit** is supposed to be overridden, it has been declared as abstract in **TBinaryProperty**.

That's half the job already done! Who says property editors are hard to build?

SetValue, as you can probably guess, is responsible for the other half of the job: text-to-integer conversion. This time, instead of returning a string like **GetValue** did, it accepts one directly from the Object Inspector and translates it character by character into an integer assigned to the corresponding property:

```
procedure TBinaryProperty.SetValue(const Value:String);
var
  i:Integer;
  OrdValue:Word;
  ValueLength:Word;
  ValueStr:String;
begin
  OrdValue:=0;
  ValueStr:=Trim(Value);
  ValueLength:=Length(ValueStr);
  for i:=ValueLength downto 1 do
  begin
    if ValueStr[i] = '1' then
      inc(OrdValue,1 shl (ValueLength-i));
  end;
  SetOrdValue(OrdValue);
end;
```

Similar to how **GetOrdValue** retrieves the property's value, **SetOrdValue**, assigns it to the value that is passed as a parameter. While we're on the topic, in addition to **SetOrdValue** there are the **GetFloatValue**, **GetMethodValue**, and **GetStrValue** methods that are useful if the base type of the property is something other than ordinal.

The only remaining step required to get the property editor up and running is to register it by placing a call to **RegisterPropertyEditor** into the **Register** procedure:

```
procedure RegisterPropertyEditor(PropertyType:PTypeInfo;
  ComponentClass:TClass; const PropertyName:string;
  EditorClass: TPropertyEditorClass);
```

Making this call is the most important task that has to be done when creating a property editor. Essentially, it tells the Object Inspector what property editor to use whenever it encounters a type represented by the information passed to **PropertyType**. I say "information" for a good reason; the function does not accept the type directly, and instead it requires the **TypeInfo** function to be used in combination with the type to get the value it needs.

The **ComponentClass** parameter specifies the component that the property editor is to be used with. If **nil** is passed, all components become a suitable candidate for the editor. The third parameter, **PropertyName** is the name of the property that is to use the property editor. This makes it possible to have several properties of the same type but register different property editors to edit their values. If, however, its value is an empty string ('), all properties of the appropriate type will use the same editor. The final parameter, **EditorClass**, accepts the type of the property editor to be used, **TBin8Property** and **TBin16Property**, in our example.

Here is what our final code looks like:

Listing 9.1 BINPROP.PAS

```
unit BinProp;

interface

uses DsgnIntf,SysUtils;
```

```
type
  TBin8=Byte;
  TBin16=Word;

  TBinaryProperty=class(TPropertyEditor)
    function GetValue:String;override;
    procedure SetValue(const Value:String);override;
    function GetEditLimit:Integer;override;abstract;
  end;

  TBin8Property=class(TBinaryProperty)
    function GetEditLimit:Integer;override;
  end;

  TBin16Property=class(TBinaryProperty)
    function GetEditLimit:Integer;override;
  end;

procedure Register;

implementation

function TBinaryProperty.GetValue:String;
var
  i:Integer;
  OrdValue:Word;
begin
  OrdValue:=GetOrdValue;
  for i:=GetEditLimit-1 downto 0 do
  begin
    if OrdValue and (1 shl i) <> 0 then
      Result:=Result+'1'
    else
      Result:=Result+'0';
  end;
end;

procedure TBinaryProperty.SetValue(const Value:String);
```

```
var
  i:Integer;
  OrdValue:Word;
  ValueLength:Word;
  ValueStr:String;
begin
  OrdValue:=0;
  ValueStr:=Trim(Value);
  ValueLength:=Length(ValueStr);
  for i:=ValueLength downto 1 do
  begin
    if ValueStr[i] = '1' then
      inc(OrdValue,1 shl (ValueLength-i));
  end;
  SetOrdValue(OrdValue);
end;

function TBin8Property.GetEditLimit:Integer;
begin
  GetEditLimit:=8;
end;

function TBin16Property.GetEditLimit:Integer;
begin
  GetEditLimit:=16;
end;

procedure Register;
begin
  RegisterPropertyEditor(TypeInfo(TBin8),nil,'',TBin8Property);
  RegisterPropertyEditor(TypeInfo(TBin16),nil,'',TBin16Property);
end;

end.
```

You have undoubtedly noticed the similarity between creating a component and creating a property editor. This goes even one step farther because to get Delphi to know about the property editor, it must be installed just like a component. To do this, select **Components, Install** from the main menu. The Install dialog box will open. Click on **Add**, **Browse** and hunt down the **BINPROP.PAS** file in the **\DC\CHAP9** directory. When you find it, click on **Open** and then **OK**. This will add the property editor to the VCL, allowing any component that uses either the **TBin8** or **TBin16** types as properties to have them editable as binary numbers.

After the property editor has been installed, you can start creating components that use it. To demonstrate the **TBin8Property** property editor, I have written a small example component, **TBinaryLights**—the code follows—that displays eight circles and colors them according to how the **State** property—editable as a binary number—is set. To see the property editor in action, you will need to drop the component onto a form and edit the **State** field. I didn't provide an example for **TBin16Property** because its operation is practically identical. Only the bit length differs. However, if you're curious enough, it would be a great exercise to make a 16-bit version of **TBinaryLights**.

Listing 9.2 BINARYLIGHTS.PAS

```
unit BinaryLights;

interface

uses
  Windows, Messages, SysUtils, Classes, Graphics, Controls, Forms,
Dialogs,BinProp;

const
  HeightDefault=17;
  WidthDefault=153;
  OnColorDefault=clRed;
  OffColorDefault=clMaroon;

type
  TBinaryLights = class(TGraphicControl)
```

```
private
  FState:Byte;
  FOnColor:TColor;
  FOffColor:TColor;
  procedure DrawLight(Index:Byte);
  procedure SetState(AState:Byte);
  procedure SetOnColor(AOnColor:TColor);
  procedure SetOffColor(AOffColor:TColor);
protected
  procedure Paint;override;
  constructor Create(AOwner:TComponent);override;
published
  property State:TBin8 read FState write SetState;
  property OnColor:TColor read FOnColor write SetOnColor;
  property OffColor:TColor read FOffColor write SetOffColor;
  property Height default HeightDefault;
  property Width default WidthDefault;
end;

procedure Register;

implementation

procedure TBinaryLights.DrawLight(Index:Byte);
var
  XPos,YPos,Radius:Integer;
begin
  if FState and (1 shl Index) <> 0 then
    Canvas.Brush.Color:=FOnColor
  else
    Canvas.Brush.Color:=FOffColor;

  if Height>Width then
  begin
    YPos:=MulDiv(8-Index,Height,9);
    XPos:=Width div 2;
```

```
    Radius:=Height div 24;
  end
  else
  begin
    XPos:=MulDiv(8-Index,Width,9);
    YPos:=Height div 2;
    Radius:=Width div 24;
  end;

  Canvas.Ellipse(XPos-Radius,YPos-Radius,XPos+Radius,YPos+Radius);
end;

procedure TBinaryLights.SetState(AState:Byte);
var
  i:Integer;
  LastState:Byte;
begin
  LastState:=FState;
  FState:=AState;
  for i:=0 to 7 do
  begin
    if (LastState xor AState) and (1 shl i) <> 0 then
      DrawLight(i);
  end;
end;

procedure TBinaryLights.SetOnColor(AOnColor:TColor);
begin
  FOnColor:=AOnColor;
  Repaint;
end;

procedure TBinaryLights.SetOffColor(AOffColor:TColor);
begin
  FOffColor:=AOffColor;
  Repaint;
```

```
end;

procedure TBinaryLights.Paint;
var
  i:Byte;
begin
  for i:=0 to 7 do
    DrawLight(i);
end;

constructor TBinaryLights.Create(AOwner:TComponent);
begin
  inherited Create(AOwner);
  Height:=HeightDefault;
  Width:=WidthDefault;
  FOnColor:=OnColorDefault;
  FOffColor:=OffColorDefault;
end;

procedure Register;
begin
  RegisterComponents('additional', [TBinaryLights]);
end;

end.
```

Form-Based Property Editors

When a property is excessively complex, a class for example, it is often beneficial to forgo the notion of restricting the user to text-only data entry. The alternative is to provide the same information in a visual format by using a form-based property editor. First, we'll take a look at what Delphi offers in the way of built-in editors, and then we'll see how go about it ourselves.

Built-In Form-Based Property Editors

You may recall the problem that we encountered a few chapters back with our **TCheckGrid** component. The properties responsible for interfacing with the column and row text were declared as arrays, and therefore unable to be published because there is no provision for modifying arrays built in to the Object Inspector. We finally had to settle with a mechanism that parsed a pair of comma-delimited strings. Wouldn't it be much more useful, however, if we were able to edit the array through the Object Inspector directly without having to fool around with this string parsing nonsense? Of course it would, which is where using a built-in form-based property editor enters the thick of things.

Delphi has several built-in form-based property editors, most of which you are probably familiar with such as the **TFont** editor and the **TColor** editor to name two. If you have played around with list-oriented components, **TMemo** or **TListBox**, for instance, you have undoubtedly run across another type of property editor for the class **TStrings**. This property editor, shown in Figure 9.2, permits strings to be added, deleted, and moved about with ease.

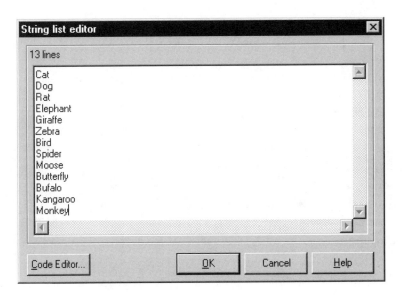

Figure 9.2 The **TStrings** property editor.

The **TStrings** class works much like a conventional string array, but with a few key differences. First, its size is not fixed; the number of elements may grow or shrink dynamically, resulting in potentially enormous memory savings over a fixed size conventional array. Second, it provides methods and properties that actually manipulate and work with the data it contains, such as the **Sorted** property, which ensures that the strings are stored in alphabetical order, and the **Find** method, which searches all the strings for a match. Finally, **TStrings** knows how to save and recall its data from disk using the **SaveToFile** and **LoadFromFile** methods. With features like this, it's hard to make a case against using **TStrings**.

TStrings itself is an abstract class. It provides no storage for the strings, but merely acts as a consistent inheritable interface for its descendants that do, such as **TStringList**, **TMemoStrings**, **TComboBoxStrings**, and **TListBoxStrings**. You will often see the following when you encounter something that uses a **TStrings** derived class:

```
type
  TMyComp = class(TComponent)
  private
    FMyList:TStrings;
    procedure SetMyList(AMyList:TStrings);
  public
    constructor Create(AOwner:TComponent);override;
  published
    property MyList:TStrings read FMyList write SetMyList;
  end;

constructor TMyComp.Create(AOwner:TComponent);
begin
  inherited Create(AOwner);
  FMyList:=TStringList.Create;
end;

procedure TMyComp.SetMyList(AMyList:TStrings);
begin
  FMyList.Assign(AMyList);
end;
```

Of immediate interest in the preceding bit of code is the way **FMyList** is declared and created. In the declaration for it, notice that it is of type **TStrings**. However, I just told you that **TStrings** is an abstract class that provides no storage capability for the data. This is true, which is why when it comes time to initialize **FMyList**, it is done as an instance of type **TStringList**, which is indeed capable of storing the data. The question that comes up is why bother declaring **FMyList** as **TStrings** when we really want the functionality of **TStringList**? Suppose for a moment that we were to declare **FMyList** as type **TStringList**.

The nasty thing you would discover is that you no longer have full compatibility with every other string list that exists in the entire VCL. Although this would work

```
Memo1.Lines:=MyComp1.MyList;
```

This would not

```
MyComp1.MyList:=Memo1.Lines;
```

Of course, this wrinkle could be ironed out with some creative typecasting:

```
MyComp1.MyList:=TStringList(Memo1.Lines);
```

But this would just provide confusion for what should be an intuitive experience.

Modifying **TCheckGrid** to work with a string list instead of traditional arrays is really quite trivial. The type of the variables **FColumnText** and **FRowText**, as well as the properties **ColumnText** and **RowText** need to be changed to **TStrings**. Along with this change, the **SetColumnText** and **SetRowText** methods need to be updated:

```
procedure TCheckGrid.SetColumnText(AColumnText:TStrings);
begin
  FColumnText.Assign(AColumnText);
  if FColumnText.Count=0 then
    FColumnText.Add('Column 1');
  CalculateRects;
  Invalidate;
```

```
end;

procedure TCheckGrid.SetRowText(ARowText:TStrings);
begin
  FRowText.Assign(ARowText);
  if FRowText.Count=0 then
    FRowText.Add('Row 1');
  CalculateRects;
  Invalidate;
end;
```

As you can see, the **Assign** method is employed to copy the contents of the **TStrings** parameter passed to each procedure to both **FColumnText** or **FRowText**.

There is also no need to maintain the variables **FColumns** and **FRows**, used previously to indicate how many items were in each array, because the **TStrings** class does this for us automatically by providing a **Count** property. So they get the ax, and any reference to them is changed accordingly to either **FColumnText.Count** or **FRowText.Count**. In the preceding code segment, you can see how the **Count** property is used to check if the assigned string list has zero elements, in which case it will add one because it is nonsensical to have zero rows or columns for the **TCheckGrid** component.

Another thing that must be accounted for is that the first element of a **TString** list starts at zero rather than one as it did with the arrays. The fix for this is to subtract one each time an element is referenced. This is an opportune moment to mention that accessing individual elements of a **TString** list is identical to accessing elements of a traditional array:

```
type
  MyArray:array[0..1] of String;
  MyStrings:TStrings;

begin
  {Traditional array element access}
```

```
  MyArray[0]:='Hello ';
  MyArray[1]:='Delphi';
  writeln(MyArray[0]+MyArray[1]);

  {TStrings element access}
  MyStrings:=TStringList.Create;
  MyStrings.Add('Hello ');
  MyStrings.Add('Delphi');
  writeln(MyStrings[0]+MyStrings[1]);
  MyStrings.Free;
end;
```

Notice how the elements of **MyStrings** are accessed using square brackets, just like the **MyArray** array. This feature is possible because the **Strings** property of **TStrings** is declared as the default property for the class. You may recall from way back in **Chapter 1** that the default property may be accessed without specifying the property name. However, if you were inclined to do so, you could provide a fully qualified identifier:

```
writeln(MyStrings.Strings[0]+MyStrings.Strings[1]);
```

Only a couple of minor changes need to be made. All **FColumnString** and **FRowString** references can be removed because there is no longer a need to use them as a parsed list. Finally, in the original code, we simply went ahead and initialized the entire **FColumnText** and **FRowText** arrays to the values Column x and Row x, where x ranges from one to **ColumnsMax** and **RowsMax**. Well, we still have to do this initialization, but if we were to initialize for every column and row, our default, freshly-plopped-on-the-form check grid component would contain 20 columns and 20 rows, which at the initial default component size is somewhat crowded. The reason this happens at all is because the **Add** method needs to be called to get a string into our string lists. Each call to **Add** increases the value of the **Count** property accordingly. The **Count** property is used all over as the value of how many rows or columns there are. So by restricting the number of times **Add** is called, we thereby restrict the initial density of the component.

The code for the changes we just discussed appears later in this chapter because we're not quite finished modifying the component. Before getting on to that, let's first talk about making your own form-based property editor.

Creating Your Own Form-Based Editor

Using a built-in form-based editor is fine and dandy, but not every property you program will have a suitable ready-to-use editor. Therefore, you have no choice but to roll up your sleeves and make your own. In Chapter 4, we talked about embedding a dialog box in a component. You already know that a property editor is not significantly different from a component—only the ancestor class and the registration call differ. So, by using the same techniques for componentizing a dialog box, we can easily do the same for a property editor.

In the last chapter, we created the spiffy **TPrintGrid** component. One of the properties it forces you to deal with is **PrintSettings**, a fairly complex class that is used to provide information on what the printout will look like. It is also an ideal candidate for a form-based property editor.

Unlike the hack and slash job we just finished doing to **TCheckGrid**, we won't have to edit a single line of code in the three units that compose **TPrintGrid**. Instead, we'll create a single unit that "hooks" into the type **TPrintSettings**, just like the **TBinaryProperty** editor does, and performs the dirty work from there.

The easiest way to start making the property editor is close any open project in Delphi and select **New Form** from the **File** menu. A blank form appears, and through some hard work you could dress it up to look like the one shown in Figure 9.3. Looking at the figure, you may notice a component that we have not talked about, **TFontStyle**, for selecting a font and its style. This component is an excellent example of how to embed components inside a component. Unfortunately, we won't be discussing it in any detail, nor will you find its source code in print; but if you're interested, the code can be found in the **\DC\CHAP9** directory as **FONTSTYL.PAS**.

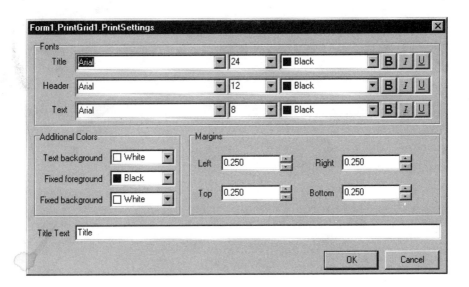

Figure 9.3 Print Settings form.

After the cosmetic surgery to the form has been finished, or even before, if you want—you can always come back to it later. The necessary property editor code can be added:

```
implementation

.

.

.

type
  TPrintSettingsProperty=class(TClassProperty)
    function GetAttributes:TPropertyAttributes;override;
    procedure Edit;override;
  end;

procedure Register;

interface
```

```
      .

      .

      .

function TPrintSettingsProperty.GetAttributes:TPropertyAttributes;
begin

  GetAttributes:=[paDialog,paSubProperties];
end;

procedure TPrintSettingsProperty.Edit;
begin

    .

    .

    .

end;

procedure Register;
begin
  RegisterPropertyEditor(TypeInfo(TPrintSettings),TPrintGrid,
    'PrintSettings',TPrintSettingsProperty);
end;

    .

    .

    .
```

Don't worry about the gaping holes; they represent where code relating to the form is located, which will be presented in full later.

The **GetAttributes** method of **TPrintSettingsProperty** has been overridden so it can tell the Object Inspector two important things about the property editor: that it has a corresponding dialog box, indicated by the **paDialog** member; and that the individual subproperties of **TPrintSettings** can still be edited as text, specified by the **paSubProperties** member.

The only other method that needs to be overridden to pull this thing off is **Edit**. It is called when the user double-clicks on the edit portion of the property in the Object Inspector or clicks on the small button marked with an ellipsis. The proper action to perform in **Edit** is to display the dialog box and accept user input. Here's a deeper peek into its contents:

```
procedure TPrintSettingsProperty.Edit;
var
  PrintSettingsDlg:TPrintSettingsDlg;
  PrintSettings:TPrintSettings;
begin
  PrintSettings:=TPrintSettings(GetOrdValue);
  Application.CreateForm(TPrintSettingsDlg, PrintSettingsDlg);

PrintSettingsDlg.TitleFontStyle.SelectedFont:=PrintSettings.TitleFont;
  PrintSettingsDlg.Caption:=GetComponent(0).Owner.Name+'.'+
    GetComponent(0).Name+'.'+GetName;
  .

  .

  .

  if PrintSettingsDlg.ShowModal = mrOk then
  begin
    PrintSettings.TitleFont:=
      PrintSettingsDlg.TitleFontStyle.SelectedFont;
    .

    .

    .

  end;
  PrintSettingsDlg.Free;
end;
```

Before we can even think of popping up the dialog box, we need a way to extract the data from the property we are editing. That's what is accomplished by typecasting **GetOrdValue** to **TPrintSettings**. Recall that **GetOrdValue** returns the ordinal value associated with the property. In the case of a class, the ordinal value associated with it is a pointer, so by doing the typecast, we end up with a perfectly functional reference to the class that contains the properties we're interested in. Because we end up using this reference a lot, it is assigned to the variable **PrintSettings**.

Now that we can get to our data, we can create the dialog box, but not display it, by calling **Application.CreateForm**. At this stage, the dialog box is alive, as are all its components, which we can start assigning values to using the properties of **PrintSettings**. Shown in the preceding code is one such assignment, **PrintSettings.TitleFont** to **PrintSettingsDlg. TitleFontStyle.SelectedFont**, properly setting the **SelectedFont** property of the **TitleFontStyle** component.

After all the remaining properties have been set in a similar manner, the only remaining task to be performed before displaying the dialog box is to set its caption. The accepted format for a form-based property editor's caption is *FormName.ComponentName.PropertyName*. Retrieving the form and component names requires that you know exactly what component you are editing. This information can be retrieved by calling the **GetComponent** method and passing it a index value of zero, indicating the first, and in our case only, component. This returns a pointer to the component being edited. The form name can be extracted through the property **Owner** and its property **Name**. Using the same pointer, the component's name is accessed using the **Name** property. Finally, to get the name of the property, the **GetName** method of **TPrintSettingsProperty** is called. All resulting strings are then concatenated with periods in between each to construct the fully qualified name of the property. The actual process for all this is shown in the preceding code segment.

It is finally time to display the dialog box by calling **PrintSettings Dlg.ShowModal**. At this point, the user gets the opportunity to fuss with various fields in an attempt to get the printout looking "just right." When the fussing is over and they click on **OK** or they've decided they were being too fussy and click on **Cancel**, the dialog box vanishes. If **OK** was clicked, the return value of **PrintSettingsDlg. ShowModal** will be **mrOK**, and data in the components of the dialog box is transferred to the properties of **PrintSettings**. If **Cancel** is clicked, nothing is transferred. Regardless of what is clicked, the dialog box is then removed from memory by calling **PrintSettingsDlg.Free**.

That's the scoop on custom form-based property editors. The complete code for the **TPrintSettingsProperty** can be found in the **\DC\CHAP9** directory as **PRINTGRIDPROP.PAS**. For your convenience, however, it is also shown here:

```
unit PrintGridProp;

interface

uses
```

```
  Windows, Messages, SysUtils, Classes, Graphics, Controls, Forms,
  Dialogs, StdCtrls, ComCtrls, DsgnIntf, ColorDrop,
FontStyl,PrintGrid;

type
  TPrintSettingsProperty=class(TClassProperty)
    function GetAttributes:TPropertyAttributes;override;
    procedure Edit;override;
  end;

type
  TPrintSettingsDlg = class(TForm)
    FontGroupBox: TGroupBox;
    TitleFontStyle: TFontStyle;
    HeaderFontStyle: TFontStyle;
    TextFontStyle: TFontStyle;
    TitleFontLabel: TLabel;
    HeaderFontLabel: TLabel;
    TextFontLabel: TLabel;
    ColorGroupBox: TGroupBox;
    TextBackColorDrop: TColorDrop;
    FixedForeColorDrop: TColorDrop;
    FixedBackColorDrop: TColorDrop;
    FixedForeColorLabel: TLabel;
    FixedBackColorLabel: TLabel;
    TextBackColorLabel: TLabel;
    MarginGroupBox: TGroupBox;
    MarginLeftLabel: TLabel;
    MarginRightLabel: TLabel;
    MarginTopLabel: TLabel;
    MarginBottomLabel: TLabel;
    MarginLeftEdit: TEdit;
    MarginRightEdit: TEdit;
    MarginTopEdit: TEdit;
    MarginBottomEdit: TEdit;
    MarginTopUpDown: TUpDown;
    MarginRightUpDown: TUpDown;
    MarginBottomUpDown: TUpDown;
    TitleTextLabel: TLabel;
```

```
    TitleTextEdit: TEdit;

    OKButton: TButton;

    CancelButton: TButton;

    MarginLeftUpDown: TUpDown;

    procedure MarginLeftUpDownClick(Sender: TObject;
       Button: TUDBtnType);

    procedure MarginRightUpDownClick(Sender: TObject;
       Button: TUDBtnType);

    procedure MarginTopUpDownClick(Sender: TObject;
       Button: TUDBtnType);

    procedure MarginBottomUpDownClick(Sender: TObject;
       Button: TUDBtnType);
  private
    function GetMarginValue(MarginEdit:TEdit):Integer;
    procedure MarginChange(MarginEdit:TEdit;Button:TUDBtnType);
    procedure SetMarginValue(MarginEdit:TEdit;Value:Integer);
  public

  end;

procedure Register;

implementation

{$R *.DFM}

function TPrintSettingsProperty.GetAttributes:TPropertyAttributes;
begin
  GetAttributes:=[paDialog,paSubProperties];
end;

procedure TPrintSettingsProperty.Edit;
var
  PrintSettingsDlg:TPrintSettingsDlg;
  PrintSettings:TPrintSettings;
begin
  PrintSettings:=TPrintSettings(GetOrdValue);
```

```
Application.CreateForm(TPrintSettingsDlg, PrintSettingsDlg);
PrintSettingsDlg.TitleFontStyle.SelectedFont:=
  PrintSettings.TitleFont;
PrintSettingsDlg.HeaderFontStyle.SelectedFont:=
  PrintSettings.HeaderFont;
PrintSettingsDlg.TextFontStyle.SelectedFont:=
  PrintSettings.TextFont;
PrintSettingsDlg.TextFontStyle.SelectedFont:=
  PrintSettings.TextFont;
PrintSettingsDlg.TextBackColorDrop.SelectedColor:=
  PrintSettings.TextBackColor;
PrintSettingsDlg.FixedForeColorDrop.SelectedColor:=
  PrintSettings.FixedForeColor;
PrintSettingsDlg.FixedBackColorDrop.SelectedColor:=
  PrintSettings.FixedBackColor;
PrintSettingsDlg.SetMarginValue(PrintSettingsDlg.MarginLeftEdit,
  PrintSettings.MarginLeft);
PrintSettingsDlg.SetMarginValue(PrintSettingsDlg.MarginRightEdit,
  PrintSettings.MarginRight);
PrintSettingsDlg.SetMarginValue(PrintSettingsDlg.MarginTopEdit,
  PrintSettings.MarginTop);
PrintSettingsDlg.SetMarginValue(PrintSettingsDlg.MarginBottomEdit,
  PrintSettings.MarginBottom);
PrintSettingsDlg.TitleTextEdit.Text:=PrintSettings.TitleText;
PrintSettingsDlg.Caption:=GetComponent(0).Owner.Name+'.'+
  GetComponent(0).Name+'.'+GetName;
if PrintSettingsDlg.ShowModal = mrOk then
begin
  PrintSettings.TitleFont:=
    PrintSettingsDlg.TitleFontStyle.SelectedFont;
  PrintSettings.HeaderFont:=
    PrintSettingsDlg.HeaderFontStyle.SelectedFont;
  PrintSettings.TextFont:=
    PrintSettingsDlg.TextFontStyle.SelectedFont;
  PrintSettings.TextFont:=
    PrintSettingsDlg.TextFontStyle.SelectedFont;
```

```
      PrintSettings.TextBackColor:=
        PrintSettingsDlg.TextBackColorDrop.SelectedColor;
      PrintSettings.FixedForeColor:=
        PrintSettingsDlg.FixedForeColorDrop.SelectedColor;
      PrintSettings.FixedBackColor:=
        PrintSettingsDlg.FixedBackColorDrop.SelectedColor;
      PrintSettings.MarginLeft:=

PrintSettingsDlg.GetMarginValue(PrintSettingsDlg.MarginLeftEdit);
      PrintSettings.MarginRight:=

PrintSettingsDlg.GetMarginValue(PrintSettingsDlg.MarginRightEdit);
      PrintSettings.MarginTop:=
        PrintSettingsDlg.GetMarginValue(PrintSettingsDlg.MarginTopEdit);
      PrintSettings.MarginBottom:=
        PrintSettingsDlg.GetMarginValue(
        PrintSettingsDlg.MarginBottomEdit);
      PrintSettings.TitleText:=
        PrintSettingsDlg.TitleTextEdit.Text;
    end;
    PrintSettingsDlg.Free;
end;

procedure Register;
begin
  RegisterPropertyEditor(TypeInfo(TPrintSettings),TPrintGrid,
    'PrintSettings',TPrintSettingsProperty);
end;

function TPrintSettingsDlg.GetMarginValue(MarginEdit:TEdit):Integer;
var
  i:Integer;
  Text:String;
begin
  Text:='';
  for i:=1 to Length(MarginEdit.Text) do
  begin
```

```
      if MarginEdit.Text[i] in ['0'..'9','.'] then
        Text:=Text+MarginEdit.Text[i];
    end;
    if Text='' then
      Text:='0';
    GetMarginValue:=Trunc(StrToFloat(Text)*1000);
  end;


procedure TPrintSettingsDlg.SetMarginValue(MarginEdit:TEdit;
  Value:Integer);
begin
  if Value<0 then
    Value:=0
  else if Value>3000 then
    Value:=3000;
  MarginEdit.Text:=Format('%2.3f',[Value / 1000]);
end;


procedure TPrintSettingsDlg.MarginChange(MarginEdit:TEdit;
  Button:TUDBtnType);
var
  MarginValue:Integer;
begin
  MarginValue:=GetMarginValue(MarginEdit);
  if Button = btPrev then
    dec(MarginValue,10)
  else
    inc(MarginValue,10);
  SetMarginValue(MarginEdit,MarginValue);
end;


procedure TPrintSettingsDlg.MarginLeftUpDownClick(Sender: TObject;
  Button: TUDBtnType);
begin
  MarginChange(MarginLeftEdit,Button);
end;
```

```
procedure TPrintSettingsDlg.MarginRightUpDownClick(Sender: TObject;
  Button: TUDBtnType);
begin
  MarginChange(MarginRightEdit,Button);
end;

procedure TPrintSettingsDlg.MarginTopUpDownClick(Sender: TObject;
  Button: TUDBtnType);
begin
  MarginChange(MarginTopEdit,Button);
end;

procedure TPrintSettingsDlg.MarginBottomUpDownClick(Sender: TObject;
  Button: TUDBtnType);
begin
  MarginChange(MarginBottomEdit,Button);
end;

end.
```

Component Editors

Custom property editors are only half of the story; often you will find that it is desirable to edit a conponent as a whole instead of just manipulating individual properties. This is easily acheivable under Delphi through the use of custom component editors.

Intercepting the Component Double-Click

The primary annoyance of **TCheckGrid** is its inability to allow the state of the cells to be set during design time. This was not an oversight; rather, it is a limitation of what the Object Inspector permits. We were able to "trick" it into accepting parsed strings for the column and row text—simple one-dimensional arrays; but it is wholly unrealistic to try the same thing with the two-dimensional array needed to store the checked state of each cell. So we left the **Checked** property unpublished and thereby restricted it to being usable only from a code level.

The time has come to blow away this final restriction and allow the cell states to be set at design time in the most intuitive way possible—visually. There are two possible ways to approach this idea. The **Checked** property could be changed from an array type to a class, allowing it to be published, and thereby permitting a form-based property editor to be used on it. Or, we could construct a component editor for **TCheckGrid**, one that appears whenever the user double-clicks on the component. The appeal of a component editor is that it has the ability to edit all the component's properties, not just one as with a property editor. Even though we're not going to include the capability to edit properties other than **Checked** in this discussion, it leaves open a giant window of opportunity to expand the capabilities of the editor later on.

Saving Additional Data in the Form File

I told you earlier that some more changes needed to be made to **TCheckGrid**, and it's now time to talk about that. Before we can write an editor that allows the state of the cells to be set at design time, we need some way to make the state persistent. That is, if we have a form with a **TCheckGrid** component on it, check a few cells, and then save the form and close it, when it is reopened, the state of each cell should be the same as we left it. However, this is currently not the situation because the component has no way of storing the data in the form file.

To remedy this, the **DefineProperties** method of **TCheckGrid**, inherited ultimately from **TPersistent**, needs to be overridden. This method provides a way to store data that is normally not stored automatically:

```
procedure DefineProperties(Filer: TFiler);
```

When this procedure is called, its **Filer** parameter is passed either a **TWriter** instance when data is being written to a form file or a **TReader** instance when it is being read from a form file. Regardless of which is passed, the process of indicating there is extra data is the same and involves calling the **DefineProperty** method of **Filer**:

```
procedure DefineProperty(const Name: string; ReadData: TReaderProc;
  WriteData: TWriterProc;HasData: Boolean); virtual; abstract;
```

The **Name** parameter specifies a string of text that is used to identify the property in the form file, and although it need not be the same as the property's name, convention dictates that it is a good idea. The **ReadData** parameter points to the procedure that does the actual reading of data from the form file. The **WriteData** parameter is similar, but it points to the procedure that writes the data to the form file. The final parameter, **HasData**, is used to determine whether the **WriteData** procedure will be called. If **HasData** is **True**, it means "Yes, I have data to store." Otherwise, it means "This data is the same as the default state, so don't bother storing it."

In the following code, you can see how the **DefineProperites** method is set up, as well as the function **AnyChecked,** which determines if there is at least one checked cell and passes the result to **DefineProperty**:

```
function TCheckGrid.AnyChecked:Boolean;
var
  i,j:Byte;
begin
  AnyChecked:=False;
  for i:=1 to FColumnText.Count do
  begin
    for j:=1 to FRowText.Count do
    begin
      if Checked[i,j] then
      begin
        AnyChecked:=True;
        exit;
      end;
    end;
  end;
end;
```

```
procedure TCheckGrid.DefineProperties(Filer:TFiler);
begin
  inherited DefineProperties(Filer);
  Filer.DefineProperty('Checked',ReadChecked,WriteChecked,AnyChecked);
end;
```

Writing the Data

When the **WriteData** procedure, **WriteChecked**, is called, it has to first tell the **TWriter** class to start a new section in the form file by calling **ReadListBegin**. Next, the data can be stored. If we were to just go ahead and store the entire array, we would end up wasting a lot of space because the maximum size is 20 cells by 20 cells, an admittedly improbable situation when using the **TCheckGrid** component. It is far better to store only what needs to be stored. Although there are many possibilities for storing the data, I chose a method that makes it readable by a human who happens to be browsing through the form file when viewed as text:

```
procedure TCheckGrid.WriteChecked(Writer:TWriter);
var
  X,Y:Byte;
  LastY:Byte;
begin
  Writer.WriteListBegin;
  for Y:=1 to FRowText.Count do
  begin
    for X:=1 to FColumnText.Count do
    begin
      if Checked[X,Y] then
      begin
        if Y=LastY then
          Writer.WriteString(Format('%d',[X]))
        else
        begin
          Writer.WriteString(Format('%d, %d',[X,Y]));
          LastY:=Y;
```

```
        end;
      end;
    end;
  end;
  Writer.WriteListEnd;
end;
```

After that data has all been written, the **WriteListEnd** property has to be called to properly end the section.

Reading the Data

Reading the data from the form file is very similar to writing it, except that the process is reversed. In the code for writing the data, a string was created containing the coordinates of each cell that contains a check mark and then stored. To retrieve the individual coordinates, the string must be read by calling the **ReadString** property of **Writer** and then parsed into the two comma-delimited values. However, before any of this can occur, the read procedure, **ReadChecked**, must indicate that it is expecting a new section of the form file by calling **ReadListBegin**. Each string is then read in one by one and parsed, and the appropriate elements of the **Checked** property are set to **True**. When there is no more data to be read, the **Reader.EndOfList** function returns **True**, at which point **ReadListEnd** is called to stop the reading process. All this is illustrated in the following code:

```
procedure TCheckGrid.ReadChecked(Reader:TReader);
var
  Coord:String;
  CommaPos:Byte;
  X,Y:Byte;
begin
  Reader.ReadListBegin;
  while not Reader.EndOfList do
  begin
    Coord:=Trim(Reader.ReadString);
    CommaPos:=Pos(',',Coord);
    X:=StrToInt(Copy(Coord,1,CommaPos-1));
```

```
      Y:=StrToInt(Trim(Copy(Coord,CommaPos+1,Length(Coord)-CommaPos)));
      Checked[X,Y]:=True;
    end;
  Reader.ReadListEnd;
end;
```

This also marks the end of the changes needed to make **TCheckGrid** compatible with the property editor we're about to construct, so now is a good time to present the final listing for the component, **CHKGRID.PAS**, which you can also find in the **\DC\CHAP9** directory:

Listing 9.3 CHKGRID.PAS

```pascal
unit Chkgrid;

interface

uses
  SysUtils, WinTypes, WinProcs, Messages, Classes, Graphics,
  Controls, Forms, Dialogs, StdCtrls;

const
  RowsMax=20;
  ColumnsMax=20;

type
  TColumns=1..ColumnsMax;
  TRows=1..RowsMax;
  TMode=(moNormal,moColumnExclusive,moRowExclusive);

const
  RowsDefault=5;
  ColumnsDefault=5;
  ModeDefault=moNormal;
  ColorDefault=clBtnText;
  BackgroundColorDefault=clBtnFace;
  FontNameDefault='Arial';
  FontSizeDefault=10;
```

```
type
  TChangeEvent=procedure(Column:TColumns;Row:TRows;
    State:Boolean) of Object;

  TCheckGrid = class(TCustomControl)
  private
    ColumnTextRect:TRect;
    RowTextRect:TRect;
    CheckGridRect:TRect;

    ColumnPos:array[1..ColumnsMax+1] of Integer;
    RowPos:array[1..RowsMax+1] of Integer;

    CheckXOffset:Word;
    CheckYOffset:Word;

    ColumnTextHeight:array[1..ColumnsMax] of Word;
    RowTextWidth:array[1..RowsMax] of Word;

    ColumnTextOffset:Word;
    RowTextOffset:Word;

    CurrentColumn:Byte;
    CurrentRow:Byte;

    HasFocus:Boolean;
    CheckThickness:Word;
    HasBeenCalculated:Boolean;

    FChecked:array[1..ColumnsMax,1..RowsMax] of Boolean;
    FMode:TMode;
    FColor:TColor;
    FBackgroundColor:TColor;
    FRowText:TStrings;
    FColumnText:TStrings;
    FOnChange:TChangeEvent;
```

```
    procedure RotateFont(Angle:Integer);
    procedure CalculateRects;
    procedure DrawCell(Column:TColumns;Row:TRows);
    procedure CheckCell(Column:TColumns;Row:TRows);
    procedure SetMode(AMode:TMode);
    procedure SetColor(AColor:TColor);
    procedure SetBackgroundColor(ABackgroundColor:TColor);
    procedure SetColumnText(AColumnText:TStrings);
    procedure SetRowText(ARowText:TStrings);
    procedure SetChecked(Column:TColumns;Row:TRows;
      AChecked:Boolean);
    function GetChecked(Column:TColumns;Row:TRows):Boolean;
    procedure WMSize(var Message:TWMSIZE); message WM_SIZE;
    procedure WMSetFocus(var Message: TWMSetFocus);
      message WM_SETFOCUS;
    procedure WMKillFocus(var Message: TWMKillFocus);
      message WM_KILLFOCUS;
    procedure WMGetDlgCode(var Message: TWMGetDlgCode);
      message WM_GETDLGCODE;
    procedure ChangeFont(Sender:TObject);
    procedure ChangeText(Sender:TObject);
    procedure ReadChecked(Reader:TReader);
    procedure WriteChecked(Writer:TWriter);
    function AnyChecked:Boolean;
    procedure DefineProperties(Filer:TFiler);override;
protected
    procedure MouseDown(Button:TMouseButton;Shift:TShiftState;
      X,Y:Integer);override;
    procedure Paint;override;
    procedure KeyDown(var Key: Word; Shift: TShiftState);override;
public
    constructor Create(AOwner:TComponent);override;
    property Checked[Column:TColumns;Row:TRows]:Boolean
      read GetChecked write SetChecked;
published
```

```
property Mode:TMode read FMode write SetMode
  default ModeDefault;
property Color:TColor read FColor write SetColor
  default ColorDefault;
property BackgroundColor:TColor read FBackgroundColor
  write SetBackgroundColor default BackgroundColorDefault;
property OnChange: TChangeEvent read FOnChange
  write FOnChange;
property ColumnText:TStrings read FColumnText
  write SetColumnText;
property RowText:TStrings read FRowText
  write SetRowText;
property DragCursor;
property DragMode;
property Enabled;
property Font;
property ParentFont;
property ParentShowHint;
property ShowHint;
property TabOrder;
property TabStop;
property Visible;
property OnClick;
property OnDragDrop;
property OnDragOver;
property OnEndDrag;
property OnEnter;
property OnExit;
property OnKeyDown;
property OnKeyPress;
property OnKeyUp;
property OnMouseDown;
property OnMouseMove;
property OnMouseUp;
end;
```

```pascal
procedure Register;

implementation

procedure TCheckGrid.RotateFont(Angle:Integer);
var
  LogFont:TLogFont;
begin
  GetObject(Canvas.Font.Handle,SizeOf(TLogFont),@LogFont);
  LogFont.lfEscapement:=Angle;
  Canvas.Font.Handle:=CreateFontIndirect(LogFont);
end;

procedure TCheckGrid.CalculateRects;
var
  i:Byte;
  ColumnHeightMax:Word;
  RowWidthMax:Word;
  WidthSize,HeightSize:Word;
begin
  if csLoading in ComponentState then exit;
  HasBeenCalculated:=True;
  Canvas.Font:=Font;
  RowTextRect.Left:=0;
  RowTextRect.Bottom:=Height-1;
  ColumnTextRect.Top:=0;
  ColumnTextRect.Right:=Width-1;

  RowWidthMax:=0;
  for i:=1 to FRowText.Count do
  begin
    WidthSize:=Canvas.TextWidth(FRowText[i-1]);
    RowTextWidth[i]:=WidthSize;
    if WidthSize>RowWidthMax then RowWidthMax:=WidthSize;
  end;
  RowTextRect.Right:=RowWidthMax+10;
```

```
ColumnTextRect.Left:=RowWidthMax;

ColumnHeightMax:=0;
for i:=1 to FColumnText.Count do
begin
  HeightSize:=Canvas.TextWidth(FColumnText[i-1]);
  ColumnTextHeight[i]:=HeightSize;
  if HeightSize>ColumnHeightMax then
    ColumnHeightMax:=HeightSize;
end;

RowTextRect.Top:=ColumnHeightMax;
ColumnTextRect.Bottom:=ColumnHeightMax+10;

CheckGridRect.Left:=RowTextRect.Right;
CheckGridRect.Top:=ColumnTextRect.Bottom;
CheckGridRect.Right:=Width-1;
CheckGridRect.Bottom:=Height-1;

for i:=1 to FColumnText.Count+1 do
  ColumnPos[i]:=MulDiv(CheckGridRect.Right-CheckGridRect.Left,
    i-1,FColumnText.Count)+CheckGridRect.Left;

for i:=1 to FRowText.Count+1 do
  RowPos[i]:=MulDiv(CheckGridRect.Bottom-CheckGridRect.Top,i-1,
    FRowText.Count)+CheckGridRect.Top;

CheckXOffset:=(ColumnPos[2]-ColumnPos[1]) div 4;
CheckYOffset:=(RowPos[2]-RowPos[1]) div 4;
CheckThickness:=(CheckXOffset+CheckYOffset) div 4;

ColumnTextOffset:=(ColumnPos[2]-ColumnPos[1]+Font.Height) div 2;
RowTextOffset:=(RowPos[2]-RowPos[1]+Font.Height) div 2;
end;

procedure TCheckGrid.DrawCell(Column:TColumns;Row:TRows);
var
```

```
    i:Byte;
  FocusRect:TRect;
begin
  if FChecked[Column,Row] then
    Canvas.Pen.Color:=FColor
  else
    Canvas.Pen.Color:=FBackgroundColor;

  Canvas.MoveTo(ColumnPos[Column]+CheckXOffset,RowPos[Row]+
    CheckYOffset);
  Canvas.LineTo(ColumnPos[Column+1]-CheckXOffset,RowPos[Row+1]-
    CheckYOffset);

  Canvas.MoveTo(ColumnPos[Column+1]-CheckXOffset,RowPos[Row]+
    CheckYOffset);
  Canvas.LineTo(ColumnPos[Column]+CheckXOffset,RowPos[Row+1]-
    CheckYOffset);

  if (Column=CurrentColumn) and (Row=CurrentRow) then
  begin
    FocusRect.Left:=ColumnPos[CurrentColumn]+2;
    FocusRect.Top:=RowPos[CurrentRow]+2;
    FocusRect.Right:=ColumnPos[CurrentColumn+1]-1;
    FocusRect.Bottom:=RowPos[CurrentRow+1]-1;
    Canvas.Brush.Color:=FBackgroundColor;
    Canvas.FrameRect(FocusRect);

    if HasFocus then
      Canvas.DrawFocusRect(FocusRect);
  end;
end;

procedure TCheckGrid.CheckCell(Column:TColumns;Row:TRows);
var
  i:Byte;
begin
  Canvas.Pen.Width:=CheckThickness;
```

```
  case FMode of
    moNormal:
      DrawCell(Column,Row);
    moColumnExclusive:
    begin
      for i:=1 to FRowText.Count do
      begin
        FChecked[Column,i]:=i=Row;
        DrawCell(Column,i);
      end;
    end;
    moRowExclusive:
    begin
      for i:=1 to FColumnText.Count do
      begin
        FChecked[i,Row]:=i=Column;
        DrawCell(i,Row);
      end;
    end;
  end;
end;

procedure TCheckGrid.SetMode(AMode:TMode);
begin
  FMode:=AMode;
end;

procedure TCheckGrid.SetColor(AColor:TColor);
begin
  FColor:=AColor;
  Paint;
end;

procedure TCheckGrid.SetBackgroundColor(ABackgroundColor:TColor);
begin
  FBackgroundColor:=ABackgroundColor;
```

```
    Paint;
  end;

procedure TCheckGrid.ChangeFont(Sender:TObject);
begin
  CalculateRects;
  Invalidate;
end;

procedure TCheckGrid.ChangeText(Sender:TObject);
begin
  CalculateRects;
  Invalidate;
end;

procedure TCheckGrid.ReadChecked(Reader:TReader);
var
  Coord:String;
  CommaPos:Byte;
  X,Y:Byte;
begin
  Reader.ReadListBegin;
  while not Reader.EndOfList do
  begin
    Coord:=Trim(Reader.ReadString);
    CommaPos:=Pos(',',Coord);
    X:=StrToInt(Copy(Coord,1,CommaPos-1));
    Y:=StrToInt(Trim(Copy(Coord,CommaPos+1,Length(Coord)-
      CommaPos)));
    Checked[X,Y]:=True;
  end;
  Reader.ReadListEnd;
end;

procedure TCheckGrid.WriteChecked(Writer:TWriter);
var
```

```
  X,Y:Byte;
  LastY:Byte;
begin
  Writer.WriteListBegin;
  for Y:=1 to FRowText.Count do
  begin
    for X:=1 to FColumnText.Count do
    begin
      if Checked[X,Y] then
        Writer.WriteString(Format('%d, %d',[X,Y]));
    end;
  end;
  Writer.WriteListEnd;
end;

function TCheckGrid.AnyChecked:Boolean;
var
  i,j:Byte;
begin
  AnyChecked:=False;
  for i:=1 to FColumnText.Count do
  begin
    for j:=1 to FRowText.Count do
    begin
      if Checked[i,j] then
      begin
        AnyChecked:=True;
        exit;
      end;
    end;
  end;
end;

procedure TCheckGrid.DefineProperties(Filer:TFiler);
begin
  inherited DefineProperties(Filer);
```

```
  Filer.DefineProperty('Checked',ReadChecked,WriteChecked,
    AnyChecked);
end;

procedure TCheckGrid.SetColumnText(AColumnText:TStrings);
begin
  FColumnText.Assign(AColumnText);
  if FColumnText.Count=0 then
    FColumnText.Add('Column 1');
  CalculateRects;
  Invalidate;
end;

procedure TCheckGrid.SetRowText(ARowText:TStrings);
begin
  FRowText.Assign(ARowText);
  if FRowText.Count=0 then
    FRowText.Add('Row 1');
  CalculateRects;
  Invalidate;
end;

procedure TCheckGrid.SetChecked(Column:TColumns;Row:TRows;
    AChecked:Boolean);
begin
  FChecked[Column,Row]:=AChecked;
  CheckCell(Column,Row);
end;

function TCheckGrid.GetChecked(Column:TColumns;Row:TRows):Boolean;
begin
  GetChecked:=FChecked[Column,Row];
end;

constructor TCheckGrid.Create(AOwner:TComponent);
var
  i,j:Byte;
```

```
begin
  inherited Create(AOwner);
  FColumnText:=TStringList.Create;
  FRowText:=TStringList.Create;
  FMode:=ModeDefault;
  FColor:=ColorDefault;
  FBackgroundColor:=BackgroundColorDefault;
  Font.Name:=FontNameDefault;
  Font.Size:=FontSizeDefault;
  Font.OnChange:=ChangeFont;
  FOnChange:=nil;
  CurrentColumn:=1;
  CurrentRow:=1;
  HasFocus:=False;
  HasBeenCalculated:=False;

  for i:=1 to ColumnsMax do
  begin
    for j:=1 to RowsMax do
    begin
      FChecked[i,j]:=False;
    end;
  end;

  for i:=1 to 5 do
    FRowText.Add('Row '+IntToStr(i));

  for i:=1 to 5 do
    FColumnText.Add('Column '+IntToStr(i));

  TStringList(FColumnText).OnChange:=ChangeText;
  TStringList(FRowText).OnChange:=ChangeText;
end;

procedure TCheckGrid.Paint;
var
  i,j:Byte;
begin
  if not HasBeenCalculated then CalculateRects;
```

```
Canvas.Font:=Font;

Canvas.Pen.Color:=Color;

Canvas.Pen.Width:=1;

Canvas.Brush.Color:=FBackgroundColor;

Canvas.Brush.Style:=bsSolid;


Canvas.Rectangle(CheckGridRect.Left,CheckGridRect.Top,
  CheckGridRect.Right,CheckGridRect.Bottom);


Canvas.Brush.Style:=bsClear;


RotateFont(-900);

for i:=1 to FColumnText.Count do

begin
  Canvas.TextOut(ColumnPos[i+1]-ColumnTextOffset,
    ColumnTextRect.Bottom-ColumnTextHeight[i]-10,
      FColumnText[i-1]);
  Canvas.MoveTo(ColumnPos[i],CheckGridRect.Top);
  Canvas.LineTo(ColumnPos[i],CheckGridRect.Bottom);
end;


RotateFont(0);

for i:=1 to FRowText.Count do

begin
  Canvas.TextOut(RowTextRect.Right-RowTextWidth[i]-10,RowPos[i]+
    RowTextOffset,FRowText[i-1]);
  Canvas.MoveTo(CheckGridRect.Left,RowPos[i]);
  Canvas.LineTo(CheckGridRect.Right,RowPos[i]);
end;


Canvas.Pen.Width:=CheckThickness;

for i:=1 to FColumnText.Count do

begin
  for j:=1 to FRowText.Count do
    DrawCell(i,j);
  end;
end;


procedure TCheckGrid.MouseDown(Button:TMouseButton;
```

```
      Shift:TShiftState;X,Y:Integer);
var
  i,j:Byte;
  FoundBox:Boolean;
begin
  FoundBox:=False;
  i:=0;
  repeat
    inc(i);
    if (X>=ColumnPos[i]) and (X<=ColumnPos[i+1]) then
    begin
      j:=0;
      repeat
        inc(j);
        if (Y>=RowPos[j]) and (Y<=RowPos[j+1]) then
        begin
          if TabStop or HasFocus then
          begin
            SetFocus;
            HasFocus:=False;
            DrawCell(CurrentColumn,CurrentRow);
            HasFocus:=True;
          end;
          CurrentColumn:=i;
          CurrentRow:=j;
          FChecked[i,j]:=not FChecked[i,j];
          CheckCell(i,j);
          if Assigned(FOnChange) then
            FOnChange(CurrentColumn,CurrentRow,
              FChecked[CurrentColumn,CurrentRow]);
          FoundBox:=True;
        end;
      until (j>FRowText.Count) or FoundBox;
    end;
  until (i>FColumnText.Count) or FoundBox;
  inherited MouseDown(Button,Shift,X,Y);
end;
```

```
procedure TCheckGrid.WMSize(var Message:TWMSIZE);
begin
  CalculateRects;
  Invalidate;
end;

procedure TCheckGrid.WMSetFocus(var Message: TWMSetFocus);
var
  FocusRect:TRect;
begin
  HasFocus:=True;
  DrawCell(CurrentColumn,CurrentRow);
  inherited;
end;

procedure TCheckGrid.WMKillFocus(var Message: TWMKillFocus);
begin
  HasFocus := False;
  DrawCell(CurrentColumn,CurrentRow);
  inherited;
end;

procedure TCheckGrid.KeyDown(var Key: Word; Shift: TShiftState);
begin
  inherited KeyDown(Key,Shift);
  case Key of
    VK_LEFT:
    begin
      HasFocus:=False;
      DrawCell(CurrentColumn,CurrentRow);
      dec(CurrentColumn);
      if CurrentColumn=0 then CurrentColumn:=FColumnText.Count;
      HasFocus:=True;
      DrawCell(CurrentColumn,CurrentRow);
    end;
    VK_RIGHT:
    begin
```

```
      HasFocus:=False;
      DrawCell(CurrentColumn,CurrentRow);
      inc(CurrentColumn);
      if CurrentColumn>FColumnText.Count then CurrentColumn:=1;
      HasFocus:=True;
      DrawCell(CurrentColumn,CurrentRow);
    end;
  VK_DOWN:
  begin
    HasFocus:=False;
    DrawCell(CurrentColumn,CurrentRow);
    inc(CurrentRow);
    if CurrentRow>FRowText.Count then CurrentRow:=1;
    HasFocus:=True;
    DrawCell(CurrentColumn,CurrentRow);
  end;
  VK_UP:
  begin
    HasFocus:=False;
    DrawCell(CurrentColumn,CurrentRow);
    dec(CurrentRow);
    if CurrentRow=0 then CurrentRow:=FRowText.Count;
    HasFocus:=True;
    DrawCell(CurrentColumn,CurrentRow);
  end;
  VK_SPACE:
  begin
    FChecked[CurrentColumn,CurrentRow]:=
      not FChecked[CurrentColumn,CurrentRow];
    CheckCell(CurrentColumn,CurrentRow);
    if Assigned(FOnChange) then
      FOnChange(CurrentColumn,CurrentRow,FChecked[CurrentColumn,
      CurrentRow]);
  end;
  end;
end;


procedure TCheckGrid.WMGetDlgCode(var Message: TWMGetDlgCode);
```

```
begin
  Message.Result := DLGC_WANTARROWS;
end;

procedure Register;
begin
  RegisterComponents('Additional', [TCheckGrid]);
end;

end.
```

Implementing the Component Editor

After the lengthy diversion of getting **TCheckGrid** up to par, we can finally get back to our component editor. It starts its life out just like the form-based property editor—selecting **New Form** from the **File** menu. After being decorated with the needed components, it ends up looking like Figure 9.4.

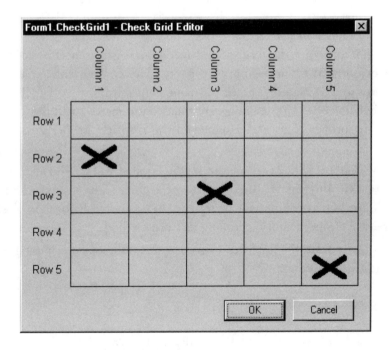

9.4 The **TCheckGrid** component editor.

The big difference between a property editor and a component editor is the class that they are derived from. For a component editor, it is usually **TComponentEditor**, but it can also be **TDefaultEditor** if you want to inherit the ability to double-click on a component and have the default event handler for in appear in the code editor. For our component editor, **TCheckGridEditor**, we want the double-click action to pop up the dialog box that allows us to set the check states.

It may surprise you to learn that the double-click-and-pop-up-a-form action I just described requires that we override only one member of **TComponentEditor**, the **Edit** method. When **Edit** is called, it first creates an instance of the dialog box and transfers the state of each cell from the **TCheckGrid** component being edited to the **TCheckGrid** on the dialog box. It must also transfer the **ColumnText** and **RowText** properties because they determine the number of rows and columns to display. Besides, it is less confusing to have the actual text displayed in the dialog box.

The caption of the dialog box must also be set. This, too, is similar to a property editor, except the format is somewhat different, being *FormName.ComponentName - EditorName*. The name of the form—the design form, not the form of our dialog box—is retrieved by accessing the **Component.Owner.Name** property. The component name is simply **Component.Name**. The editor name comes from the original caption of the dialog box. All the strings are then concatenated, with the "." and " - " in the proper place and assigned to the **Caption** property of the dialog box.

The dialog box is displayed by the familiar call to **ShowModal**, and if the **OK** button is clicked, the cell states are transferred to the **TCheckGrid** component being edited. After the dialog box closes, it is released from memory by calling its **Free** method.

After **Edit**, the final step to getting this thing up and running is its registration procedure:

```
procedure Register;
begin
  RegisterComponentEditor(TCheckGrid,TCheckGridEditor);
end;
```

The heart of the beast is the call to **RegisterComponentEditor:**

```
procedure RegisterComponentEditor(ComponentClass:TComponentClass;
  ComponentEditor:TComponentEditorClass);
```

The **ComponentClass** parameter accepts the type for the component that we want to provide an editor for, **TCheckGrid**, in our case. The second parameter, **ComponentEditor**, tells which editor to use, which for us is **TCheckGridEditor.**

And there you go, a complete component editor. The calorie-light code for this is right here:

```
unit CheckGridEditor;

interface

uses
  Windows, Messages, SysUtils, Classes, Graphics, Controls, Forms,
  Dialogs,Chkgrid,DsgnIntf, StdCtrls, ColorDrop, ExtCtrls,StrEdit;

type
  TCheckGridEditor=class(TComponentEditor)
    procedure Edit;override;
  end;

  TCheckGridDlg = class(TForm)
    CheckGrid1: TCheckGrid;
    OKButton: TButton;
    CancelButton: TButton;
  end;

procedure Register;

implementation

{$R *.DFM}

procedure TCheckGridEditor.Edit;
```

```
var
  EditGrid:TCheckGrid;
  CompGrid:TCheckGrid;
  CheckGridDlg:TCheckGridDlg;
  i,j:Byte;
begin
  Application.CreateForm(TCheckGridDlg,CheckGridDlg);
  EditGrid:=CheckGridDlg.CheckGrid1;
  CompGrid:=TCheckGrid(Component);
  CheckGridDlg.Caption:=Component.Owner.Name+'.'+Component.Name+
    ' - '+CheckGridDlg.Caption;
  for i:=1 to CompGrid.ColumnText.Count do
  begin
    for j:=1 to CompGrid.RowText.Count do
    begin
      EditGrid.Checked[i,j]:=CompGrid.Checked[i,j];
    end;
  end;
  EditGrid.ColumnText:=CompGrid.ColumnText;
  EditGrid.RowText:=CompGrid.RowText;

  if CheckGridDlg.ShowModal=mrOK then
  begin
    for i:=1 to EditGrid.ColumnText.Count do
    begin
      for j:=1 to EditGrid.RowText.Count do
      begin
        TCheckGrid(Component).Checked[i,j]:=
          CheckGridDlg.CheckGrid1.Checked[i,j];
      end;
    end;
    Designer.Modified;
  end;
  CheckGridDlg.Free;
end;

procedure Register;
```

```
begin
  RegisterComponentEditor(TCheckGrid,TCheckGridEditor);
end;

end.
```

Adding Items to the Context Menu

When you right-click on a component at design time, a menu pops up. Normally, this menu contains odds and ends for aligning components, specifying the creation order, and so on. However, it can also be put to your advantage by automating actions for your components that would otherwise prove to be tedious to do through the Object Inspector.

This is perhaps the simplest type of editor to implement that we have looked at so far, except maybe for the text-based property editors, because it doesn't require a dialog box. This is not to say that it can't have one—or several—however, it's just not required as a convention.

This type of component editor uses the same base component editor classes we looked at before, either **TComponentEditor** or **TDefaultEditor**. The implication that arises here is that a context menu based editor can be located in the same class that contains the double-click editor, with no need to have multiple component editors.

To demonstrate how a context menu based editor can be put to use, we'll construct a simple component editor for the **TLedGauge** class of Chapter 5. It will provide menu items that allow the component to be flipped from horizontal to vertical and vice versa, as well as permit the setting of the shape of the LEDs.

The first step is to create a new unit for the editor. The easiest way to do this is to select **Component, New** from the main menu; for the class name enter **TLedGaugeEditor**; and for the ancestor name enter **TComponentEditor**. We're using the **TComponentEditor** class rather than **TDefaultEditor** because **TLedGauge** has no events, so double-clicking on it and expecting to see one in the code editor window and not getting anything is confusing. By using **TComponentEditor** as the ancestor, an interesting feature is revealed: In the absence of an **Edit** method, the first context menu item is executed, which just happens to be the command to flip the gauge.

Getting back to creating the unit, don't worry about the **Palette Page** field of the Component Expert because the registration procedure has to be changed anyway from a component registration to a component editor registration. Click on **OK**, and in the blink of an eye, a unit will appear in the code editor window.

Three key methods of **TComponentEditor** need to be overridden. The first is **GetVerbCount**:

```
function GetVerbCount: Integer;
```

This function returns a value indicating how many menu items (verbs) there are to be. For instance, if you want three menu items, you should be returning a value of three from this function.

The next method is **GetVerb**:

```
function GetVerb(Index:Integer): string;
```

This function is called with a zero-based index and should return a string that contains the text for the corresponding menu item. Typically, the **case** statement is used to do this.

The final method that has to be overridden is **ExecuteVerb**:

```
procedure ExecuteVerb(Index:Integer);
```

This procedure is called whenever one of the added menu items is actually selected. The **Index** parameter contains the zero-base index identifying which menu item caused the call. Again, a **case** statement can be used to differentiate among the various indexes and execute the appropriate code.

It is also important to change the registration procedure so that it calls **RegisterComponentEditor** instead of **RegisterComponent**. This, as well as the methods we have just overridden, is shown in the following complete listing for the **TLedGaugeEditor** component editor:

Listing 9.4 LEDGAUGEEDITOR.PAS

```pascal
unit LedGaugeEditor;

interface

uses
  Windows, Messages, SysUtils, Classes, Graphics, Controls, Forms,
  Dialogs,DsgnIntf,LedGauge;

type
  TLedGaugeEditor = class(TDefaultEditor)
    function GetVerbCount:Integer;override;
    function GetVerb(Index:Integer):String;override;
    procedure ExecuteVerb(Index:Integer);override;
  end;

procedure Register;

implementation

function TLedGaugeEditor.GetVerbCount:Integer;
begin
  GetVerbCount:=4;
end;

function TLedGaugeEditor.GetVerb(Index:Integer):String;
begin
  case Index of
    0:GetVerb:='&Flip Gauge';
    1:GetVerb:='Re&ctangular';
    2:GetVerb:='&Round';
    3:GetVerb:='Ro&unded Rectangular';
  end;
end;
```

```
procedure TLedGaugeEditor.ExecuteVerb(Index:Integer);
var
  Temp:Integer;
begin
  case Index of
    0:
      begin
        Temp:=TLedGauge(Component).Width;
        TLedGauge(Component).Width:=TLedGauge(Component).Height;
        TLedGauge(Component).Height:=Temp;
      end;
    1:TLedGauge(Component).Shape:=shRectangular;
    2:TLedGauge(Component).Shape:=shRound;
    3:TLedGauge(Component).Shape:=shRoundedRect;
  end;
  Designer.Modified;
end;

procedure Register;
begin
  RegisterComponentEditor(TLedGauge,TLedGaugeEditor);
end;

end.
```

INDEX •